Greek

An Essential Grammar of the Modern Language

Greek: An Essential Grammar of the Modern Language is a concise and user-friendly reference guide to the most important aspects of Modern Greek.

It presents a fresh and accessible description of the language in short, readable sections. Explanations are clear and supported by examples throughout.

The *Grammar* is ideal for learners of all levels and is suitable for those involved in independent study and for students in schools, colleges, universities and adult classes of all types.

Features include:

- Variety of examples
- Clear explanations of grammatical terms
- Discussion of points which often cause problems
- Highlighted Greek/English comparisons and contrasts

Greek: An Essential Grammar of the Modern Language will help you read, speak and write with greater confidence.

David Holton is Reader in Modern Greek at the University of Cambridge and a Fellow of Selwyn College. **Peter Mackridge** is Professor of Modern Greek at the University of Oxford and a Fellow of St Cross College. **Irene Philippaki-Warburton** is Professor of Linguistics at Reading University.

Routledge Essential Grammars

Essential Grammars are available for the following languages:

Chinese
Danish
Dutch
English
Finnish
Hungarian
Modern Hebrew
Norwegian
Polish
Portuguese
Swedish
Thai
Urdu

Other titles of related interest published by Routledge:

Greek: A Comprehensive Grammar of the Modern Language
By David Holton, Peter Mackridge and Irene Philippaki-Warburton

Colloqual Greek
By Niki Watts

Greek

An Essential Grammar of the Modern Language

**David Holton,
Peter Mackridge and
Irene Philippaki-Warburton**

Routledge
Taylor & Francis Group
LONDON AND NEW YORK

First published 2004
by Routledge
2 Park Square, Milton Park, Abingdon, Oxon OX14 4RN

Simultaneously published in the USA and Canada
by Routledge
771 Third Ave, New York, NY 10017

Routledge is an imprint of the Taylor & Francis Group, an informa business

© 2004 David Holton, Peter Mackridge and Irene Philippaki-Warburton

Typeset in Sabon and Gill
by Florence Production Ltd, Stoodleigh, Devon
Printed and bound in Great Britain
by the MPG Books Group

All rights reserved. No part of this book may be reprinted or
reproduced or utilised in any form or by any electronic, mechanical,
or other means, now known or hereafter invented, including
photocopying and recording, or in any information storage or
retrieval system, without permission in writing from the publishers.

British Library Cataloguing in Publication Data
A catalogue record for this book is available from the British Library

Library of Congress Cataloging in Publication Data
A catalog record for this book has been requested

ISBN 10: 0–415–23210–4 (pbk)
     10: 0–415–23209–0 (hbk)

     13: 978–0–415–23210–4 (pbk)
     13: 978–0–415–23209–8 (hbk)

Contents

Preface   xi
Abbreviations and symbols   xiii

Chapter 1   The alphabet and pronunciation   1

     1.1   The Greek alphabet   1

     Pronunciation   3
     1.2   Vowels   3
     1.3   Combinations of vowels   4
     1.4   Consonants   4
     1.5   Combinations of consonants   7
     1.6   Phonological phenomena across word boundaries   9

     Stress and intonation   10
     1.7   Word stress   10
     1.8   Enclisis   11
     1.9   Intonation   11

Chapter 2   The writing system   14

     2.1   Accents (the monotonic system)   14
     2.2   Other diacritics   15
     2.3   The use of capital and lower-case letters   15
     2.4   Punctuation   16
     2.5   The transcription of foreign names   18

Chapter 3   The noun and the noun phrase   19

     3.1   Constituents of the noun phrase   19
     3.2   Functions of the noun phrase   20

Gender, number and case — 22
- 3.3 Gender — 22
- 3.4 Number — 24
- 3.5 Case — 24

The articles — 25
- 3.6 The forms of the definite article — 25
- 3.7 The forms of the indefinite article — 26

Nouns — 27
- 3.8 Declensions: an overview — 27

Masculine nouns — 28
- 3.9 Nouns in -ας (parisyllabic) — 28
- 3.10 Nouns in -ης (parisyllabic) — 31
- 3.11 Nouns in -ος — 31
- 3.12 Nouns in -έας — 34
- 3.13 Imparisyllabic nouns in -άς, -ας, -ής, -ης, -ές, -ούς — 34

Feminine nouns — 36
- 3.14 Nouns in -α (parisyllabic) — 36
- 3.15 Nouns in -η with plural -ες — 38
- 3.16 Nouns in -ος — 39
- 3.17 Nouns in -η with plural -εις — 40
- 3.18 Imparisyllabic nouns in -ά and -ού — 40
- 3.19 Nouns in -ω — 41

Nouns of common gender — 42
- 3.20 Nouns which may be either masculine or feminine — 42

Neuter nouns — 44
- 3.21 Nouns in -ο — 44
- 3.22 Nouns in -ί — 45
- 3.23 Nouns in -ι — 46
- 3.24 Nouns in -ος — 47
- 3.25 Nouns in -μα — 47
- 3.26 Nouns in -ιμο — 48
- 3.27 Other neuter nouns in -ς — 49
- 3.28 Other neuter nouns ending in vowels — 50
- 3.29 Nouns in -ν — 51

Special types of noun — 52
- 3.30 Nouns with a change of gender in the plural — 52
- 3.31 Indeclinable nouns — 53

Adjectives — 54
- 3.32 Adjectives in outline — 54

The forms of adjectives		54
3.33	Adjectives in -ος, -η, -ο	54
3.34	Adjectives in -ος, -α, -ο	55
3.35	Adjectives in -ος, -ια, -ο	56
3.36	Adjectives in -ύς, -ιά, -ύ	56
3.37	Adjectives in -ής, -ιά, -ί	57
3.38	The adjective (quantifier) πολύς	57
3.39	Adjectives in -ης, -ες	59
3.40	Adjectives with neuter in -ικο	60
3.41	Adjectives in -ων, -ουσα, -ον	62
3.42	Indeclinable adjectives	63
Comparison of adjectives		63
3.43	Overview	63
3.44	The comparative	63
3.45	The relative superlative	64
3.46	The absolute superlative	65
3.47	Irregular comparatives and superlatives	65
The use of noun phrases and of adjectives		67
3.48	Agreement within the noun phrase	67
3.49	The use of the cases: introduction	68
3.50	The use of the nominative	69
3.51	The use of the accusative	69
3.52	The use of the genitive	72
3.53	The use of the vocative	77
3.54	The use of the definite article	77
3.55	The use of the indefinite article	81
3.56	Absence of article	81
3.57	The use of adjectives	83

Chapter 4 Pronouns and determiners — 87

4.1	Personal pronouns: weak (clitic) forms	87
4.2	Personal pronouns: emphatic forms	91
4.3	Demonstrative pronouns and determiners	92
4.4	Possessive pronouns and determiners	94
4.5	Interrogative pronouns and determiners	95
4.6	Indefinite pronouns and determiners	96
4.7	Relative and correlative pronouns and determiners	99
4.8	The universal pronouns καθένας and καθετί and the distributive determiner κάθε	101

4.9	Other pronouns and determiners	101
4.10	Quantifiers	103

Chapter 5 Numerals — 105

5.1	Table of cardinal and ordinal numerals	105
5.2	The declined forms of cardinal numerals	108
5.3	Multiplicative numerals	109
5.4	Collective numerals	110
5.5	Numerals in expressions of time, space and quantity	110

Chapter 6 The verb and the verb phrase — 112

6.1	Introduction to the verb phrase	112
6.2	Preliminary notes on the verb system	116
6.3	Person and number	117
6.4	Tense, aspect, voice and mood	118
6.5	The use of the tenses and other verb forms	120
6.6	Defective, impersonal and deponent verbs	125

The basic forms — 125

6.7	The verb 'to be'	126
6.8	First-conjugation verbs	126
6.9	Second-conjugation verbs (type A)	130
6.10	Second-conjugation verbs (type B)	134
6.11	Second-conjugation verbs with passive only	137
6.12	Verbs with contracted active present forms	138
6.13	Verbs with irregular form of active dependent	140

The formation of active and passive perfective stems — 141

6.14	Perfective stems of first-conjugation verbs	141
6.15	Perfective stems of second-conjugation verbs	146
6.16	The passive perfect participle	147

The formation of other tenses and verb forms — 149

6.17	The perfective and imperfective futures	149
6.18	The perfect tenses and the auxiliary verb έχω	150
6.19	The conditional and perfect conditional	151
6.20	The subjunctive forms	151

Augment — 152

6.21	Syllabic augment	152
6.22	Vocalic augment	152
6.23	Internal augment	153

Irregular verbs 154
6.24 Definition of an irregular verb 154
6.25 Table of irregular verbs 154

Chapter 7 The adverb and the adverbial phrase 169

7.1 Types of adverb: manner, place, time, quantity, etc. 169
7.2 The use of adverbs and adverbial phrases 173

The formation of adverbs from adjectives 177
7.3 Adverbs in -α 177
7.4 Adverbs in -ως 178
7.5 Other adverbs formed from adjectives 179
7.6 Comparison of adverbs 179

Chapter 8 The preposition and the prepositional phrase 181

8.1 Introduction to prepositions and prepositional phrases 181
8.2 The uses of individual prepositions 182
8.3 Compound prepositions; adverbs used as prepositions 189

Chapter 9 Conjunctions and particles 193

9.1 Co-ordinating conjunctions 193
9.2 Subordinating conjunctions 194
9.3 Particles 195

Chapter 10 The clause 203

10.1 Types of clause 203

Main clauses 203
10.2 Statements 203
10.3 Suggestions, wishes, requests, promises etc. 204
10.4 Commands and prohibitions 204
10.5 Yes/no questions 205
10.6 Wh- questions 206
10.7 Negation 207
10.8 Exclamations 211

Subordinate clauses 212
10.9 Relative clauses 212
10.10 Indirect questions 216

Contents

10.11	Indirect commands	218
10.12	Complement clauses	218
10.13	Conditional constructions	223
10.14	Concessive clauses	225
10.15	Temporal clauses	226
10.16	Clauses of manner	227
10.17	Clauses of purpose (final clauses)	227
10.18	Clauses of result	227
10.19	Clauses of cause	228

Other syntactic phenomena — 229

10.20	Word order, topicalization and focusing	229
10.21	Co-ordination	232
10.22	Comparison	234
10.23	Reflexive expressions	237
10.24	Reciprocal expressions	238
10.25	Impersonal uses of verbs	239

Chapter 11 Word formation — 241

11.1	Suffixation	241
11.2	Prefixation	244
11.3	Compound formation	246

Chapter 12 Conversational features — 248

12.1	Politeness and familiarity	248
12.2	Proper names and pet names	251
12.3	Greetings and wishes	255

Appendices — 258

1	Correspondence table of pronouns, determiners and adverbs	258
2	Some abbreviations in common use	260

Glossary of grammatical terms — 263
Some recommended books for further study — 271
Index of grammatical categories and concepts — 274
Index of Greek words — 278

Preface

The aim of this book is to provide a concise, but sufficiently detailed, description of the Greek language as spoken and written in Greece today. Greek is a highly inflected language, and consequently we have had to devote considerable space to the basic patterns of declension and conjugation which learners need to master. However, we also give close attention to the structure of phrases and sentences, i.e. to the syntax of the language, which other grammars have tended to treat rather cursorily. Throughout the book, our intention is to provide a reliable guide to Greek grammar and usage, up to date in terms of both its linguistic approach and the linguistic material we use to exemplify the various aspects of the language.

The book is intended to serve the needs of adult learners, both those attending classes and those studying alone, of school students up to A level, and of first-year university students, particularly beginners or near-beginners. The terminology used is to a great extent traditional, although we have made certain innovations in the interests of greater transparency and precision (as we did in the *Comprehensive Grammar* which we co-authored). For example, we talk about the simple past tense rather than the 'aorist', a term inherited from descriptions of Ancient Greek grammar, but no longer meaningful for the modern language. All linguistic terms are fully explained in the text, as well as in the glossary. We frequently contrast Greek with English, in order to aid the learner in understanding the linguistic concepts and categories involved. Attention is paid to particular points of difficulty for English-speaking learners and to the most important differences between the two languages. All the linguistic features we discuss are illustrated by appropriate examples of their use in whole phrases or sentences. We give priority to the everyday spoken language, and this is reflected in the idiomatic language of the English translations given for all examples. More formal spoken and written usages, whether of grammatical forms or of sentence structures, are also noted and signalled as such.

Preface

This grammar is intended to serve as a work of reference. It does not provide a graded course of study, for which we assume the learner will use other materials. (Some suggestions of suitable works are given at the end of the book.) What the book does offer, in comparison with most 'methods', is more detailed and systematically organized information about the linguistic features which the learner will encounter. Users can consult the grammar in order to supplement the basic information presented in course books, and thus acquire a fuller understanding of the grammatical structure of Greek and patterns of contemporary usage.

Some comparison should be made with our *Greek: A Comprehensive Grammar of the Modern Language*. The present volume is not simply a shortened version of the earlier one, omitting the less common features of the language. While it is true that we have omitted a good many morphological features that are not commonly used in the spoken language, the *Essential Grammar* is structured in a quite different way: grammatical forms and their usage are generally covered together (rather than being separated in different parts of the book). As far as possible we have avoided repetition of the same material, such as examples of usage. The presentation of grammatical phenomena in the present work takes into account the different needs of its users, and, as already mentioned, there is more explicit comparison with English. On the other hand, the two books have much in common as regards the analysis presented and the terminology used. Users of this book who wish to continue their study of Greek to a more advanced level will be able to progress to the *Comprehensive Grammar*, where they will find further and more detailed information about forms and structures which native speakers employ in spoken and written registers.

Finally, a note on pronunciation: in the sections that deal with the sounds of Greek and with stress patterns, the underlying sounds are given between slashes (/ /). These sounds may have different variants in pronunciation. The actual pronunciation is given in square brackets ([ ]), using a simplified version of the International Phonetic Alphabet (IPA). Learners who are not familiar with the IPA are advised to study the sections describing the pronunciation of individual vowels and consonants, and either to consult a native speaker or to listen to suitable cassettes, in order to acquire a sure grasp of the pronunciation of Greek, particularly of those sounds which are not found in English.

David Holton
Peter Mackridge
Irene Philippaki-Warburton
April 2003

Abbreviations and symbols

acc.	accusative (case)
adj.	adjective
def. art.	definite article
dep.	dependent (verb form)
F *or* fem.	feminine
gen.	genitive (case)
imp.	imperative (mood)
imperf.	imperfect (tense)
indef. art.	indefinite article
lit.	literally
M *or* masc.	masculine
N *or* neut.	neuter
nom.	nominative (case)
pass.	passive (voice)
pl.	plural
sg.	singular
voc.	vocative (case)
†	indicates a verb which has no passive perfective forms
/ /	around letters or groups of letters indicates underlying sounds
[ ]	around letters or groups of letters indicates actual pronunciation, using an adapted version of the International Phonetic Alphabet
ʹ	after a letter indicates that the sound is palatalized
/	indicates alternatives

Chapter 1

The alphabet and pronunciation

In this section we focus on letters, while in sections 1.2–1.8 we concentrate on sounds.

1.1 The Greek alphabet

The Greek alphabet consists of twenty-four letters. The table on page 2 presents each letter (in upper and lower case) in alphabetical order, its Greek name, and its basic pronunciation (for further details of pronunciation see sections 1.2–1.6).

Anyone who knows how to pronounce the Greek letters can pronounce any written word in the language; this is unlike English, where we often don't know how a word is pronounced unless we have heard it spoken. On the other hand, as in English, it is often impossible to tell how to spell a word that we have heard spoken.

Taken on their own, seven letters of the alphabet represent vowel sounds (α, ε, η, ι, ο, υ, ω), and seventeen represent consonant sounds (all the rest). But when some letters are combined together, they are pronounced differently. Each of the following combinations represents a single sound:

αι /e/
ει /i/
οι /i/
ου /u/
υι /i/

The combination **αυ** is pronounced [af] at the end of a word and before the following consonants: π, τ, κ, φ, θ, χ, σ, ξ, ψ, but [av] before a vowel or any other consonant (i.e. β, δ, γ, ζ, λ, ρ, μ, ν). Similarly, **ευ** is pronounced [ef]

The Greek alphabet

Form	Name	Pronunciation		Form	Name	Pronunciation	
Α α	άλφα	[álfa]	a	Ν ν	νι	[ni]	n
Β β	βήτα	[víta]	v	Ξ ξ	ξι	[ksi]	ks (x in 'wax')
Γ γ	γάμα	[γáma]	γ*, y	Ο ο	όμικρον	[ómikron]	o
Δ δ	δέλτα	[δélta]	th in 'this'	Π π	πι	[pi]	p
Ε ε	έψιλον	[épsilon]	e	Ρ ρ	ρο	[ro]	r
Ζ ζ	ζήτα	[zíta]	z	Σ σ	σίγμα	[síγma]	s
Η η	ήτα	[íta]	i	(ς at end of word)			
Θ θ	θήτα	[θíta]	th in 'thin'	Τ τ	ταυ	[taf]	t
Ι ι	γιώτα	[jóta]	i	Υ υ	ύψιλον	[ípsilon]	i
Κ κ	κάπα	[kápa]	k	Φ φ	φι	[fi]	f
Λ λ	λάμδα	[lámδa]	l	Χ χ	χι	[x'i]	x*
Μ μ	μι	[mi]	m	Ψ ψ	ψι	[psi]	ps
				Ω ω	ωμέγα	[oméγa]	o

*These two sounds do not correspond to anything in English; see section 1.4.

or [ev] in the same positions, and the rare combination ηυ is pronounced [if] or [iv].

Pairs of identical consonants are pronounced like a single consonant, except γγ, which is pronounced [(ŋ)g] or [(ŋ)g'] (see section 1.4). In addition, the following combinations of letters representing consonants are pronounced in a special way:

γκ   like γγ (see above)
μπ   [(m)b]
ντ   [(n)d]
τζ   [dz]

Finally, σ is pronounced [z] before a voiced consonant (β, γ, δ, λ, ρ, μ, ν).

Pronunciation

1.2 Vowels

The Greek sound system has five distinct vowels: /i, e, a, o, u/.

The vowel /i/ is pronounced between the English vowel in 'bit' and that in 'beat'. The Greek vowel /i/ corresponds to six different spellings: ι, η, υ, οι, ει and υι, e.g. το παιδί [to peðí] 'the child', Ελένη [eléni] 'Helen', πολύ [polí] 'very, much', οι κόποι [i kópi] 'the labours', μπορεί [borí] 'maybe', υιοθετώ [ioθetó] 'I adopt'.

The vowel /e/ is pronounced like the English vowel /e/ in 'kept' but it is pronounced slightly longer and with lips more open. The Greek /e/ corresponds to two different spellings: ε and αι, e.g. λένε [léne] 'they say', κλαίνε [kléne] 'they cry'.

The vowel /a/ is similar to the *a* in 'father'. It corresponds to the spelling α, e.g. η Μαρία [i maría] 'Mary'.

The vowel /o/ is pronounced between the English vowel in 'pot' and that in 'bought' but the lips are slightly more closed and more rounded. The vowel /o/ corresponds to two different spellings: ο and ω, e.g. το δώρο [to δóro] 'the present'.

The vowel /u/ is somewhere between the vowels in the English words 'put' and 'boot'. It corresponds to the spelling ου, e.g. του παιδιού [tu peðjú] 'of the child'.

I The alphabet and pronunciation

The vowel /i/ may lose its vowel quality and become non-syllabic if unstressed and followed by another vowel.

Non-syllabic /i/ is pronounced as [j] (like the *y* in 'yes') if it follows a voiced consonant [b, d, g, v, δ, γ, z, r, m], as in **παιδιά** [peδjá] 'children' (contrast **παιδεία** [peδía] 'education'), or as voiceless [x'] (pronounced like the *h* in 'huge') if it follows a voiceless consonant [p, t, k, f, θ, x, s], as in **ράφια** [ráfx'a] 'shelves'. This general reduction of /i/ to [j], or [x'] does not apply to words from the more formal vocabulary: compare **βιολί** [vjolí] 'violin' with **βιολόγος** [viológos] 'biologist'.

1.3 Combinations of vowels

Combinations of two or three vowels are possible, e.g. **νεαρός** [nearós] 'young man', **νεοελληνικός** [neoelinikós] 'modern Greek'. In words like **ρολόι** /rolói/ 'clock, watch', **πάει** /pái/ 'it goes' and **λέει** /léi/ '(s)he/it says', where the unstressed /i/ follows a vowel, it may be pronounced like the *y* in the English words 'toy', 'spy', 'stay', etc.

1.4 Consonants

There are twenty-five consonant sounds, which we represent by the following symbols: p, t, k, b, d, g, f, θ, x, v, δ, γ, k', x', g', j, s, z, l, l', r, m, n, ŋ, ɲ.

	Bilabial		Labiodental		Dental		Alveolar		Velar		Palatal	
	VL	VD	VL	VD	VL	VD	VL	VD	VL	VD	VL	VD
Plosive	p	b			t	d			k	g	k'	g'
Nasal		m						n		ŋ		ɲ
Flap								r				
Fricative			f	v	θ	δ			x	γ	x'	j
Sibilant							s	z				
Liquid								l				l'

VL: voiceless
VD: voiced

Consonants

[The voiceless plosives [p], [t] and [k] are pronounced like their English equivalents in 'spot', 'stay' and 'scot' respectively. However, unlike their English counterparts, these Greek consonants remain without aspiration (expulsion of breath) even in initial position before a vowel. [p] corresponds to the spelling π, e.g. ο πατέρας [opatéras] 'the father', κάπως [kápos] 'somewhat'.

The voiced bilabial plosive [b] corresponds to the spelling μπ. It is optionally preceded by a short [m] when it is within a word, e.g. κουμπάρος [ku(m)báros] 'best man'. This preceding nasal is generally absent when [b] occurs at the beginning of a word, e.g. μπότα [bóta] 'boot'.

The voiceless dental plosive [t] corresponds to the spelling τ, e.g. το ποτό [topotó] 'the drink'.

The voiced dental plosive [d] corresponds to the spelling ντ and is optionally preceded by a short nasal [n] when it occurs within a word, e.g. αντίπαλος [a(n)dípalos] 'opponent'. This preceding nasal is generally absent when [d] occurs at the beginning of a word, e.g. ντύνω [díno] 'I dress (someone)'.

The voiceless velar plosive [k] corresponds to the spelling κ, e.g. καλός [kalós] 'good', ακόμη [akómi] 'still'. [k] has a variant [k'], which is pronounced like the first consonant in the English word 'queue', before the vowels /e/ and /i/, e.g. κέφι [k'éfi] 'good mood', εκείνος [ek'ínos] 'that one'.

The voiced velar plosive [g] corresponds to the spellings γγ and γκ, and is optionally preceded by a nasal [ŋ] (pronounced like the *ng* in English 'anger'), e.g. εγκώμιο [e(ŋ)gómio] 'praise', εγγονός [e(ŋ)gonós] 'grandson'. [g] has a variant [g'], pronounced like the *g* in 'singular', when it precedes either [e] or [i], e.g. έγκυος [é(ŋ)g'ios] 'pregnant'.

The voiceless labiodental fricative [f] is pronounced like the English *f* in 'fat' and it corresponds to the spelling φ, e.g. φάρος [fáros] 'lighthouse', νέφος [néfos] 'smog'. The letter υ is also pronounced as [f] in the combination αυ or ευ when it is followed by one of the following sounds [p, t, k, f, θ, x], e.g. αυτός [aftós] 'he', ευχή [efx'í] 'wish', ευθύνη [efθíni] 'responsibility'.

The voiceless dental fricative [θ] is pronounced like the *th* in the word 'think' and it corresponds to the spelling θ, e.g. θέλω [θélo] 'I want', έθνος [éθnos] 'nation'.

The voiceless velar fricative [x] is pronounced like the *ch* in the Scottish word 'loch'. [x] corresponds to the spelling χ, e.g. χορός [xorós] 'dance', τρέχω [tréxo] 'I run'. [x] has a variant [x'] before the vowels [e] and [i], which is pronounced like the *h* in 'huge', e.g. χέρι [x'éri] 'hand', αρχή [arx'í] 'beginning'.

The voiced labiodental fricative [v] is pronounced like the *v* in 'vain' and corresponds to the spelling β, e.g. βάρκα [várka] 'boat', αβγό [avγó] 'egg'. [v] also corresponds to the υ in ευ and αυ when this combination is followed by a vowel or one of the following sounds [v, δ, γ, m, n, z, l, r], e.g. μαγειρεύω [majirévo] 'I cook', ευγνωμοσύνη [evγnomosíni] 'gratitude', παύω [pávo] 'I stop'.

The voiced dental fricative [δ] is pronounced like *th* in 'this' and corresponds to the spelling δ, e.g. δίνω [δíno] 'I give', άδεια [áδia] 'permission'.

The voiced velar fricative [γ] is pronounced like [x] except that it is voiced (i.e. with vibration of the vocal chords). [γ] corresponds to the spelling γ, e.g. γάτα [γáta] 'cat', γουρούνι [γurúni] 'pig', αγώνας [aγónas] 'struggle'. When [γ] precedes either [e] or [i], it is pronounced [j] (like the *y* in 'yes'), e.g. γείτονας [jítonas] 'neighbour', πηγαίνω [pijéno] 'I go'. [j] is also the result of the combination γ + unstressed /i/ + vowel, e.g. γιατρός [jatrós] 'doctor'.

The voiceless dental sibilant [s] is pronounced like the English *s* in 'simple' but with the front of the tongue touching the back of the teeth. It corresponds to the spellings σ and (at the end of the word) ς, e.g. σειρά [sirá] 'row, series', δάσος [δásos] 'forest'.

The voiced dental sibilant [z] is pronounced like the English *z* but with the front of the tongue touching the back of the lower teeth. It corresponds to the spelling ζ, e.g. ζώνη [zóni] 'belt', λούζω [lúzo] 'I wash hair'. The sound [z] also corresponds to the spelling σ when it is followed by one of the consonants [v, γ, m, n], e.g. σμήνος [zmínos] 'swarm', σβήνω [zvíno] 'I erase'.

The dental liquid [l] is pronounced like the English *l* in 'fellow' and it corresponds to the spelling λ, e.g. λόγος [lóγos] 'word, speech', πολλά [polá] 'many'. The combination of λ + unstressed /i/ + vowel gives the pronunciation [l'], where the middle of the top of the tongue touches the middle of the roof of the mouth, as in ελιά [el'á] 'olive, olive tree'.

The voiced alveolar flap [r] is pronounced like the Scottish [r]. The front of the tongue taps the front of the roof of the mouth once or twice. It corresponds to the spelling ρ, e.g. νερό [neró] 'water', κύριος [k'írios] 'mister'.

The bilabial nasal [m] corresponds to the spelling μ, e.g. μήλο [mílo] 'apple', θέμα [θéma] 'theme'.

The alveolar nasal [n] corresponds to the spelling ν, e.g. **νόμος** [nómos] 'law', **Άννα** [ána] 'Ann'. The variant [ɲ] (pronounced like *n* in British English 'new'), where the middle of the tongue touches the middle of the roof of the mouth, is the result of the combination ν + unstressed /i/ + vowel, e.g. **εννιά** [eɲá] 'nine'. The variant [ŋ] (pronounced like the *n* in anger), where the back of the tongue touches the back of the mouth, is found before one of the consonants /x, γ, k, g /, e.g. **αγκώνας** [a(ŋ)gónas] 'elbow', **άγχος** [áŋxos] 'anxiety'.

1.5 Combinations of consonants

Greek has a rich system of consonant clusters (consisting of up to three consonants) at the beginning of a word and an even richer one (up to four consonants) in the middle of a word.

The pronunciation of combinations of consonants is straightforward. It normally corresponds to the spelling, except that the double consonants that appear in the spelling are pronounced as single consonant sounds: **γράμμα** [γráma] 'letter', **αλλά** [alá] 'but'. The only exception is the combination γγ, which is pronounced as [(ŋ)g]: **φεγγάρι** [fe(ŋ)gári] 'moon'. Most of the English consonant combinations also occur in Greek. Below we list those two-consonant combinations of Greek which do not occur at the beginning of a word in English.

ps	**ψάρι** [psári]	fish
ts	**τσέπη** [tsépi]	pocket
ks	**ξένος** [ksénos]	foreigner
dz	**τζάκι** [dzáki]	fireplace
pn	**πνεύμα** [pnévma]	spirit
kn	**κνησμός** [knizmós]	itching
tm	**τμήμα** [tmíma]	section
kt	**κτήνος** [ktínos]	beast
pt	**πτήση** [ptísi]	flight
mn	**μνήμη** [mními]	memory
θl	**θλίψη** [θlípsi]	sadness
δr	**δρόμος** [δrómos]	road
xl	**χλομός** [xlomós]	pale
xr	**χρόνος** [xrónos]	time, year
vl	**βλάκας** [vlákas]	stupid
vr	**βράδυ** [vráδi]	evening
γr	**γράμμα** [γráma]	letter

Combinations of consonants

1 The alphabet and pronunciation

γλ	γλυκός [γlikós]	sweet
ft	φτωχός [ftoxós]	poor
sθ	σθένος [sθénos]	strength
sx	σχολείο [sxolío]	school
vδ	βδομάδα [vδomáδa]	week
vγ	βγάζω [vγázo]	I take out
γδ	γδύνω [γδíno]	I undress (someone)
fθ	φθάνω [fθáno]	I arrive
ft	φτερό [fteró]	wing
xθ	χθεσινός [xθesinós]	yesterday's
γn	γνώμη [γnómi]	opinion
xn	χνάρι [xnári]	trace
zm	σμήνος [zmínos]	swarm
zv	σβήνω [zvíno]	I erase
zγ	σγουρός [zγurós]	curly

Note that the **σ** in the spellings **σμ, σβ, σγ** of the last three examples above is pronounced [z].

There are combinations of three consonants, most of which also occur in English. We give below the three-consonant combinations which are not found at the beginning of a word in English.

skl	σκληρός [sklirós]	hard
skn	σκνίπα [sknípa]	gnat, midge
sfr	σφραγίζω [sfrajízo]	I stamp

An interesting characteristic of Greek is that many words may be found with two different consonant clusters, differing in both spelling and pronunciation, as in the following examples:

οχτώ [oxtó]	**οκτώ** [októ]	eight
χτες [xtes]	**χθες** [xθes]	yesterday
εφτά [eftá]	**επτά** [eptá]	seven
φτάνω [ftáno]	**φθάνω** [fθáno]	I arrive
άσκημος [ásk'imos]	**άσχημος** [ásx'imos]	ugly
θα πειστώ [θapistó]	**θα πεισθώ** [θapisθó]	I will be persuaded

The difference between the forms of the above two columns is stylistic: the forms in the first column are normally used in colloquial speech, while those in the second are normally used in formal writing.

1.6 Phonological phenomena across word boundaries

Some adaptations of pronunciation occur between words which form a single phrase, namely: between an article and the following word; between a weak pronoun and the following verb; between the negative particles **δεν** and **μην** and the following verb; or between a preposition and the item governed by that preposition.

The final /n/ of the definite articles **τον** and **την** or of the weak pronouns **τον** and **την** or of the negative particles **δεν** and **μην**, when followed by a word beginning with a /p/, is either pronounced [m] or is not pronounced at all. At the same time the initial /p/ of the following word is pronounced [b]: **τον πατέρα** /ton patéra/ → [to(m)batéra] 'the father' (acc. sg.), **τον πήραμε** /ton pírame/ → [to(m)bírame] 'we took him', **μην πάτε** /min páte/ → [mi(m)báte] 'don't go'.

The initial consonant /t/ of a word following a final /n/ is pronounced [d], while the nasal sound /n/ may be deleted: **τον τρελό** /ton treló/ → [to(n)dreló] 'the madman' (acc. sg.), **την τίμησαν** /tin tímisan/ → [ti(n)dímisan] 'they honoured her', **δεν τολμώ** /den tolmó/ → [δe(n)dolmó] 'I don't dare'.

The initial consonant /k/ of a word following a final /n/ is pronounced [g] while the /n/ reduces to [ŋ] or may be omitted: **τον κάλεσαν** /ton kálesan/ → [to(ŋ)gálesan] 'they invited him', **δεν ξέρω** /den kséro/ → [δe(ŋ)gzéro] 'I don't know'. (Note that when /k/ becomes [g] the following /s/ becomes voiced [z], as in the last example.)

The final /s/ of an article, a weak pronoun or the particle **ας** 'let' is pronounced [z] if the word that immediately follows has a voiced initial consonant: **της δώσανε** /tis δósane/ → [tizδósane] 'they gave her', **ας γελάσω** /as jeláso/ → [azjeláso] 'let me laugh'.

The final /n/ of the feminine article and weak pronoun **την** is normally deleted in both speech and writing when immediately followed by a word with initial /f, θ, x, v, δ, γ, j, s, z, l, r, m, n /: **τη(ν) λέξη** /tin léksi/ → [tiléksi] 'the word', **τη(ν) σεβάστηκαν** /tin sevástikan/ → [tisevástikan] 'they respected her', **τη(ν) φιλοξένησα** /tin filoksénisa/ → [tifiloksénisa] 'I gave her hospitality'. The final -ν of the negative particle **μην** behaves in the same way: **μη με λυπάσαι** 'don't pity me', **μη βλέπεις** 'don't look', **μη θυμώνεις** 'don't get angry'.

When a weak pronoun or particle ends in a vowel and the following verb begins with the same vowel, the first vowel may be omitted: **θα αγοράσω** [θααγοράso] or **θ' αγοράσω** [θαγοráso]. When the vowels are different, one of the two vowels, irrespective of their relative position, may be deleted. /i/ and /e/ may be deleted if they are next to an /o/, /u/ or /a/: **το είπα** [toípa] or **το 'πα** [tópa] 'I said it', **το έδωσα** [toédosa] or **το 'δωσα** [tódosa] 'I gave it', **τα είδα** [taída] or **τα 'δα** [táda] 'I saw them', **σου έδωσα** [suédosa] or **σου 'δωσα** [súdosa] 'I gave you', **θα έχω** [θaécho] or **θα 'χω** [θáchο] 'I shall have'. /o/ and /u/ may be deleted if they are next to an /a/: **μου απάντησε** [muapá(n)dise] or **μ' απάντησε** [mapá(n)dise], '(s)he replied to me'.

The final /o/ or /a/ of the neuter definite article may be deleted before a word beginning with /a/: **το αγόρι** [toaγóri] or **τ' αγόρι** [taγóri] 'the boy', **τα αγόρια** [taaγórja] or **τ' αγόρια** [taγórja] 'the boys'.

The final vowel of the prepositions **σε** /se/ 'in, at' (obligatorily) and **από** /apó/ 'from' (optionally) is deleted before a following definite article: **σε + το Λονδίνο → στο Λονδίνο** [stolondíno] 'in London', **από + την Αθήνα → απ' την Αθήνα** [aptinaθína] 'from Athens'.

The final /e/ of a two-syllable singular perfective imperative may be deleted if followed by a neuter weak pronoun or a noun with a definite article: **φέρε το** /fére to/ → **φέρ' το** [férto] 'bring it', **φέρε το βιβλίο** /fére to vivlío/ → **φέρ' το βιβλίο** [fértovivlío] 'bring the book', **κόψε τα** /kópse ta/ → **κόψ' τα** [kópsta] 'cut them'.

Stress and intonation

1.7 Word stress

Every Greek word of two or more syllables has stress on one of its vowels. The vowel that carries the stress is pronounced at a higher pitch and is slightly longer and louder; compare the English word 'polish', where the stress falls on the first vowel, with 'police', where the stress falls on the second.

The stress of a word may occur either on the last syllable, the last but one syllable, or the third syllable from the end: **αγαπητός** [aγapitós] 'likeable', **ταχυδρόμος** [taxiðrómos] 'postman', **άγριος** [áγrios] 'wild'. Among the words that inflect, only the adjectives retain the stress on the same syllable in all their inflected forms (see sections 3.33–3.38 and 3.40).

In some classes of nouns the stress may move one or two syllables to the right, e.g. **μάθημα** [máθima] 'lesson', gen. sg. **μαθήματος** [maθímatos], gen.

pl. **μαθημάτων** [maθimáton]; **δάσκαλος** [δáskalos] 'teacher', gen. sg. **δασκάλου** [δaskálu], gen. pl. **δασκάλων** [δaskálon]; **θάλασσα** [θálasa] 'sea', gen. pl. **θαλασσών** [θalasón] (see sections 3.29–3.9).

In some verbs the stress may move to the left in past tenses: **σπουδάζω** [spuδázo] 'I am studying', imperfect **σπούδαζα** [spúδaza] 'I was studying'. When the inflectional ending creates three unstressed syllables at the end of the verb form the original stress moves one syllable to the right: **δέχομαι** [δéxome] 'I accept', **δεχόμαστε** [δexómaste] 'we accept' (see Chapter 6).

1.8 Enclisis

Enclisis of stress (the development of a second stress) applies within a phrase which consists of one or more weak pronouns and the preceding word which these pronouns are associated with. Such combinations are: verbs followed by weak object pronouns; nouns or adjectives followed by possessive pronouns; and adverbs followed by weak pronouns. In these combinations, where the basic stress falls more than three syllables from the end an additional stress is added to the second vowel to the right of the original stress, e.g.

κάλεσε + τον /kálese ton/ → **κάλεσέ τον** [káleséton] 'invite him'
πάρε + του + το /páre tu to/ → **πάρε τού το** [páretúto] 'take it from him'
δίνοντας + σου + τα /δínontas su ta/ → **δίνοντάς σου τα** [δíno(n)δásuta] 'giving them to you'
ο δάσκαλος + μας /o δáskalos mas/ → **ο δάσκαλός μας** [o δáskalózmas] 'our teacher'
απέναντι + σας /apénanti sas/ → **απέναντί σας** [apéna(n)dísas] 'opposite you'

1.9 Intonation

The intonation associated with statements is similar to that of English. There are, however, differences in the intonation of questions.

The main intonation contours are as follows:

- In yes/no questions the pitch of the voice rises and then slightly falls to a mid level at the end of the utterance:

I The alphabet and pronunciation

          1   2   3 2
1   Θα τον δεις τον Νίκο αύριο;
    Will you see Nick tomorrow?

- An abrupt rise and fall conveys surprise:

    2   3 2
2   Ήρθε κι ο Γιάννης;
    So John came too?

- To show surprise and ask for more information the pitch rises and remains high at the end of an utterance:

        3   3   4
3   Θα δεις αύριο τον Νίκο!;
    What! You are going to see Nick tomorrow!?

- To express doubt the pitch falls at the end of an utterance and then immediately rises:

    1   2   2   1   2
4   Ίσως να πάρει εκείνο το δάνειο.
    (S)he may get that loan.

- A stable falling intonation at the end of the utterance indicates conclusion:

         1   1   2   1
5   Και ζήσανε αυτοί καλά κι εμείς καλύτερα.
    And they lived happily ever after (lit. 'And they lived well and we even better').

The intonation peak (the word pronounced with the highest pitch) of a sentence normally falls on the last stressed word in the verb phrase because this word represents informationally the most important item:

6   Η Άννα θα φέρει μαζί της *τον Νίκο*.
    Ann will be bringing *Nick* with her.

7   Η Άννα θα φύγει *απόψε*.
    Ann will be leaving *tonight*.

The words **τον Νίκο** and **απόψε** are the most significant elements of these utterances in terms of information and carry the main stress of the utterance.

It is possible to place emphasis on one of the elements in a sentence when you want to express surprise or to convey contrast (see section 10.20). The emphasized element often occurs at the beginning of the utterance, though it may occur in other places too. It is always associated with rising pitch followed by a fall.

Intonation

8a *Τον Νίκο θα φέρει μαζί της η Άννα.*
    Nick is the person Anna will be bringing with her (not somebody else).

b   *Η Άννα θα φέρει μαζί της τον Νίκο.*
    Anna will be bringing *Nick* (not somebody else).

Chapter 2

The writing system

2.1 Accents (the monotonic system)

The rules given here apply to the monotonic (single-accent) system taught in Greek schools since 1982. For details of the older polytonic system, which is still used by many writers, see *Comprehensive Grammar*, pp. 34–37.

An acute accent is placed over the stressed vowel in any word of more than one syllable, e.g. χώρος [xóros] 'space, place', χορός [xorós] 'dance'. The accent is placed before an initial capital letter representing a stressed vowel ('Όμηρος [ómiros] 'Homer'), but no accent is written when the word is written entirely in capitals. When a stressed vowel sound is written as two letters, the accent is placed over the second letter: τοίχος [tíxos] 'wall'. Similarly, in the combinations αυ and ευ (when pronounced [af], [av], [ef] or [ev]), the accent is placed on the second letter, e.g. παύω [pávo] 'I stop'. However, when two letters are pronounced as separate vowels, the accent is placed on the first one if that is the stressed vowel, e.g. γάιδαρος [γájδaros] 'donkey'. When a word is stressed on two syllables as a result of enclisis (see Section 1.8), the accent is written over each of the stressed vowels: ο εξάδελφός μου [oeksáδelfózmu] 'my cousin'.

In general, the accent is not written on words of one syllable. It is however retained on words that have become monosyllabic as a result of vowel deletion, e.g. φέρ' το (short for φέρε το) 'bring it'. In addition, the accent is written on three single-syllable words to distinguish them from other words that are otherwise written the same:

- the conjunction ή 'or', to distinguish it from the feminine nominative singular form of the article η
- the question words πού 'where' and πώς 'how', to distinguish them from the relative and complementizer που and the complementizer πως

It is recommended that the accent be written on the weak personal pronoun when it functions as the object of a following verb, in cases where otherwise it might be read as a possessive modifying a preceding noun: thus

1a **Η μητέρα μού είπε**
The mother told me (μού is the indirect object of the verb είπε)

b **Η μητέρα μου είπε**
My mother said (μου is a possessive pronoun modifying the noun μητέρα)

Finally, the accent is also used after Greek capital letters denoting ordinal numerals, e.g. **Γεώργιος Β'** 'George II' (see section 5.1).

2.2 Other diacritics

Apart from the accent, two other diacritics are used, the diaeresis and the apostrophe.

The diaeresis is written on the second of two adjacent vowels to indicate that they are pronounced separately, e.g. **γαϊδάρου** [γajδáru] 'donkey' (gen. sg.). The diaeresis is not used when the first of the two vowels is stressed, e.g. **γάιδαρος** [γájδaros] 'donkey' (nom. sg.). Where a diaeresis appears on a stressed vowel, the diaeresis and accent are written thus: **καΐκι** [kaík'i] 'caique', where the **α** and the following **ι** are pronounced separately.

The apostrophe indicates that a vowel has been deleted, e.g. **θα 'ρθω** 'I'll come', **θ' ανέβω** 'I'll come up'. When the apostrophe is used, the two words are separated by a space, as shown in the above examples.

2.3 The use of capital and lower-case letters

As in English, a capital letter is used at the beginning of a sentence and at the beginning of names of people, places, the days of week, the months, and religious festivals. Although usage varies, words derived from such nouns are usually written with a lower-case initial letter:

1a ένας Έλληνας
a Greek

b η ελληνική μουσική
Greek music

Titles before proper names usually begin with a lower-case letter:

2   η κυρία Μητσάκη
Mrs Mitsaki

Usage varies in titles of books, etc., some writers preferring to use an initial capital only for the first word, others for every word:

3a «Το τρίτο στεφάνι»
b «Το Τρίτο Στεφάνι»
The Third Wedding

2.4 Punctuation

Greek generally follows the same rules as English regarding punctuation. We first list the chief punctuation marks, then we confine ourselves to the main differences between Greek and English usage.

The chief punctuation marks are:

- full stop (UK) or period (USA) (τελεία): .
- comma (κόμμα): ,
- raised point (άνω τελεία): ·
- colon (διπλή τελεία/άνω και κάτω τελεία): :
- question mark (ερωτηματικό): ;
- exclamation mark (θαυμαστικό): !
- parentheses or brackets (παρενθέσεις): ( )

The full stop is used chiefly

- to indicate the end of a sentence
- to indicate an abbreviation: π.χ. 'e.g.', π.Χ. 'B.C.'
- to indicate clock times: **11.40**
- to divide large numbers into groups of three figures; thus Greek **1.234.567** corresponds to British and US 1,234,567.

The comma is used to separate clauses or phrases within a sentence. It is also used to separate an integer from a decimal where English uses the full stop (decimal point); thus Greek **34,45** corresponds to British and American 34.45. In addition, the comma is written in the pronoun and determiner **ό,τι** (without a space after the comma) to distinguish it from the complementizer **ότι**.

The raised point corresponds to the English semicolon, i.e. to a break less significant than one indicated by a full stop but more significant than one indicated by a comma.

The colon is used especially to introduce a list of items and to introduce direct speech.

The question mark looks the same as the English semicolon, with which the foreign learner must be careful not to confuse it. It is used at the end of a sentence expressing a direct question.

The exclamation mark is used at the end of a sentence expressing an exclamation or consisting of a vocative noun phrase, or a command or prohibition, e.g. **Γιάννη! Έλα δω!** 'John! Come here!'

Parentheses are used to isolate a word or phrase that is interpolated into a phrase, clause or sentence.

In addition, the hyphen (**ενωτικό**) is used to join words together (**μια επίσκεψη-αστραπή** 'a lightning visit'), while the dash (**παύλα**) is used, sometimes with a space either side, to separate phrases, e.g.:

1   Ο Γιάννης θα έρθει – ελπίζω! – αύριο.
    John will come – I hope! – tomorrow.

In practice, however, many writers confuse the two. The dash is also used to introduce the speech of each character in a dialogue (see below).

There are two different conventions for indicating direct speech. According to the first, each character's speech is introduced by a dash, with no indication of the boundary between the speech and the narrative. Alternatively, the speech can be contained within quote marks (**εισαγωγικά**).

2a – Δυστυχώς, της είπα, ήρθες αργά.
 b «Δυστυχώς» της είπα «ήρθες αργά».
    'Unfortunately,' I told her, 'you've come too late.'

Quote marks are also used for titles and for quoting any piece of language word for word:

3   οι «Τάιμς»
    the *Times*

4   ο λεγόμενος «τρίτος δρόμος»
    the so-called 'third way'

Finally, suspension points (**αποσιωπητικά**) are often used to indicate either an incomplete sentence or thought, or to lead up to a word or phrase that is intended to come as a surprise to the reader:

5   Θα 'ταν ωραία να . . .
    It would be nice to . . .

6   Αχ! να μπορούσες να έρθεις . . .
    Oh, if only you could come . . .

7   Ξαφνικά, ενώ καθόμουν στη θέση μου, μπήκε . . .
    ο πρωθυπουργός!
    Suddenly, as I was sitting in my seat, in came the prime minister!

2.5 The transcription of foreign names

This is a topic about which there is considerable disagreement. Some older foreign names have been naturalized in Greek in forms that inflect according to the Greek system, e.g. **ο Δαρβίνος** '[Charles] Darwin', **η Οξφόρδη** 'Oxford'. Other names are transcribed according to their pronunciation, or as close to the original pronunciation as it is possible to get with the Greek alphabet, e.g. **ο Μπους** 'Bush' (pronounced like northern English 'bus'), **το Λος Άντζελες** [tolosádzeles] 'Los Angeles'. In the past, attempts were often made to achieve a compromise between the pronunciation and the spelling of the word in the original language, e.g. **ο Πήτερ** 'Peter', **το Καίμπριτζ** 'Cambridge'. In recent years some linguists have recommended that all foreign names should be spelt as simply as possible in Greek, ignoring the foreign spelling and recommending transcriptions such as **Πίτερ** and **Κέμπριτζ**, but these modern versions are still controversial. On the other hand, it is very common for foreign names that do not have an established transcription in Greek to be written in the Roman alphabet.

Chapter 3

The noun and the noun phrase

3.1 Constituents of the noun phrase

A noun is a word that names a person, thing or concept (e.g. 'John', 'woman', 'plate', 'hope'). A noun phrase is normally a phrase whose chief constituent is a noun. It may consist of a noun alone (e.g. 'John'), or it may consist of a noun accompanied by various modifiers (article, adjective, etc., e.g. 'a busy woman', 'some new plates', 'false hopes'). Sometimes a noun phrase consists of an adjective or pronoun (e.g. 'me', 'someone') rather than a noun. In Greek, a noun phrase may also consist of a phrase or clause preceded by the definite article **το**.

Here are some examples of noun phrases in Greek (for the sake of simplicity, these examples are all in the nominative case, but bear in mind that within a noun phrase, all other declinable words must agree with the noun in gender, number and case (see section 3.48)):

1 ο Γιάννης (def. art. + noun (masc. sg.))
   John

2 ένα άσπρο σπίτι (indef. art. + adj. + noun (neut. sg.))
   a white house

3 δύο άσπρα σπίτια (numeral + adj. + noun (neut. pl.))
   two white houses

4 αυτό το σπίτι (demonstrative + def. art. + noun (neut. sg.))
   this house

5 αυτό το άσπρο σπίτι (demonstrative + def. art. + adj. + noun)
   this white house

6 όλα αυτά τα άσπρα σπίτια (quantifier + demonstrative + def. art. + adj. + noun)
   all these white houses

3 The noun and the noun phrase

7   ποιο άσπρο σπίτι; (interrogative + adj. + noun)
    which white house?

8   το σπίτι μου (def. art. + noun + possessive pronoun)
    my house

9   ένας νέος (indef. art. + adj.)
    a young [man]

10 εγώ (emphatic pronoun)
    I, me (subject)

11 το ότι έχασαν τις εκλογές (def. art. + clause)
    the [fact] that they lost the elections

A noun phrase may include another noun phrase in the genitive (12), or a prepositional phrase (13), or a clause (14–15):

12 το σπίτι *του Γιάννη*
    John's house (lit. 'the house *of-the John*')

13 το σπίτι *στη γωνία*
    the corner house (lit. 'the house *at-the corner*')

14 το σπίτι *που αγόρασα* (relative clause)
    the house *(which) I bought*

15 το γεγονός *ότι ο πρωθυπουργός μίλησε* (complement clause)
    the fact *that the prime minister spoke*

3.2 Functions of the noun phrase

The chief functions of the noun phrase are

- to act as the subject of a verb (in the nominative: 1);
- to act as the direct object of a verb (in the accusative: 2);
- to act as the indirect object of a verb (in the genitive: 2);
- to act as a subject predicate (3);
- to act as an object predicate (4);
- to be the object of a preposition (5);
- to address someone (in the vocative: 6).

1   *Ο Στέφανος* (nom.) θα έρθει αύριο.
    Stephen will come tomorrow.

> **Functions of the noun phrase**

2 Αύριο θα του δώσουμε *του Στέφανου* (gen.) *τα ρούχα του* (acc.).
Tomorrow we'll give *Stephen* (indirect object) *his clothes* (direct object).

3 Ο Γιάννης είναι *δάσκαλος* (nom.).
John's *a teacher.*

4 Τον διόρισαν *δάσκαλο* (acc.).
They appointed him *a teacher.*

5 Η Μαρία ήρθε από *τη Θεσσαλονίκη* (acc.).
Mary came from *Thessaloniki.*

6 Στέφανε! (voc.)
Stephen!

More frequently, however, the indirect object expressed by a noun phrase is linked to the rest of the clause by the preposition **σ[ε]** (+ accusative):

7 Αύριο θα δώσουμε *στον Στέφανο* τα ρούχα του.
(same meaning as 2)

A predicate appears in the same case as the word to which it refers (nominative for a subject predicate, accusative for an object predicate).

Certain types of noun phrase in the accusative may act as an adverbial phrase of time or place (see also section 3.51):

8 τον Ιούνιο
in June

Finally, a noun phrase may depend on another noun. The dependent noun phrase may be in the genitive to indicate possession (9), or it may be in the same case as the main noun to indicate content (10–12: this last use is different from English):

9 το σπίτι *του Γιάννη*
John's house

10 ένα κιλό *πατάτες* (both noun phrases, ένα κιλό and πατάτες, are in the same case (nominative or accusative) according to their function in the clause)
a kilo *of potatoes*

11 τρία μπουκάλια *κρασί* (both noun phrases, τρία μπουκάλια and κρασί, are in the same case (nominative or accusative) according to their function in the clause)
three bottles *of wine*

3
The noun and the noun phrase

12   Τους χαρίσαμε ένα μπουκέτο *κρίνους* (the noun phrases ένα μπουκέτο and κρίνους are in the accusative because they are the direct object of the verb).
We gave them a bunch *of lilies*.

Gender, number and case

3.3   Gender

Every Greek noun belongs to one of three gender classes: masculine, feminine or neuter. These do not correspond to the division between male, female and inanimate. Nevertheless, most nouns denoting humans are masculine if the person is male, and feminine if the person is female. Thus the nouns **άντρας** 'man (male), husband' and **Γιάννης** 'John' are masculine, while **γυναίκα** 'woman, wife' and **Ελένη** 'Helen' are feminine. However, **άνθρωπος** 'person, human being' is always masculine and **παιδί** 'child' is always neuter irrespective of the sex of the person they refer to, while **κορίτσι** 'girl' and **αγόρι** 'boy' are also neuter.

Nouns denoting animals, inanimate objects, substances, natural phenomena and abstract concepts may be masculine, feminine or neuter:

- **σκύλος** 'dog' is masculine and **γάτα** 'cat' is feminine (though there is a feminine form **σκύλα** 'bitch' and a masculine form **γάτος** 'tomcat'), while two alternative forms exist for 'donkey', namely the masculine **γάιδαρος** and the neuter **γαϊδούρι**, besides the feminine **γαϊδούρα** 'female donkey'
- **μαρκαδόρος** 'marker (pen)' is masculine, **καρέκλα** 'chair' is feminine and **τραπέζι** 'table' is neuter
- **υδράργυρος** 'mercury' is masculine, **κιμωλία** 'chalk' is feminine and **ξύλο** 'wood' is neuter
- **αέρας** 'air, wind' is masculine, **βροχή** 'rain' is feminine and **χαλάζι** 'hail' is neuter
- **πόλεμος** 'war' is masculine, **ελευθερία** 'freedom' is feminine and **κέφι** 'high spirits' is neuter (in fact the majority of abstract nouns are feminine)

The gender of a noun has to be learned at the same time as the noun. This is not difficult, since a noun in the nominative singular form can almost always be readily assigned to one of the three genders: all masculine nouns end in -ς (see sections 3.9–3.13), almost all feminine nouns end in either

-α or -η (see sections 3.14–3.19), and most neuter nouns end in -ο, -ι or -μα (see sections 3.21–3.29).

Many nouns – most of them denoting people who practise certain professions – are of common gender, e.g. [ο or η] πρόεδρος '[the] president'. Although their endings follow the declension patterns of masculine nouns, they may be masculine or feminine (and are therefore accompanied by masculine or feminine articles, adjectives, etc.) according to the sex of the person denoted (see section 3.20).

Articles, adjectives and other modifiers that agree with a noun in the same noun phrase do so with the gender of the noun rather than the sex of the pronouns and person or animal denoted: thus in the sentence

1 Η (fem.) Μαρία (fem.) είναι *καλός* (masc.) *άνθρωπος* (masc.).
   Mary is *a nice person.*

the adjective **καλός** is in the masculine form to agree with the masculine noun **άνθρωπος** 'person' rather than in the feminine form, even though Mary is female. For agreement within the noun phrase see section 3.48 and for agreement of predicates see section 6.1.

When no noun is used and the sex of the person or persons referred to is unknown, or where they consist of a mixture of males and females, the pronouns and determiners appear in the masculine form:

2 *Ποιος* (masc.) είναι;
   Who is it?

3 Αν έρθει *κανένας* (masc.) *άλλος* (masc.), πες *του* (masc.) να περιμένει.
   If *anyone else* comes, tell *them* to wait.

4 *Όλοι* (masc.) σας τον ξέρετε.
   All of you know him.

In example 2 the speaker is asking for someone's identity, irrespective of whether it is a male or a female; similarly the speaker in 3 does not know the sex of the relevant person. Example 4 may be addressed to a group of males or to a mixed group of males and females.

The neuter of numerals is used when counting. Compare example 5, where the numeral is in the neuter form because it is used simply as a number, with example 6, where the numeral is in the feminine form to agree with the feminine noun **σελίδες**, which it modifies:

5   η σελίδα τρία
    page three

6   τρεις σελίδες
    three pages

3.4 Number

Number is a category that applies to noun phrases (nouns, adjectives, pronouns and determiners) and to verbs. As in English, there are two numbers, namely singular and plural. In Greek, number is always indicated in the inflection of every one of these words (except for the very few indeclinable words, mostly nouns and adjectives, for which see sections 3.31 and 3.42). As in English, dictionaries list these words in the singular unless they are only used in the plural.

Almost all nouns, pronouns and determiners have one set of case forms for the singular and another set of case forms for the plural; a few, however, only have singular or plural forms. (For the declensions of these words see sections 3.8–3.30 and 4.1–4.10.) Similarly, verbs have one set of person forms for the singular and another for the plural; the use of the singular or plural forms of the verb depends on whether the subject is singular or plural. (For number in the verb see section 6.3.)

Normally, a noun denoting a single person, thing, etc. is in the singular form, while a noun denoting more than one person, thing, etc. is in the plural:

1   ένα σπίτι (sg.)
    one house, a house

2   δυο σπίτια (pl.)
    two houses

However, in Greek, as in French, the plural of personal pronouns and verbs is used when addressing a single person politely (see section 12.1).

3.5 Case

For each of the two numbers (singular and plural) each noun, adjective, pronoun and determiner has a set of case endings which indicate the syntactical function of the noun phrase in the clause. The cases in Greek are nominative, accusative, genitive and vocative. For the use of the cases see Case in the glossary, and sections 3.50–3.53.

The articles

Like other languages, Greek has two types of article which precede nouns and certain other words: a definite article ('the') and an indefinite one ('a', 'an'). The forms of the articles are given below. For the use of the articles see sections 3.54–3.56.

3.6 The forms of the definite article

The definite article is declined for gender, number and case and has the following forms:

	Singular			Plural		
	M	F	N	M	F	N
Nominative	o	η	το	οι	οι	τα
Accusative	τον	τη(ν)	το	τους	τις	τα
Genitive	του	της	του	των	των	των

The feminine accusative singular form must have the final -ν when the word immediately following begins with a vowel or with any of the following consonants or consonant clusters: κ, π, τ, γκ, μπ, ντ, ξ, ψ. Examples:

1   *την άνοιξη*
    (in) the spring

2   *την κυρία Αλεξίου*
    Mrs Alexiou (acc.)

Before other consonants the -ν may be omitted (and normally is not pronounced), e.g.

3   *τη Δευτέρα*
    on Monday

When the preposition σε ('to', 'at', 'in', 'on' etc.) is followed by a noun which has a definite article, the preposition combines with the article as one word: στον, στη(ν), στο, στους, στις, στα. For example:

4 στις όχθες
   on the banks

The article must agree in gender, number and case with the noun which it modifies. For further information about the use (and omission) of the definite article see sections 3.54 and 3.56.

3.7 The forms of the indefinite article

The indefinite article has only singular forms, which are declined for gender and case:

	M	F	N
Nominative	ένας	μια	ένα
Accusative	ένα(ν)	μια(ν)	ένα
Genitive	ενός	μιας	ενός

The forms of the indefinite article are almost identical to those of the numeral 'one' (see section 5.2). The only exception is that the feminine forms of the indefinite article are pronounced as one syllable, while those of the numeral can be pronounced emphatically as a two-syllable word, with stress on the first syllable (written **μία**). Compare these two examples:

1a *μια* εβδομάδα
    a week

 b μόνο *μία* εβδομάδα
    only one week

The final -ν of the accusative forms of the masculine and feminine is not obligatory, but may be used before words beginning with a vowel or any of the consonants κ, π, τ, ξ or ψ, e.g.

2 για *μιαν* άλλη γυναίκα
   for another woman

3 σ' *έναν* κύριο
   to a gentleman

The indefinite article agrees with its noun for gender and case. In phrases which link two or more nouns, the appropriate form must precede each noun in the series:

4   *ένα μαχαίρι, ένα πιρούνι* και *μια χαρτοπετσέτα*
    a knife, a fork and a paper napkin

For further information about the use (and omission) of the indefinite article see sections 3.55–3.56.

Nouns

3.8 Declensions: an overview

A noun is a word denoting a person, place, thing, abstract quality, action or condition (e.g. in English, 'woman', 'Helen', 'Greece', 'ship', 'beauty', 'peace'). Every Greek noun belongs to one of the three genders (masculine, feminine and neuter) and to a particular declension, by which we mean the pattern of different endings which mark them for number (singular and plural) and case (nominative, accusative, genitive, vocative). For gender, number and case see sections 3.3–3.5. The detailed declension patterns are set out in sections 3.9–3.29. Some nouns, particularly ones of foreign origin, are indeclinable, which means that they have a single form which does not change for number or case (see section 3.31).

In the tables that follow, nouns are classified primarily by gender, and secondarily by the ending of the nominative singular. In many instances, the ending of the nominative singular is sufficient to indicate the relevant declension. For example, all nouns with a nominative singular ending in **-o** are neuter and follow the pattern in section 3.21. But things are not always so straightforward. Nouns ending in **-ος** may be masculine (section 3.11), feminine (section 3.16) or neuter (section 3.24), with resulting differences in the way they form their other cases in the singular and plural.

We can set out some basic rules for the declension of nouns:

- Masculine nouns always end in a vowel + **-ς** in the nominative singular. In the accusative they drop the **-ς**. The genitive singular is the same as the accusative, with the exception of nouns in **-ος**, which have genitive in **-ου**.
- Feminine nouns, except for one type, have the same forms for nominative and accusative singular, which end in a vowel. For the

Masculine

Singular	Nom.	-ας	-ης	-ος	-ας	-ις	-ες-	-ους
	Acc.	-α	-η	-ο	-α	-ι	-ε	-ου
	Gen.	-α	-η	-ου	-α	-ι	-ε	-ου
	Voc.	-α	-η	-ε	-α	-ι	-ε	-ου
Plural	Nom./Voc.	-ες	-ες	-οι	-άδες	-ηδες	-έδες	-ούδες
	Acc.	-ες	-ες	-ους	-άδες	-ηδες	-έδες	-ούδες
	Gen.	-ών	-ών	-ων	-άδων	-ηδων	-έδων	-ούδων

Feminine

Singular	Nom.	-α	-α	-η	-η	-ος	-ά	-ώ
	Acc.	-α	-α	-η	-η	-ο	-ά	-ώ
	Gen.	-ας	-ας	-ης	-ης/-ιας	-ου	-άς	-ούς
Plural	Nom.	-ες	-ες	-ες	-εις	-οι	-άδες	-ούδες
	Acc.	-ες	-ες	-ες	-εις	-ους	-άδες	-ούδες
	Gen.	-ών	-ών	-ών	-εων	-ων	-άδων	-ούδων

Neuter

Singular	Nom./Acc.	-ο	-ι	-ι	-ος	-μα	-μι	-ο
	Gen.	-ου	-ιού	-ιού	-ους	-ματος	-ιμάτος	-ο
Plural	Nom./Acc.	-α	-ιά	-α	-η	-ματα	-ίματα	-ος
	Gen.	-ων	-ιών	-ιών	-ών	-μάτων	-ιμάτων (-ιμάτων)	—

genitive singular they add -ς. The nominative and accusative plural also have the same forms, ending in -ς. The exception is nouns in -ος, which follow the same pattern as masculine nouns in -ος.

- Nouns of common gender may be either masculine or feminine, depending on the sex of the person they refer to. They follow the pattern of the corresponding masculine nouns ending in -ας, -ης, -ος or -έας (see section 3.20).
- Neuter nouns have a single form for the nominative and accusative singular, and a single one for the nominative and accusative plural. The plural typically ends in -α, with the exception of nouns in -ος.
- The genitive plural of nouns of all declensions ends in -ων.

Masculine nouns

The situation is made more complicated by the position of stress, which may move, and by other peculiarities in the endings of certain declensions. However, the table on the pevious page shows, in summary form, the endings of the most common types of noun.

The vocative is not shown separately for feminine or neuter nouns, as it is the same as the corresponding nominative. (The only exception is feminine nouns in -ος, which do not normally have a vocative.)

Masculine nouns

3.9 Nouns in -*ας* (parisyllabic)

We need to make a distinction between parisyllabic nouns, which have the same number of syllables in the plural as in the singular (e.g. singular πατέρας 'father', plural πατέρες 'fathers'), and imparisyllabic nouns, which add an extra syllable in forming their plural (e.g. παπάς 'priest', plural παπάδες 'priests' – see section 3.13 for such imparisyllabic masculine nouns). Parisyllabic masculine nouns in -ας are divided into two types, according to the stress of the genitive plural: (a) those that have a genitive plural with stress on the penultimate syllable; (b) those that undergo a shift of stress to the final syllable in the genitive plural. With these exceptions, the stress remains on the same syllable as in the nominative singular.

3 The noun and the noun phrase

(a)

ο γείτονας neighbour

	Singular	Plural
Nom.	γείτονας	γείτονες
Acc./Voc.	γείτονα	γείτονες
Gen.	γείτονα	γειτόνων

Note that **γείτονας** and other nouns stressed on the third syllable from the end undergo a shift of stress in the genitive plural. Nouns stressed on the penultimate syllable, such as **αγκώνας**, have no shift of stress. Examples: **αγκώνας** 'elbow', **αγώνας** 'struggle', **αιώνας** 'century', **αναπτήρας** 'lighter', **Έλληνας** 'Greek (man)', **ήρωας** 'hero', **κανόνας** 'rule', **καύσωνας** 'heatwave', **κηδεμόνας** 'guardian', **κόρακας** 'raven', **λάρυγγας** 'throat, larynx', **μάρτυρας** 'witness', **πατέρας** 'father', **πίνακας** 'picture, board', **πράκτορας** 'agent', **πρίγκιπας** 'prince', **πρόσφυγας** 'refugee', **στρατώνας** 'barracks', **συνδετήρας** 'paper-clip', **σωλήνας** 'tube', **φύλακας** 'guard', **χειμώνας** 'winter'.

(b)

ο τουρίστας tourist

	Singular	Plural
Nom.	τουρίστας	τουρίστες
Acc./Voc.	τουρίστα	τουρίστες
Gen.	τουρίστα	τουριστών

Examples: **άντρας** (or **άνδρας**) 'man, husband', **αριβίστας** 'upstart', **βήχας** 'cough', **βλάκας** 'fool', **καρχαρίας** 'shark', **λοχίας** 'sergeant', **μήνας** 'month', and all other masculine nouns in -**ίας** and -**ίστας**.

For certain nouns, alternative forms of the genitive singular ending in -**ος** are occasionally found in formal contexts: **μηνός** (instead of **μήνα**) is often used in dates, e.g. **στις δεκαεπτά του μηνός** 'on the seventeenth of the month'.

3.10 Nouns in -ης (parisyllabic)

These nouns (apart from two exceptions given at the end of this section) always have stressed -ών in the genitive plural. Consequently those nouns that are stressed on the penultimate syllable move the stress to the final syllable in the genitive plural. (For imparisyllabic nouns in -ης, i.e. those that add an extra syllable in the plural, see section 3.13.)

ο εργάτης workman

	Singular	Plural
Nom.	εργάτης	εργάτες
Acc./Voc.	εργάτη	εργάτες
Gen.	εργάτη	εργατών

Many nouns that follow this declension end in -της. Examples include: **αναγνώστης** 'reader', **γλύπτης** 'sculptor', **διευθυντής** 'director', **εθελοντής** 'volunteer', **επιβάτης** 'passenger', **καθηγητής** 'professor, secondary-school teacher', **καθρέφτης** 'mirror', **κλέφτης** 'thief', **μαθητής** 'schoolboy, (male) pupil', **ναύτης** 'sailor', **νικητής** 'winner', **πελάτης** 'customer, client', **ποιητής** 'poet', **προδότης** 'traitor', **στρατιώτης** 'soldier', **ράφτης** 'tailor', **φοιτητής** 'student', **φράχτης** 'fence', **ψεύτης** 'liar'. Other nouns that follow this pattern (with shift of stress in the genitive plural) include **βιβλιοπώλης** 'bookseller' and **πατριάρχης** 'patriarch'.

Two other nouns, which form their plural irregularly, should be mentioned: **πρύτανης** 'vice-chancellor, rector (of a university)' and **πρέσβης** 'ambassador'. In the singular they follow the same pattern as **εργάτης**, but the plural is quite different: nominative/accusative/vocative **πρυτάνεις**, genitive **πρυτάνεων**. The plural of **πρέσβης** has these same endings, with the stress remaining on the first syllable: **πρέσβεις, πρέσβεων**.

3.11 Nouns in -ος

Nouns in this category may be stressed in the nominative singular on any of the last three syllables: **οδηγός** 'driver', **κινηματογράφος** 'cinema', **άνθρωπος** 'man, human being'. In nouns of the first two kinds, the stress remains on the same syllable throughout the declension:

3 The noun and the noun phrase

ο οδηγός driver

	Singular	Plural
Nominative	οδηγός	οδηγοί
Accusative	οδηγό	οδηγούς
Genitive	οδηγού	οδηγών
Vocative	οδηγέ	οδηγοί

This is a very large category and includes: **αδελφός/αδερφός** 'brother', **βαθμός** 'degree, mark', **γάμος** 'wedding, marriage', **γιος** 'son', **δρόμος** 'road', **εχθρός** 'enemy', **καιρός** 'time, weather', **κλάδος** 'branch (of study)', **κόσμος** 'world', **νόμος** 'law', **μαραγκός** 'carpenter', **όρος** 'term', **ουρανός** 'sky, heaven', **ποταμός** 'river', **σεισμός** 'earthquake', **σκοπός** 'purpose, tune', **σκύλος** 'dog', **τοίχος** 'wall', **τόπος** 'place', **ύπνος** 'sleep', **φίλος** 'friend', **φόβος** 'fear', **χώρος** 'space, area', **ώμος** 'shoulder'.

The third kind, nouns stressed on the third syllable from the end, presents two different patterns. In type (a) the stress moves to the penultimate syllable in the genitive singular and in the accusative and genitive plural; in type (b) the stress remains on the same syllable throughout the declension:

(a)

ο άνθρωπος man, human being

	Singular	Plural
Nominative	άνθρωπος	άνθρωποι
Accusative	άνθρωπο	ανθρώπους
Genitive	ανθρώπου	ανθρώπων
Vocative	άνθρωπε	άνθρωποι

(b)

ο καλόγερος monk

	Singular	Plural
Nominative	καλόγερος	καλόγεροι
Accusative	καλόγερο	καλόγερους
Genitive	καλόγερου	καλόγερων
Vocative	καλόγερε	καλόγεροι

Nouns in -ος

Type (a) includes many nouns which survive from Ancient Greek and other nouns which are likely to occur in more formal contexts. Examples: **άνεμος** 'wind', **αντιπρόσωπος** 'representative', **δάσκαλος** 'teacher', **διάδρομος** 'corridor', **δήμαρχος** 'mayor', **έλεγχος** 'check, control', **έμπορος** 'merchant', **θάνατος** 'death', **θόρυβος** 'noise', **Ιανουάριος** 'January' (and other names of months), **κάτοικος** 'inhabitant', **κίνδυνος** 'danger', **κύριος** 'gentleman, Mr', **όροφος** 'storey', **πλοίαρχος** 'ship's captain', **πόλεμος** 'war', **πρόλογος** 'prologue', **σιδηρόδρομος** 'railway'. Type (b) includes more recent formations, especially compounds. Examples: **ανεμόμυλος** 'windmill', **ανήφορος** 'ascent', **αντίλαλος** 'echo', **κατήφορος** 'descent', **λαχανόκηπος** 'vegetable garden', **παλιάνθρωπος** 'rogue', **παλιόκαιρος** 'foul weather', **πονόδοντος** 'toothache', **πονοκέφαλος** 'headache', **ψεύταρος** 'big liar', and also some personal names, such as **Θόδωρος**, **Στέφανος**, **Χαράλαμπος**. However, the distinction between the two types is not completely fixed: forms without shift of stress like **του σιδηρόδρομου**, or with shift of stress like **του πονοκεφάλου** are also found.

Special mention must be made of the vocative of given names. Instead of the normal -ε ending, masculine names in -ος stressed on the penultimate syllable usually have a vocative in -ο: **Αλέκο, Μάρκο, Νίκο, Πέτρο, Παύλο, Τάσο**; contrast **Αλέξανδρε, Φίλιππε, Στέφανε**, etc. A few other nouns of two syllables also have a vocative singular in -ο, e.g. **γέρο** 'old man', as do diminutives in **-άκος**: **φιλαράκο** 'little friend'.

Note also that the noun **χρόνος** 'year' has an alternative genitive plural **χρονώ(ν)** used for expressions of age (see section 5.5, examples 9 and 10). On the plural forms of this noun see further section 3.30.

Feminine nouns in -ος are considered in section 3.16; for nouns with the same ending which may be either masculine or feminine (common gender) see section 3.20.

3.12 Nouns in -έας

Nouns of this type are declined like those in -ας (section 3.9) in the singular, but have nominative, accusative and vocative plural in -είς, and genitive in -έων:

ο κουρέας barber

	Singular	Plural
Nom.	κουρέας	κουρείς
Acc./Voc.	κουρέα	κουρείς
Gen.	κουρέα	κουρέων

Examples: **αμφορέας** 'amphora, urn', **γονέας** 'father' (also sometimes γονιός, declined like nouns in section 3.11; the plural **γονείς** 'parents' is more common), **ιερέας** 'priest', **σκαπανέας** 'sapper', **τομέας** 'section, sector'.

Many nouns of this declension referring to persons are of common gender; for examples see section 3.20.

3.13 Imparisyllabic nouns in -άς, -ας, -ής, -ης, -ές, -ούς

The term 'imparisyllabic' refers to the fact that these nouns have an extra syllable in their plural forms, which always end in -δες (nominative, accusative and vocative) or -δων (genitive). In the singular they drop the -ς of the nominative in the other cases, but keep the same vowel (-α, -η, -ε or -ου). The nominative singular of such nouns may be stressed on any of the last three syllables: **γαλατάς** 'milkman', **μανάβης** 'greengrocer', **φούρναρης** 'baker'. We consider these three types below, noting certain exceptions in the formation of the plural:

(a)

ο γαλατάς milkman

	Singular	Plural
Nom.	γαλατάς	γαλατάδες
Acc./Voc.	γαλατά	γαλατάδες
Gen.	γαλατά	γαλατάδων

Imparisyllabic nouns

Examples:

- Singular in -άς, plural -άδες: **αρακάς** 'pea', **βοριάς** 'north wind', **βραχνάς** 'nightmare', **καβγάς** 'quarrel', **καλοφαγάς** 'gourmet', **κουβάς** 'bucket', **μπελάς** 'trouble', **μυλωνάς** 'miller', **παπάς** 'priest', **παράς** 'money', **σουγιάς** 'penknife', **σφουγγαράς** 'sponge fisher', **φονιάς** 'murderer', **χαλβάς** 'halva', **ψαράς** 'fisherman', **ψωμάς** 'baker', and proper names such as **Λουκάς** and **Σαμαράς**
- Singular in -ής, plural -ήδες: **ατζαμής** 'bungler', **καταφερτζής** 'smooth operator, wangler', **καφετζής** 'coffee-house keeper', **μερακλής** 'connoisseur', **μπεκρής** 'drunkard', **μπογιατζής** 'decorator', **παλιατζής** 'second-hand dealer', **παπουτσής** 'shoemaker', **ταξιτζής** 'taxi driver', and proper names such as **Κωστής**, **Ραγκαβής**, **Χατζής**
- Singular in -ές, plural -έδες: **γλεντζές** 'fun-lover', **καναπές** 'sofa', **καφές** 'coffee', **κεφτές** 'meatball', **λεκές** 'spot, stain', **μεζές** 'hors d'oeuvre, titbit', **μενεξές** 'violet', **μιναρές** 'minaret', **πανσές** 'pansy', **πουρές** 'puré, mash', **τενεκές** 'tin', **χαφιές** 'informer'
- Singular in -ούς, plural -ούδες: **παππούς** 'grandfather', mash

(b)

ο μανάβης greengrocer

	Singular	Plural
Nom.	μανάβης	μανάβηδες
Acc./Voc.	μανάβη	μανάβηδες
Gen.	μανάβη	μανάβηδων

Examples:

- Singular in -ης, plural -ηδες: **βαρκάρης** 'boatman', **καβαλάρης** 'horseman', **λεβέντης** 'brave young man', **μπακάλης** 'grocer', **νοικοκύρης** 'landlord, householder', **παππούλης** 'granddad', **τιμονιέρης** 'helmsman', **χασάπης** 'butcher', and proper names such as **Βασίλης, Μανόλης, Παυλάκης, Τρικούπης**. These nouns are always stressed on the third syllable from the end in the plural, e.g. **χασάπηδες** 'butchers'.
- Singular in -ας, plural -άδες: **μπάρμπας** 'uncle, old man'. Note that the stress moves one syllable forward in the plural.

Note also nouns in -άκιας which have a plural in -άκηδες: **γυαλάκιας** 'bespectacled person, four-eyes", **κορτάκιας** 'womanizer, flirt', **τσαντάκιας** 'bag snatcher', **τυχεράκιας** 'lucky devil'.

(c)

ο φούρναρης baker		
	Singular	Plural
Nom.	φούρναρης	φουρνάρηδες
Acc./Voc.	φούρναρη	φουρνάρηδες
Gen.	φούρναρη	φουρνάρηδων

Examples:

- Singular -ης, plural -ηδες (with stress on the third syllable from the end): **γούναρης** 'furrier'.
- Singular -ας, plural -άδες (with stress on the penultimate syllable): **τσέλιγκας** 'chief shepherd'.

Feminine nouns

3.14 Nouns in -α (parisyllabic)

The distinction between parisyllabic (same number of syllables in singular and plural forms) and imparisyllabic (an additional syllable in the plural) which was made for masculine nouns in -ας (sections 3.9 and 3.13) is valid here too. (For imparisyllabic nouns in -ά see section 3.18.) Similarly, we must also divide the parisyllabic feminine nouns in -α into two types according to the stress of the genitive plural. Type (a) nouns have the stress on the penultimate syllable in the genitive plural. Type (b) move the stress to the final syllable in the genitive plural (if they are not stressed on the final syllable throughout their declension).

Feminine nouns

(a)

η ελπίδα hope		
	Singular	Plural
Nom./Acc./Voc.	ελπίδα	ελπίδες
Gen.	ελπίδας	ελπίδων

Examples:

- With stress on the same syllable throughout: **ακτίνα** 'ray of light, radius', **εβδομάδα** 'week', **εικόνα** 'picture, image', **εφημερίδα** 'newspaper', **μητέρα** 'mother', **ομάδα** 'group, team', **πατρίδα** 'fatherland', **σελίδα** 'page', **σταγόνα** 'drop', **σταφίδα** 'raisin', and many other nouns in -άδα or -ίδα.
- With movement of stress to the penultimate syllable in the genitive plural: **κλίμακα** 'scale', **σάλπιγγα** 'trumpet', **σήραγγα** 'tunnel', **δυνατότητα** 'possibility', **ικανότητα** 'ability', **ταυτότητα** 'identity, identity card', **ταχύτητα** 'speed, gear' and all other nouns in -ότητα or -ύτητα.

Some nouns have an alternative genitive singular in -ος, which is sometimes used in formal contexts, e.g. **Ελλάδος** 'Greece' (instead of **Ελλάδας**).

(b)

η θάλασσα sea		
	Singular	Plural
Nom./Acc./Voc.	θάλασσα	θάλασσες
Gen.	θάλασσας	θαλασσών

Examples: **άγκυρα** 'anchor', **αίθουσα** 'hall', **άμυνα** 'defence', **αξία** 'value', **απεργία** 'strike', **απόπειρα** 'attempt', **βελόνα** 'needle', **γέφυρα** 'bridge', **γλώσσα** 'tongue, language', **γραβάτα** 'necktie', **γυναίκα** 'woman, wife', **δουλειά** 'work', **έρευνα** 'research', **ιδέα** 'idea', **καρδιά** 'heart', **κεραία** 'antenna, aerial', **κυρία** 'lady, Mrs', **μάζα** 'mass, lump', **μέλισσα** 'bee', **(η)μέρα** 'day' (genitive plural always **ημερών** – other forms with **η-** are regarded as more formal), **μοίρα** 'fate, degree (of a circle)', **μοτοσικλέτα** 'motor-cycle', **ντομάτα** 'tomato', **νύχτα** (or **νύκτα**) 'night', **οικογένεια** 'family', **ορχήστρα** 'orchestra', **πλατεία** 'square', **ρίζα** 'root', **σημαία** 'flag', **ταινία** 'film, tape', **τράπεζα** 'bank', **τρύπα** 'hole', **χώρα** 'country', **ώρα** 'hour'. Similarly all feminine nouns with the suffixes **-τρια** (e.g. **μαθήτρια** 'schoolgirl, (female) pupil') or **-ισσα** (e.g. **βασίλισσα** 'queen'), and abstract nouns in **-εια, -ιά,** or **-οια** (e.g. **έννοια** 'meaning'). Also the plural place names **Βρυξέλλες** 'Brussels', **Ινδίες** 'India, Indies', **Σεϋχέλλες** 'Seychelles', all of which have genitive stressed on the final syllable (e.g. **Βρυξελλών**). The place name **Αθήνα** 'Athens' can have the formal genitive plural **Αθηνών** in official names, e.g. **Πανεπιστήμιο Αθηνών** 'University of Athens'.

3.15 Nouns in -η with plural -ες

Nouns in this category, like those in **-α** in section 3.14 (b), have an obligatory shift of stress to the final syllable in the genitive plural (if they are not stressed on the last syllable throughout). They must be distinguished from other feminine nouns in **-η** which form their plural in a different way (see section 3.17).

η τέχνη art, skill		
	Singular	Plural
Nom./Acc./Voc.	τέχνη	τέχνες
Gen.	τέχνης	τεχνών

Examples: **αγάπη** 'love', **αλλαγή** 'change', **αρχή** 'beginning, principle', **βιβλιοθήκη** 'library', **βρύση** 'tap, spring (of water)', **γιορτή** 'celebration, feast, name day', **γνώμη** 'opinion', **δαπάνη** 'expense', **διακοπή** 'interruption' (plural 'holidays'), **δίκη** 'trial, lawsuit', **επιστήμη** 'science', **κόρη** 'daughter', **λάσπη** 'mud', **μηχανή** 'machine', **μύτη** 'nose', **νίκη** 'victory', **τιμή** 'price, honour', **τύχη** 'luck', **φωνή** 'voice', **ψυχή** 'soul'. Similarly the plural place names **Θερμοπύλες** 'Thermopylae', **Σπέτσες** 'Spetses'.

Some nouns exceptionally form their genitive plural in **-άδων** (similar to the imparisyllabic nouns in section 3.18): **αδελφή/αδερφή** 'sister', **(ε)ξαδέλφη/(ε)ξαδέρφη** '(female) cousin', **νύφη** 'bride, daughter-in-law, sister-in-law'.

3.16 Nouns in *-ος*

Feminine nouns in this category have exactly the same endings as masculine nouns in **-ος** (section 3.11), but are of course accompanied by the feminine forms of the articles. Nouns stressed on the third syllable from the end move the stress to the penultimate syllable in the genitive singular and the accusative and genitive plural. These feminine nouns do not normally have a vocative.

η μέθοδος method

	Singular	Plural
Nominative	μέθοδος	μέθοδοι
Accusative	μέθοδο	μεθόδους
Genitive	μεθόδου	μεθόδων

Examples: **άβυσσος** 'abyss', **άμμος** 'sand', **άνοδος** 'ascent', **Βίβλος** 'Bible', **διάλεκτος** 'dialect', **διάμετρος** 'diameter', **είσοδος** 'entrance', **έξοδος** 'exit', **επέτειος** 'anniversary', **ήπειρος** 'continent', **θαλαμηγός** 'yacht', **κάθοδος** 'descent', **καπνοδόχος** 'chimney', **λεωφόρος** 'avenue', **νήσος** 'island', **οδός** 'street', **παράγραφος** 'paragraph', **πάροδος** 'side street', **περίμετρος** 'perimeter', **περίοδος** 'period', **πρόοδος** 'progress', **σορός** 'coffin, corpse', **χερσόνησος** 'peninsula'. There are also many names of towns, regions, countries and islands which follow this declension in the singular (they have no plural): e.g. **Αίγυπτος** 'Egypt', **Άνδρος**, **Βηρυτός** 'Beirut', **Επίδαυρος**, **Ήπειρος**, **Κόρινθος** 'Corinth', **Κύπρος** 'Cyprus', **Νάξος**, **Οδησσός** 'Odessa', **Πελοπόννησος** 'Peloponnese', **Χίος** and, in fact, almost all names of islands ending in **-ος**.

3.17 Nouns in -η with plural -εις

Nouns in this category generally follow the declension of other feminine nouns in -η in the singular (see section 3.15), but the plural forms are quite different. The stress of two-syllable words remains on the same syllable throughout the declension (e.g. γνώση 'knowledge', plural γνώσεις). The stress of words of more than two syllables moves one syllable forward in the plural forms. In the genitive singular, these nouns also have an alternative form which can be used in more formal contexts, with the same movement of stress as in the plural.

η κυβέρνηση government	Singular	Plural
Nom./Acc./Voc.	κυβέρνηση	κυβερνήσεις
Gen.	κυβέρνησης or κυβερνήσεως	κυβερνήσεων

Examples: δύναμη 'force, strength', πίστη 'faith', πόλη 'city', and almost all nouns ending in -ση, -ξη or -ψη: e.g. αίτηση 'application', απόφαση 'decision', άποψη 'view, opinion', γέννηση 'birth', γνώση 'knowledge', δήλωση 'declaration', διασκέδαση 'enjoyment', εκμετάλλευση 'exploitation', έκφραση 'expression', ένωση 'union', θέση 'position, place', κατάσταση 'condition, situation', κίνηση 'movement', μετάφραση 'translation', όρεξη 'appetite', παράδοση 'tradition', παράσταση 'performance', ποίηση 'poetry', σκέψη 'thought', στάση 'stop', σχέση 'relation(ship)', τηλεόραση 'television', υπόθεση 'hypothesis, affair', ψύξη 'freezing'. Similarly the place names Ακρόπολη 'Acropolis', Κωνσταντινούπολη 'Constantinople, Istanbul', Νεάπολη 'Naples', and the plurals Άνδεις 'Andes', Άλπεις 'Alps'.

3.18 Imparisyllabic nouns in -ά and -ού

These feminine nouns add an extra syllable in their plural, just like the masculine imparisyllabic nouns discussed in section 3.13. Their plural always ends in -δες (nominative, accusative and vocative) or -δων (genitive), and this ending is added directly to the nominative singular, which always ends in a stressed vowel, either -ά or -ού. Like other feminine nouns, they have a genitive singular in -ς.

η γιαγιά grandmother		
	Singular	Plural
Nom./Acc./Voc.	γιαγιά	γιαγιάδες
Gen.	γιαγιάς	γιαγιάδων

Examples: **κυρά** 'missus, madam', **μαμά** 'mummy', **νονά** 'godmother', **νταντά** 'nursemaid'.

η αλεπού fox		
	Singular	Plural
Nom./Acc./Voc.	αλεπού	αλεπούδες
Gen.	αλεπούς	αλεπούδων

Examples: **γλωσσού** 'gossiping woman', **μαϊμού** 'monkey', **παραμυθού** 'story-teller', **πολυλογού** 'chatterbox', **υπναρού** 'sleepy-head', and many other words referring to females and often corresponding to a masculine noun in -άς or -ής, e.g. **φωνακλού** 'loud-mouthed woman', compare **φωνακλάς** 'loud-mouthed man'.

3.19 Nouns in -ω

Feminine nouns ending in -ω include many personal (given) names, often diminutives; they do not usually have a plural. There are two types, which differ in the formation of their genitive. The stress remains on the same syllable as in the nominative.

η Φρόσω Froso (diminutive of Ευφροσύνη)	
Nom./Acc./Voc.	Φρόσω
Gen.	Φρόσως

Examples: **Αργυρώ, Αργώ** 'the Argo' (but there is an alternative genitive **Αργούς**), **Δέσπω, Ηρώ, Καλυψώ, Μάρω** and most diminutives in -ω from female given names.

η ηχώ echo (no plural)

Nom./Acc./Voc.   ηχώ
Gen.   ηχούς

Examples: **πειθώ** 'persuasion', **φειδώ** 'thrift', and the proper names **Ιεριχώ** 'Jericho', **Λητώ** 'Leto' (with an alternative genitive **Λητώς**).

Nouns of common gender

3.20 Nouns which may be either masculine or feminine

Many nouns referring to persons, particularly nouns that denote occupations, are of common gender. In other words, the same forms of the noun are used for both male and female persons, but the article and any other words which modify it (such as adjectives) indicate whether the noun denotes a male or female person or persons in the specific context. For example:

1a ένας καλός ηθοποιός
   a good actor

b μια καλή ηθοποιός
   a good actress

Nouns of common gender follow the declension patterns of masculine nouns, but with masculine or feminine article etc. as appropriate. Some examples:

- Like masculine nouns in -ας (section 3.9): **ο/η επαγγελματίας** 'professional man/woman', **ο/η επιστήμονας** 'scientist, scholar', **ο/η μάρτυρας** 'witness', **ο/η ταμίας** 'cashier'
- Like masculine nouns in -ης (section 3.10): **ο/η βουλευτής** 'member of parliament', **ο/η δικαστής** 'judge', **ο/η καλλιτέχνης** 'artist', **ο/η ληστής** 'robber', **ο/η πολίτης** 'citizen'

- Like masculine nouns in -ος (section 3.11): **ο/η γιατρός** 'doctor', **ο/η δημοσιογράφος** 'journalist', **ο/η δικηγόρος** 'lawyer', **ο/η ζωγράφος** 'painter', **ο/η μαθηματικός** 'mathematician', **ο/η μουσικός** 'musician', **ο/η οικονομολόγος** 'economist', **ο/η πρόεδρος** 'president', **ο/η σύζυγος** 'spouse', **ο/η υπάλληλος** 'employee', **ο/η υπουργός** 'government minister', **ο/η φωτογράφος** 'photographer', **ο/η ψυχολόγος** 'psychologist'
- Like masculine nouns in -έας (section 3.12): **ο/η γραμματέας** 'secretary', **ο/η διερμηνέας** 'interpreter', **ο/η εισαγγελέας** 'public prosecutor', **ο/η συγγραφέας** 'writer, author'. When referring to females, the genitive singular of these nouns has the ending -έως, e.g. **της γραμματέως**

Nouns which may be either masculine or feminine

However, many masculine nouns referring to people form a corresponding feminine noun by adding a suffix or different ending, e.g. **ο καθηγητής** 'male professor', **η καθηγήτρια** 'female professor', **ο δάσκαλος** 'male teacher', **η δασκάλα** 'female teacher', but the list of those that use the same form as the masculine for female referents, as in the above examples, is growing as a result of women entering more professions (for the formation of feminine nouns from masculine ones see section 11.1).

There is one other type of noun of common gender, with singular in -ής and plural in -είς. Strictly speaking, these are adjectives used as nouns (corresponding to the adjectives in section 3.39), but their singular endings are identical with those of the masculine nouns in section 3.10 (except for the alternative genitive form).

ο/η συγγενής male/female relative		
	Singular	Plural
Nom.	συγγενής	συγγενείς
Acc./Voc.	συγγενή	συγγενείς
Gen.	συγγενή or συγγενούς	συγγενών

Other examples: **ασθενής** 'sick person, patient', **ευγενής** 'nobleman or noblewoman'. In these two cases the genitive singular form in -ούς is the more common one (while for **συγγενής** it is the form in -ή).

3 The noun and the noun phrase

Neuter nouns

3.21 Nouns in -*o*

Nouns in this category may have stress on any of the last three syllables. As in the case of masculine nouns in -ος (section 3.11), we must distinguish two types for nouns of more than two syllables stressed on the third syllable from the end, according to whether the stress moves in the genitive singular and plural. In nouns of type (a) the stress moves to the penultimate syllable in the genitive, whereas in type (b) it remains on the third syllable from the end throughout.

(a)

το θέατρο theatre		
	Singular	Plural
Nom./Acc./Voc.	θέατρο	θέατρα
Gen.	θεάτρου	θεάτρων

Examples: **άλογο** 'horse', **αυτοκίνητο** 'car', **άτομο** 'person, individual', **διαβατήριο** 'passport', **δωμάτιο** 'room', **εισιτήριο** 'ticket', **έξοδο** 'expense' (usually in the plural), **έπιπλο** 'piece of furniture', **εστιατόριο** 'restaurant', **ημερολόγιο** 'calendar, diary', **κείμενο** 'text', **κίνητρο** 'motive', **κτήριο** 'building', **μέτωπο** 'forehead, front', **όργανο** 'instrument', **πανεπιστήμιο** 'university', **πρόσωπο** 'face, person', **τηλέφωνο** 'telephone', and place names such as **Μέτσοβο** and those which have plural forms only, e.g. **Ιωάννινα** (normally **Γιάννινα** or **Γιάννενα**, but genitive plural always **Ιωαννίνων**), **Καλάβρυτα**, **Τρίκαλα**, **Φάρσαλα**. Other nouns which have only plural forms include: **γενέθλια** 'birthday', **δίδακτρα** 'tuition fees', **εντόσθια** 'entrails', **περίχωρα** 'environs', **συγχαρητήρια** 'congratulations', **Χριστούγεννα** 'Christmas'.

(b)

το αντρόγυνο married couple		
	Singular	Plural
Nom./Acc./Voc.	αντρόγυνο	αντρόγυνα
Gen.	αντρόγυνου	αντρόγυνων

Examples (with stress remaining on the same syllable): **απομεσήμερο** 'afternoon', **δάχτυλο** 'finger', **κάρβουνο** 'coal', **κάστανο** 'chestnut', **κόκκαλο** 'bone', **κόσκινο** 'sieve', **λάχανο** 'lettuce', **μάγουλο** 'cheek', **μανάβικο** 'greengrocer's shop', **ξέφωτο** 'clearing (in forest)', **πόμολο** 'door knob', **ροδάκινο** 'peach', **σίδερο** 'iron', **σύννεφο** 'cloud', **τραπεζομάντιλο** 'tablecloth', **τριαντάφυλλο** 'rose', **χαμόγελο** 'smile', **χασάπικο** 'butcher's shop', **χιονόνερο** 'sleet', and all nouns ending in **-άδικο, -άρικο,** or **-όπουλο,** as well as many compounds.

The division between nouns of three or more syllables that have fixed stress and those that move the stress has some flexibility: in formal contexts some type (b) nouns may shift the stress to the penultimate syllable in the genitive singular and plural. Nouns that can have both types include: **αμύγδαλο** 'almond', **ατμόπλοιο** 'steamship', **βούτυρο** 'butter', **γόνατο** 'knee', **ποδήλατο** 'bicycle', **πρόβατο** 'sheep', **σωσίβιο** 'life-jacket, lifebelt'.

In nouns stressed on the last or penultimate syllable, the stress remains on the same syllable throughout: **αεροπλάνο** 'aeroplane', **βιβλίο** 'book', **βουνό** 'mountain', **δέντρο** 'tree', **θρανίο** 'desk', **μπάνιο** 'bath', **νερό** 'water', **ξύλο** 'wood', **πλοίο** 'ship', **ποσό** 'amount', **φτερό** 'feather', **χωριό** 'village'.

3.22 Nouns in -*ί*

Neuter nouns in stressed **-ί** have the same endings in the genitive singular and in the plural cases as the nouns in **-ο**. They keep the stress on the final syllable throughout. In all forms except the nominative, accusative and vocative singular the **-ι-** loses its syllabic value (see section 1.2).

το παιδί child	Singular	Plural
Nom./Acc./Voc.	παιδί	παιδιά
Gen.	παιδιού	παιδιών

Examples: **αρνί** 'lamb', **αφτί** 'ear', **ζουμί** 'juice', **κλειδί** 'key', **κρασί** 'wine', **μαγαζί** 'shop', **μαλλί** 'wool' (plural 'hair'), **νησί** 'island', **πουλί** 'bird', **φιλί** 'kiss', **χαρτί** 'paper', **ψωμί** 'bread', and all other nouns in **-ί** stressed on the final syllable, except for words of foreign origin such as **ταξί** 'taxi', which are normally indeclinable (see section 3.31). The noun **πρωί** 'morning' has genitive singular **πρωινού**, nominative and accusative plural **πρωινά**, genitive plural **πρωινών**. Note that the plural place names **Χανιά** 'Chania' and **Σφακιά** 'Sfakia' are stressed on the penultimate syllable in the genitive: **Χανίων, Σφακίων**.

3.23 Nouns in -ι

These nouns are always stressed on the penultimate syllable (with one exception, for which see below). In the genitive singular and plural they move the stress to the final syllable, with the -ι- losing its syllabic value (compare the nouns in section 3.22).

το αγόρι boy

	Singular	Plural
Nom./Acc./ Voc.	αγόρι	αγόρια
Gen.	αγοριού	αγοριών

Examples: **αλάτι** 'salt', **δόντι** 'tooth', **κορίτσι** 'girl', **κρεβάτι** 'bed', **λουλούδι** 'flower', **μολύβι** 'pencil', **παντελόνι** 'trousers', **παπούτσι** 'shoe', **πόδι** 'foot, leg', **σπίτι** 'house', **τραπέζι** 'table', **χέρι** 'hand', and all other neuter nouns in -ι. There is one noun which is stressed on the third syllable from the end: **φίλντισι** 'ivory', genitive **φιλντισιού** (no plural). Diminutives in -άκι and -ούλι, e.g. **παιδάκι** 'little boy', have no genitive forms, either singular or plural.

A few nouns end in -υ (instead of -ι). They are: **βράδυ** 'evening' (but genitive singular **βραδιού**, nominative and accusative plural **βράδια**, genitive plural **βραδιών**), **δίχτυ** 'net', **στάχυ** 'ear of corn'. An exception is **δάκρυ** 'tear', spelt with **υ** in all its forms: singular **δάκρυ** (the genitive is not normally used), nominative and accusative plural **δάκρυα**, genitive **δακρύων**. For other neuter nouns in -υ see section 3.28.

Neuter nouns in -άι or -όι add a **γ** before the endings in all forms other than the nominative and accusative singular, e.g. **τσάι** 'tea', genitive **τσαγιού**. Similarly **κομπολόι** 'worry beads', **ρολόι** 'clock, watch', **σόι** 'family, lineage'.

3.24 Nouns in -ος

Neuter nouns in -ος may be of either two syllables (like **κράτος** 'state') or three syllables (like **έδαφος** 'ground, territory'). They are all stressed on the first syllable in the nominative and accusative singular and move the stress to the final syllable in the genitive plural. Three-syllable words move the stress to the penultimate syllable in the genitive singular and the nominative and accusative plural (the vocative case is rarely used).

το κράτος state	Singular	Plural
Nom./Acc.	κράτος	κράτη
Gen.	κράτους	κρατών

Examples: **βάρος** 'weight', **γένος** 'gender', **δάσος** 'forest', **έθνος** 'nation', **κέρδος** 'profit', **κόστος** 'cost' (no plural forms), **λάθος** 'mistake', **λίπος** 'fat', **μέλος** 'member', **μέρος** 'place, part', **μήκος** 'length', **μίσος** 'hatred', **όρος** 'mountain', **τέλος** 'end', **ύφος** 'style, manner', **χρέος** 'duty, debt'.

το έδαφος ground, territory	Singular	Plural
Nom./Acc.	έδαφος	εδάφη
Gen.	εδάφους	εδαφών

Examples: **μέγεθος** 'size', **πέλαγος** 'sea'.

3.25 Nouns in -μα

These nouns may be of two syllables, like **κύμα** 'wave' (stressed on the first syllable), or of three or more syllables, like **αποτέλεσμα** 'result' (stressed on the third syllable from the end). The endings of the genitive singular and all plural cases involve an additional syllable, which has implications for the position of the stress. The genitive singular and the nominative and accusative plural of these nouns are always stressed on the third syllable from the end; the genitive plural always has the stress on the penultumate syllable. The vocative is the same as the nominative but is rarely found.

το αποτέλεσμα result

	Singular	Plural
Nom./Acc.	αποτέλεσμα	αποτελέσματα
Gen.	αποτελέσματος	αποτελεσμάτων

Examples: **άγαλμα** 'statue', **αίμα** 'blood', **γράμμα** 'letter', **διάβασμα** 'reading', **διάλειμμα** 'interval', **διάστημα** 'space', **δράμα** 'drama', **κλίμα** 'climate', **μάθημα** 'lesson', **μυθιστόρημα** 'novel', **ξημέρωμα** 'daybreak', **όνομα** 'name', **ποίημα** 'poem', **πράγμα** 'thing', **πρόβλημα** 'problem', **σύστημα** 'system', **σχεδίασμα** 'sketch', **σώμα** 'body', **χρώμα** 'colour', and all other nouns ending in -μα (with two exceptions: **κρέμα** 'cream' and **λάμα** 'blade', which are feminine). Some nouns occur only in the plural, e.g. **γεράματα** 'old age', **τρεχάματα** 'running around', **χαιρετίσματα** 'greetings'.

3.26 Nouns in -ιμο

These nouns are all derived from verbs and denote an action. Their nominative singular ends in **-σιμο**, **-ξιμο**, or **-ψιμο**, with the stress on the third syllable from the end. In the genitive singular and all cases in the plural they have endings like those of nouns in **-μα** (section 3.25), with the same pattern of stress. The genitive plural of these nouns is rarely used.

το πλύσιμο (act of) washing

	Singular	Plural
Nom./Acc.	πλύσιμο	πλυσίματα
Gen.	πλυσίματος	(πλυσιμάτων)

Examples: **γράψιμο** 'writing', **δέσιμο** 'tying', **κόψιμο** 'cutting', **ντύσιμο** 'dressing, dress', **σπάσιμο** 'breaking', **τρέξιμο** 'running', **φέρσιμο** 'behaviour', **φταίξιμο** 'fault, blame'.

3.27 Other neuter nouns in -ς

A few neuter nouns end in -ς, but are distinguished from nouns in -ος (section 3.24) by the different vowel of the last syllable, or by the position of the stress in the nominative singular. The endings of the other cases (-τος etc.) are similar to those of neuter nouns in -μα (section 3.25), but without the syllable -μα-. The position of stress varies. In the first example, the stress of the genitive singular and the nominative and accusative plural is on the third syllable from the end; in the genitive plural it moves to the penultimate syllable (compare neuter nouns in -μα).

το κρέας meat

	Singular	Plural
Nom./Acc.	κρέας	κρέατα
Gen.	κρέατος	κρεάτων

Examples: **πέρας** 'end, conclusion' and **τέρας** 'monster'. These are the only other nouns which follow this pattern.

Other neuter nouns in -ς have the same endings added to the last vowel (ω or ο). They keep the stress on the same syllable as in the nominative singular. First we give **φως**, which is irregular in that the stress of its genitive singular is on the last syllable.

το φως light

	Singular	Plural
Nom./Acc.	φως	φώτα
Gen.	φωτός	φώτων

Examples (with no shift of stress): **γεγονός** 'event, fact', **καθεστώς** 'régime, status quo'. The following have no plural forms: **αεριόφως** 'gaslight', **ημίφως** 'half-light, twilight', **λυκόφως** 'dusk'.

3.28 Other neuter nouns ending in vowels

A few other neuter nouns present certain irregularities. First, there are two nouns which have a genitive singular in -τος:

το γάλα milk

	Singular	Plural
Nom./Acc.	γάλα	γάλατα
Gen.	γάλατος	(γαλάκτων)
	or γάλακτος	

The genitive plural of this noun is very rarely used. Similarly, **μέλι** 'honey', genitive **του μέλιτος** or **μελιού** (no plural).

Second, there are two neuter nouns ending in -υ which have a genitive singular in -εος, but with different stress:

το οξύ acid

	Singular	Plural
Nom./Acc.	οξύ	οξέα
Gen.	οξέος	οξέων

το ήμισυ half (no plural forms)

Nom./Acc.	ήμισυ
Gen.	ημίσεος

For other neuter nouns ending in -υ see section 3.23.

3.29 Nouns in -ν

In this category are a number of nouns which derive from participles, and two other words which have slightly different endings. First we give the nouns originally derived from the neuter forms of participles (compare the adjective declensions in section 3.41). They keep the stress on the same syllable as in the nominative singular, except for the genitive plural, which is always stressed on the penultimate syllable.

το ενδιαφέρον interest

	Singular	Plural
Nom./Acc.	ενδιαφέρον	ενδιαφέροντα
Gen.	ενδιαφέροντος	ενδιαφερόντων

Examples: **καθήκον** 'duty', **μέλλον** 'future', **ον** 'being, creature', **παρελθόν** 'past', **παρόν** 'present', **περιβάλλον** 'environment, surroundings', **προϊόν** 'product', **προσόν**, 'qualification, advantage', **συμβάν** 'event', **σύμπαν** 'universe' (no plural), **συμφέρον** 'personal interest, advantage', **φωνήεν** 'vowel'.

The noun **παν** 'everything' has a similar declension to the above, except that it is stressed on the final syllable in the genitive singular:

το παν everything

	Singular	Plural
Nom./Acc.	παν	πάντα
Gen.	παντός	πάντων

Finally in this category, the noun **μηδέν** 'zero' has the following singular forms, but no plural:

το μηδέν zero

Nom./Acc.	μηδέν
Gen.	μηδενός

Special types of noun

3.30 Nouns with a change of gender in the plural

The list below shows nouns which are masculine in the singular, but have a plural of neuter gender. Sometimes a masculine plural form also exists, but may have a different meaning:

ο **αδελφός/αδερφός** 'brother', pl. οι **αδελφοί/αδερφοί** 'brothers', τα **αδέλφια/αδέρφια** 'siblings'

ο **βάτος** 'bush', pl. οι **βάτοι** or τα **βάτα**

ο **βράχος** 'rock', pl. οι **βράχοι** or τα **βράχια**

ο **δεσμός** 'bond, relationship', pl. οι **δεσμοί** 'bonds' (metaphorical), τα **δεσμά** 'fetters, shackles' (literal)

ο **καπνός** 'smoke, tobacco', pl. οι **καπνοί** 'smoke', τα **καπνά** 'tobacco(s)'

ο **λαιμός** 'neck, throat', pl. οι **λαιμοί** 'necks', τα **λαιμά** 'sore throat'

ο **λόγος** 'speech, reason, word', pl. οι **λόγοι** 'speeches, reasons', τα **λόγια** 'words'

ο **πηλός** 'clay', pl. οι **πηλοί** or (non-formal only) τα **πηλά**

ο **πλούτος** 'wealth', pl. τα **πλούτη** 'riches'

ο **σανός** 'hay', pl. τα **σανά**

ο **σκελετός** 'skeleton, framework', pl. οι **σκελετοί** 'skeletons, spectacle frames', τα **σκελετά** 'shelves or frames for display of merchandise'

ο **σταθμός** 'station', pl. οι **σταθμοί** 'stations', τα **σταθμά** 'weights'

ο **χρόνος** 'time, year, tense (of verb)', pl. οι **χρόνοι** 'times, tenses', τα **χρόνια** 'years'

3.31 Indeclinable nouns

Indeclinable nouns have a single form, which serves for all cases, singular and plural. Like all other nouns, however, they have a gender: masculine, feminine or neuter. There is a large (and growing) number of nouns of foreign origin which have not been assimilated into the Greek declension system, including place names and proper names. Some common examples are given below. Also indeclinable are all the names of the letters of the Greek alphabet, which are neuter: **άλφα**, **βήτα**, etc.

Masculine:
μπάρμαν   barman

Feminine:
ελίτ	élite	**σαντιγί**	whipped cream
μπουτίκ	boutique	**σεζόν**	season
Ουάσιγκτον	Washington DC	**σπεσιαλιτέ**	speciality
πλαζ	beach	**τζαζ**	jazz

and names of football teams, e.g. η **Άρσεναλ** 'Arsenal'

Common gender:
ο/η μάνατζερ	manager	**ο/η ρεπόρτερ**	reporter
ο/η ντετέκτιβ	private detective	**ο/η σταρ**	star

Neuter:
ασανσέρ	lift	**καμουφλάζ**	camouflage
βολάν	steering-wheel	**κέικ**	cake
γκαράζ	garage	**κομπιούτερ**	computer
ευρώ	euro		also masculine; a plural **κομπιούτερς** is sometimes found
κονιάκ	cognac	**ρεπό**	day off
μακιγιάζ	make-up	**ρετιρέ**	penthouse
ματς	match	**σοκ**	shock
μετρό	metro	**ταμπλό**	picture, dashboard
μπαρ	bar		
μπάσκετ	basketball	**τανκς**	(military) tank
νάιλον	nylon	**ταξί**	taxi
παρμπρίζ	windscreen	**τιρμπουσόν**	corkscrew
πάρτι	party	**τρακ**	stage fright, nerves
πουλόβερ	sweater		
ραντεβού	appointment, date	**φερμουάρ**	zip

3 The noun and the noun phrase

Adjectives

3.32 Adjectives in outline

An adjective is a word which denotes a property or characteristic of a certain noun or noun phrase, e.g. 'white', 'short', 'difficult', 'jealous'. Almost all Greek adjectives inflect for gender, number and case. The endings have close similarities with those of various noun declensions. Unlike nouns, however, most adjectives keep the stress on the same syllable for all their forms (for the exceptions see sections 3.39 and 3.41). A few adjectives have a single invariable form, and examples of these are given in section 3.42. The use of adjectives is discussed in section 3.57.

Adjectives may also have special forms which are used to express comparison. Just as in English, there is a comparative ('bigger') and a superlative ('biggest') form for many adjectives. These forms are presented in sections 3.44–3.47.

The forms of adjectives

3.33 Adjectives in -ος, -η, -ο

This very numerous category comprises adjectives which have either a consonant or an unstressed vowel other than /i/ immediately before the ending -ος. Their endings correspond to those of nouns as follows: masculine like those of the nouns in section 3.11; feminine like nouns in section 3.15; neuter like nouns in section 3.21. The stress remains on the same syllable throughout.

ψηλός high, tall

	Singular			Plural		
	M	F	N	M	F	N
Nom.	ψηλός	ψηλή	ψηλό	ψηλοί	ψηλές	ψηλά
Acc.	ψηλό	ψηλή	ψηλό	ψηλούς	ψηλές	ψηλά
Gen.	ψηλού	ψηλής	ψηλού	ψηλών	ψηλών	ψηλών
Voc.	ψηλέ	ψηλή	ψηλό	ψηλοί	ψηλές	ψηλά

Examples:

- With stems ending in consonants: **αγγλικός** 'English', **ακριβός** 'expensive', **άρρωστος** 'ill', **γεμάτος** 'full', **έξυπνος** 'clever', **ζωντανός** 'living, lively', **καλός** 'good', **κίτρινος** 'yellow', **μεγάλος** 'big, great', **μόνος** 'alone, only', **ξερός** 'dry', **όμορφος** 'beautiful', **σωστός** 'correct', **τυχερός** 'lucky', **χρήσιμος** 'useful', and all passive perfect participles ending in -μένος, e.g. **ευχαριστημένος** 'pleased'
- With stems ending in unstressed vowels: **βέβαιος** 'sure', **βίαιος** 'violent', **δίκαιος** 'just, fair', **όγδοος** 'eighth', **στέρεος** 'solid'

3.34 Adjectives in -ος, -α, -ο

The only difference between this type and that in section 3.33 is in the vowel of the feminine singular forms: they have nominative, accusative and vocative in -**α** and genitive in -**ας**. This type includes adjectives which have /i/ or any stressed vowel before the ending -**ος**. Again the stress remains on the same syllable.

τέλειος perfect

	Singular			Plural		
	M	F	N	M	F	N
Nom.	τέλειος	τέλεια	τέλειο	τέλειοι	τέλειες	τέλεια
Acc.	τέλειο	τέλεια	τέλειο	τέλειους	τέλειες	τέλεια
Gen.	τέλειου	τέλειας	τέλειου	τέλειων	τέλειων	τέλειων
Voc.	τέλειε	τέλεια	τέλειο	τέλειοι	τέλειες	τέλεια

Examples: **άγριος** 'wild', **άδειος** 'empty', **αθώος** 'innocent', **αστείος** 'funny', **γενναίος** 'noble', **καινούριος** 'new', **κρύος** 'cold', **μέτριος** 'medium, moderate', **όρθιος** 'upright, standing', **παλιός** 'old', **πλούσιος** 'rich', **σπουδαίος** 'important', **τεράστιος** 'huge', **ωραίος** 'beautiful'.

There are some other adjectives which do not have stems ending in vowels but follow the above pattern, with feminine in -**α** rather than -**η**. Examples:

άκρος 'extreme', γκρίζος 'grey', μοντέρνος 'modern', σκούρος 'dark', and all adjectives ending in -λόγος, -ούργος, -ούχος or -φόρος, e.g. ακριβολόγος 'precise', πανούργος 'cunning', προνομιούχος 'privileged', καρποφόρος 'fruitful'.

3.35 Adjectives in *-ος, -ια, -ο*

It is the form of the feminine singular that also distinguishes this type of adjective from those in the previous two sections. The endings are **-ια** (nominative, accusative and vocative) and **-ιας** (genitive).

γλυκός sweet						
	Singular			Plural		
	M	F	N	M	F	N
Nom.	γλυκός	γλυκιά	γλυκό	γλυκοί	γλυκές	γλυκά
Acc.	γλυκό	γλυκιά	γλυκό	γλυκούς	γλυκές	γλυκά
Gen.	γλυκού	γλυκιάς	γλυκού	γλυκών	γλυκών	γλυκών
Voc.	γλυκέ	γλυκιά	γλυκό	γλυκοί	γλυκές	γλυκά

There are very few adjectives that *must* follow this pattern: apart from γλυκός, the only common one is **φρέσκος** 'fresh'. However, a number of other adjectives *may* form their feminine singular with **-ια**, as an alternative to the more usual **-η**; for example: **βρώμικος** 'dirty', **δικός (μου** etc.) '(my) own', **ελαφρός** 'light', **κακός** 'bad, wicked', **ξανθός** 'fair-haired', **φτωχός** 'poor'. The position of stress in the feminine forms is the same as in the corresponding masculine forms, e.g. **βρώμικια**, but **φτωχιά**.

3.36 Adjectives in *-ύς, -ιά, -ύ*

This type is characterized by the **-υ-** vowel of the masculine and neuter singular forms. The remaining forms have a non-syllabic **-ι-** (see section 1.2) before the endings, which are the same as those of the adjectives in section 3.34. The stress is always on the final syllable. The genitive of the masculine and neuter singular is rarely used.

βαρύς heavy						
	Singular			Plural		
	M	F	N	M	F	N
Nom.	βαρύς	βαριά	βαρύ	βαριοί	βαριές	βαριά
Acc.	βαρύ	βαριά	βαρύ	βαριούς	βαριές	βαριά
Gen.	(βαριού/ βαρύ)	βαριάς	(βαριού/ βαρύ)	βαριών	βαριών	βαριών
Voc.	βαρύ	βαριά	βαρύ	βαριοί	βαριές	βαριά

Examples: **βαθύς** 'deep', **δασύς** 'thick, dense', **ελαφρύς** 'light' (an alternative form of ελαφρός, -ή, -ό), **μακρύς** 'long', **παχύς** 'fat', **πλατύς** 'broad', **τραχύς** 'rough', **φαρδύς** 'wide'.

3.37 Adjectives in -ής, -ιά, -ί

This type is very similar to the previous one. The only difference is in the spelling of the endings: the masculine singular forms have -ή- (instead of -ύ-) and the neuter singular forms have -ί (instead of -ύ). Again the genitive singular of the masculine and neuter is rare (see table on p. 58). This category consists mostly of adjectives denoting colour or material.

Examples: **βυσσινής** 'cherry-coloured', **θαλασσής** 'sea-blue', **μαβής** 'dark blue', **μενεξεδής** 'violet', **ουρανής** 'sky-blue', **πορτοκαλής** 'orange', **σταχτής** 'ashen, grey', **χρυσαφής** 'golden'. Also **δεξής** 'right', an alternative form to δεξιός, -ά, -ό.

3.38 The adjective (quantifier) πολύς

The adjective (or quantifier) **πολύς** 'much, many' needs special attention. The endings of the nominative and accusative masculine and neuter singular are basically the same as those of the adjectives in section 3.36. The endings of the remaining forms are identical to those of adjectives in -ος, -η, -ο (section 3.33), but it is important to note that the stem of these forms ends in double λ. The genitive singular forms of the masculine and neuter are rarely used, and there is no vocative (see p. 58).

καφετής brown

	Singular			Plural		
	M	F	N	M	F	N
Nom.	καφετής	καφετιά	καφετί	καφετιοί	καφετιές	καφετιά
Acc.	καφετή	καφετιά	καφετί	καφετιούς	καφετιές	καφετιά
Gen.	(καφετιού/ καφετή)	καφετιάς	(καφετιού/ καφετί)	καφετιών	καφετιών	καφετιών
Voc.	καφετή	καφετιά	καφετί	καφετιοί	καφετιές	καφετιά

πολύς much, many

	Singular			Plural		
	M	F	N	M	F	N
Nom.	πολύς	πολλή	πολύ	πολλοί	πολλές	πολλά
Acc.	πολύ(ν)	πολλή	πολύ	πολλούς	πολλές	πολλά
Gen.	(πολλού)	πολλής	(πολλού)	πολλών	πολλών	πολλών

3.39 Adjectives in -ης, -ες

Adjectives of this type do not have separate forms for the masculine and feminine. There is one set of forms (singular and plural) for masculine and feminine genders. We give two examples below, because of their different stress patterns. In the first the stress remains on the same syllable (either the final or the penultimate syllable) for all forms. In the second the stress is on the penultimate syllable except that it moves to the third syllable from the end in the nominative and accusative of the neuter singular. Adjectives in this category do not normally have vocative forms.

ακριβής exact

	Singular		Plural	
	M/F	N	M/F	N
Nom.	ακριβής	ακριβές	ακριβείς	ακριβή
Acc.	ακριβή	ακριβές	ακριβείς	ακριβή
Gen.	ακριβούς	ακριβούς	ακριβών	ακριβών

Examples (with stress remaining on the same syllable): **αληθής** 'true', **ασφαλής** 'safe, sure', **αφελής** 'naïve', **δημοφιλής** 'popular', **διεθνής** 'international', **ειλικρινής** 'sincere', **επιμελής** 'diligent, hard-working', **ευγενής** 'noble', **πλήρης** 'full', **πολυτελής** 'luxurious', **προσεχής** 'forthcoming', **πρωτοετής** 'first-year', **σαφής** 'clear', **συνεπής** 'consistent', **συνεχής** 'continuous', **τριετής** 'lasting three years', **τριμερής** 'tripartite', **υγιής** 'healthy', **ωοειδής** 'oval' (and all other adjectives ending in -ειδής). Adjectives ending in -ώδης follow the same pattern, except that their genitive plural (all genders) has the stress on the final syllable, e.g. **φρικώδης** 'frightful', genitive plural **φρικωδών**.

συνήθης usual

	Singular		Plural	
	M/F	N	M/F	N
Nom.	συνήθης	σύνηθες	συνήθεις	συνήθη
Acc.	συνήθη	σύνηθες	συνήθεις	συνήθη
Gen.	συνήθους	συνήθους	συνήθων	συνήθων

Examples (with movement of stress to the third syllable from the end in the neuter nominative and accusative singular): **αυθάδης** 'impudent', **επιμήκης** 'oblong', **κακοήθης** 'immoral, malignant', **κλινήρης** 'bedridden'.

3.40 Adjectives with neuter in -ικο

Two sets of adjectives can be classified in this group. Those in the first set (a) mainly denote physical appearance, character or mood. Their masculine forms end in **-ης** and are declined like the corresponding nouns in section 3.13 (b); the feminine forms end in **-α** and follow the declension of the nouns in section 3.14 (but there is no genitive plural form); the neuter forms add **-ικο** to the stem and are declined like other neuter adjectives (e.g. those in section 3.33). The stress remains on the same syllable throughout (see p. 61). When they do not refer to persons, these adjectives have masculine forms in **-ικος** and feminine ones in **-ικη** (declined like adjectives in section 3.33), e.g. **μια τεμπέλικη ζωή** 'a lazy life'.

Examples: **γκρινιάρης** 'grumbling', **ζηλιάρης** 'jealous', **κατσούφης** 'scowling, sullen', **κουτσομπόλης** 'gossiping', **παραπονιάρης** 'complaining', **πεισματάρης** 'stubborn', **τσιγκούνης** 'mean, miserly', and all adjectives ending in **-ούλης**, e.g. **μικρούλης** 'tiny'. Similarly many compound adjectives in which the second element denotes a part of the body, e.g. **ξανθομάλλης** 'fair-haired', **μαυρομάτης** 'black-eyed', **ψηλομύτης** 'snobbish' (literally 'high-nosed').

The adjectives in the second set with neuter in **-ικο** (b) also mainly denote aspects of physical appearance, character or behaviour. The masculine nominative singular ends in **-άς** or **-ής**, and the plural is formed as for the corresponding nouns in section 3.13 (a). The feminine endings are the same as those of the noun declension in **-ού** in section 3.18. Just as the masculine and feminine plural forms add a **δ** to the stem of the singular, so do all the neuter forms, which consequently end in **-δικο**, etc (see p. 61). However, these adjectives also have masculine forms in **-δικος** and feminine ones in **-δικη**, which are used for nouns that do not refer to persons, e.g. **μερακλήδικος καφές** 'gourmet coffee'.

Examples: **κοιλαράς** 'fat-bellied', **πολυλογάς** 'chattering', **φωνακλάς** 'loud-mouthed'. With singular in **-ής, -ού, -ήδικο**, plural **-ήδες, -ούδες, -ήδικα: καβγατζής** 'quarrelsome', **μερακλής** 'choosy, enthusiastic'.

The masculine and feminine forms of these adjectives are also regularly used as nouns, e.g. **ο φαγάς** 'the glutton' (compare sections 3.13 and 3.18).

(a) τεμπέλης lazy

	Singular			Plural		
	M	F	N	M	F	N
Nom.	τεμπέλης	τεμπέλα	τεμπέλικο	τεμπέληδες	τεμπέλες	τεμπέλικα
Acc.	τεμπέλη	τεμπέλα	τεμπέλικο	τεμπέληδες	τεμπέλες	τεμπέλικα
Gen.	τεμπέλη	τεμπέλας	τεμπέλικου	τεμπέληδον	—	τεμπέλικον
Voc.	τεμπέλη	τεμπέλα	τεμπέλικο	τεμπέληδες	τεμπέλες	τεμπέλικα

(b) φαγάς gluttonous

	Singular			Plural		
	M	F	N	M	F	N
Nom.	φαγάς	φαγού	φαγάδικο	φαγάδες	φαγούδες	φαγάδικα
Acc.	φαγά	φαγού	φαγάδικο	φαγάδες	φαγούδες	φαγάδικα
Gen.	φαγά	φαγούς	φαγάδικου	φαγάδον	φαγούδον	φαγάδικον
Voc.	φαγά	φαγού	φαγάδικο	φαγάδες	φαγούδες	φαγάδικα

3.41 Adjectives in *-ων, -ουσα, -ον*

This is a rather small category but it includes some frequently used adjectives. In origin, they are the declined participle forms of verbs and may be compared to English adjectives in -ing, e.g. **ενδιαφέρων** 'interesting'. However, not all verbs can form adjectives in this way; in fact there are very few such words in everyday use. The masculine forms, except the nominative singular, and the neuter forms, except the nominative and accusative singular, have a stem ending in **-οντ-**. The feminine forms have a stem ending in **-ουσ-**. In the genitive plural the masculine and neuter have stress on the penultimate syllable, while the feminine moves the stress to the last syllable. The vocative is rare, but is the same as the corresponding nominative.

επείγων urgent

	Singular			Plural		
	M	F	N	M	F	N
Nom.	επείγων	επείγουσα	επείγον	επείγοντες	επείγουσες	επείγοντα
Acc.	επείγοντα	επείγουσα	επείγον	επείγοντες	επείγουσες	επείγοντα
Gen.	επείγοντος	επείγουσας	επείγοντος	επειγόντων	επειγουσών	επειγόντων

Examples: **δευτερεύων** 'secondary (in importance)', **ενδιαφέρων** 'interesting', **ιδιάζων** 'peculiar', **μέλλων** 'future', **πρωτεύων** 'primary, principal', **σπουδάζων** 'studying', **υπάρχων** 'existing'.

Other adjectives with the same endings differ in the position of stress, e.g. **παρών, παρούσα, παρόν**, plural **παρόντες, παρούσες, παρόντα** 'present'. The stress remains on the same syllable, except for the genitive plural of the feminine, which has the stress on the final syllable: **παρουσών**; similarly **απών** 'absent', **αποτυχών** 'unsuccessful', **τυχών** 'chancing to happen, ordinary'. A few others (deriving from second-conjugation verbs) have **-ούν** in the nominative and accusative neuter singular and the syllable **-ούντ-** instead of **-όντ-** in the relevant masculine and neuter forms: **διοικών, -ούσα, -ούν** 'managing', **επικρατών** 'prevailing'. Finally, there is yet another difference of vowel (-ω- throughout) in **κυβερνών, -ώσα, -ών** 'ruling'.

3.42 Indeclinable adjectives

Some adjectives, mainly loan-words from other languages, do not decline; they have a single form for all genders and cases, singular and plural. Examples: γκρι 'grey', καφέ 'brown', κομπλέ 'full, complete', μοβ 'mauve', μπλε 'blue', ριγέ 'striped', ροζ 'pink', σόκιν 'shocking', φίσκα 'full up, packed'.

Comparison of adjectives

3.43 Overview

Sections 3.33–3.42 give the basic (or positive) forms of adjectives. When we want to compare the extent to which different persons or things possess a particular property, we can use the comparative and superlative forms of adjectives: 'bigger, biggest'; 'better, best'. The comparative establishes a comparison between two persons, things or groups (e.g. 'John is kinder than Peter'). We need to make a distinction between the relative superlative ('the kindest') and the absolute superlative ('most kind', 'extremely kind'). The way such comparative and superlative forms are produced in Greek from the basic adjective forms is described in the next four sections.

3.44 The comparative

In English there are two ways of forming the comparative: we can either add the suffix -er to the positive form ('older', 'kinder', 'cleverer', etc.) or we can use the word 'more' ('more clever', 'more interesting', etc.). However, not all adjectives can use both ways of making a comparative. In addition, English has some irregular comparative forms, e.g. 'good' → 'better', 'bad' → 'worse'. Similarly in Greek there are two ways of making a comparative, but some adjectives do not have a one-word form; they can use only a form with the word πιο 'more'. There are also some irregular formations, for which see section 3.47.

All Greek adjectives can have a comparative form which simply puts πιο before the positive form: πιο όμορφος 'more beautiful', πιο φρέσκος 'fresher, more fresh', πιο τεμπέλης 'lazier', etc. The adjective is inflected for number, gender and case, just like the positive forms. The alternative, one-word comparative is formed from the nominative of the neuter singular with the addition of the suffix -τερος, e.g. σπουδαιότερος 'more important', πλατύτερος 'broader'. Such comparative forms have the stress on the third syllable from the end and are declined like the adjectives in section 3.33, i.e. with feminine singular in -η. One-word comparatives of this kind do not exist for the following: participle forms in -μένος; adjectives in -ής, -ιά, -ί or -ων, -ουσα, -ον; adjectives with neuter in -ικο; indeclinable adjectives. Such adjectives only have the comparative with πιο.

The table below lists all the adjective types presented in sections 3.33–3.37 and 3.39–3.42, with the comparative forms available for each. The dash (—) indicates that a one-word comparative form does not exist for this type.

ψηλός	πιο ψηλός	ψηλότερος	higher, taller	(section 3.33)
τέλειος	πιο τέλειος	τελειότερος	more perfect	(section 3.34)
φρέσκος	πιο φρέσκος	φρεσκότερος	fresher	(section 3.35)
βαρύς	πιο βαρύς	βαρύτερος	heavier	(section 3.36)
καφετής	πιο καφετής	—	browner	(section 3.37)
ακριβής	πιο ακριβής	ακριβέστερος	more precise	(section 3.39)
συνήθης	πιο συνήθης	συνηθέστερος	more usual	(section 3.39)
τεμπέλης	πιο τεμπέλης	—	lazier	(section 3.40)
φαγάς	πιο φαγάς	—	more gluttonous	(section 3.40)
επείγων	πιο επείγων	—	more urgent	(section 3.41)
γκρι	πιο γκρι	—	greyer	(section 3.42)

For the use of the comparative in complete sentences, and for expressions of inferiority (e.g. 'less interesting') see section 10.22.

3.45 The relative superlative

The relative superlative is used to indicate that the person or thing to which it refers possesses a particular property to the highest degree relative to others in the same group, e.g. 'the cleverest person I have ever met', 'the most important member of the team', 'the tallest building in Europe'. The relative superlative is formed in the same way as the comparative, but is preceded by the definite article. Adjectives that have a choice of two comparative forms also have two corresponding relative superlatives, declined in the same way. For convenience we give the relative superlative forms of the adjective types listed in section 3.44:

ψηλός	ο πιο ψηλός	ο ψηλότερος	the highest/tallest
τέλειος	ο πιο τέλειος	ο τελειότερος	the most perfect

φρέσκος	ο πιο φρέσκος	ο φρεσκότερος	the freshest
βαρύς	ο πιο βαρύς	ο βαρύτερος	the heaviest
καφετής	ο πιο καφετής	—	the brownest
ακριβής	ο πιο ακριβής	ο ακριβέστερος	the most precise
συνήθης	ο πιο συνήθης	ο συνηθέστερος	the most usual
τεμπέλης	ο πιο τεμπέλης	—	the laziest
φαγάς	ο πιο φαγάς	—	the most gluttonous
επείγων	ο πιο επείγων	—	the most urgent
γκρι	ο πιο γκρι	—	the greyest

The absolute superlative

3.46 The absolute superlative

Greek has a special kind of superlative called the absolute superlative, which is used to stress an exceptional property of a person or thing. Compare the English 'She is a most able teacher' or 'This news is most significant'. In such cases we are not making a direct comparison with other, less able, teachers or other, less significant, news, but merely emphasizing the exceptional ability of the teacher or the exceptional significance of the news in question. In Greek the absolute superlative is formed from the neuter of the positive adjective with the addition of the suffix **-τατος**. Like the comparative and the relative superlative, it is stressed on the third syllable from the end and declines like adjectives in **-ος, -η, -ο**. Adjectives which do not have a one-word comparative in **-τερος** cannot form an absolute superlative.

Some examples: **ωραιότατος** 'exceptionally beautiful', **φυσικότατος** 'most natural, absolutely natural', **ακριβέστατος** 'extremely precise', **βαθύτατος** 'very deep indeed, profound', **εξοχότατος** 'most eminent'. As can be seen from the translations given above, English has a variety of ways of expressing the same idea.

3.47 Irregular comparatives and superlatives

Some adjectives have comparative and/or superlative degrees that are not formed according to the patterns given in sections 3.44–3.46. The following table lists the most common irregular forms. The comparative and relative superlative forms are the same, except that the relative superlative is preceded by the definite article.

Positive	Comparative/relative superlative	Absolute superlative
απλός simple	(ο) απλούστερος simpler, simplest	απλούστατος extremely simple
κακός bad	(ο) χειρότερος worse, worst	κάκιστος most wicked
		χείριστος worst
καλός good	(ο) καλύτερος better, best	κάλλιστος finest
		άριστος excellent
κοντός short	(ο) κοντότερος shorter/est in height	—
	(ο) κοντύτερος shorter/est in length	—
λίγος little	(ο) λιγότερος less/fewer, least/fewest	ελάχιστος extremely little/few
μεγάλος big, great	(ο) μεγαλύτερος bigger, biggest	μέγιστος maximal
μικρός small	(ο) μικρότερος smaller, smallest	ελάχιστος minimal
πολύς much	(ο) περισσότερος more, most	πλείστος very much/many
πρώτος first	(ο) προυύτερος earlier, earliest	πρότιστος foremost

The following comparative, relative and absolute superlative forms do not derive from adjectives in the positive degree; some of them derive from other parts of speech, as indicated in the first column (words in brackets are not normally used today).

	Comparative/relative superlative	Absolute superlative
(άνω) above	(ο) ανώτερος superior	ανώτατος highest, supreme
κάτω below	(ο) κατώτερος inferior	κατώτατος lowest, minimum
προτιμώ I prefer	προτιμότερος preferable	—
—	(ο) προγενέστερος prior, earliest	—
—	(ο) μεταγενέστερος subsequent, latest	—
(πλησίον) near	(ο) πλησιέστερος nearer, nearest	πλησιέστατος very near

The use of noun phrases and of adjectives

3.48 Agreement within the noun phrase

As we said in section 3.1, the noun phrase typically consists of a noun (or a word substituting for a noun such as an adjective or pronoun), optionally accompanied by one or more of the following modifiers: an article, a determiner (for more on determiners see sections 4.3–4.9), an adjective, a numeral or a quantifier. All words in the same noun phrase and modifying the noun agree with the noun in gender, number and case (see also sections 3.3–3.5). This means that all declinable modifiers indicate in their inflection their gender, number and case agreement with the noun they modify:

| *Ο άλλος μικρός δρόμος είναι πιο δύσκολος.*
　The other little road is more difficult.

3 The noun and the noun phrase

In the noun phrase in example 1, since the noun **δρόμος** is masculine and appears here in the nominative singular, the article **ο**, the determiner **άλλος** and the adjective **μικρός** are all in the masculine nominative singular form. In the next example:

2   στη μέση *της άλλης μικρής πλατείας*
    in the middle *of the other little square*

the noun **πλατείας** is feminine and is being used in the genitive singular; for this reason the article **της**, the determiner **άλλης** and the adjective **μικρής** are also all in the feminine genitive singular form.

Sometimes a single modifier (normally an adjective) is used with two or more nouns. The modifier appears in the masculine plural if both nouns denote humans and both are masculine, or if one is masculine and the other feminine:

3a *Αγαπητοί μου Γιάννη και Γιώργο*
    My *dear* John and George

b   *Αγαπητοί μου Γιάννη και Μαρία*
    My *dear* John and Mary

If the nouns denote non-humans, the modifier usually appears in the gender and number of the noun nearest to it:

4   *ελληνική* (fem. sg.) *μουσική* (fem. sg.) *και τραγούδια* (neut. pl.)
    Greek music and songs

Two or more modifiers may modify a singular noun within the same noun phrase even when the noun denotes two or more entities:

5   Ο Έλληνας (sg.) και ο Τούρκος (sg.) *αντιπρόσωπος* (sg.)
    The Greek and Turkish *representatives*

3.49 The use of the cases: introduction

There are four cases in Greek:

- nominative
- accusative
- genitive
- vocative

Every declinable word (article, noun, adjective, pronoun, determiner or numeral) inflects for case, although in practice a word may not always indicate unambiguously which case it is in. Only one class of nouns, namely most masculines in -ος, has a separate form for each of the four cases, and then only in the singular. For the forms of the cases see sections 3.6–3.7 (for articles), 3.9–3.30 (for nouns), 3.33–3.42 (for adjectives), 4.1–4.10 (for pronouns and determiners) and 5.2 (for numerals).

The use of the nominative

3.50 The use of the nominative

The nominative is the basic case: dictionaries list declinable words in the nominative singular form.

The nominative is used to indicate the subject of a verb (i.e. the person, thing, etc. that does something (1), or is in a certain state (2), or undergoes a change (3), or has something done to him/her/it (4)):

1 *Η Μαρία έφυγε.*
   Mary left.

2 *Ο Παύλος κοιμάται.*
   Paul is asleep.

3 *Η Άννα έπεσε κάτω.*
   Ann fell down.

4 *Φυλακίστηκε ο κλέφτης.*
   The thief was imprisoned.

In addition, the nominative is used to indicate a subject predicate (i.e. a word or phrase referring to the same person, thing, etc., as the subject):

Η Μαρία είναι *γιατρός.*
Mary's *a doctor.*

The nominative is also used in certain more-or-less fixed expressions, e.g.:

στις τέσσερις *η ώρα*
at four o'clock

3.51 The use of the accusative

The accusative has two chief uses. The first is to indicate the direct object of a verb (i.e. the person, thing, etc. that is affected by the subject):

1a Η Μαρία έκλεισε *την πόρτα.*
   Mary shut *the door.*

b   **Η Μαρία** *την* **έκλεισε.**
    Mary shut *it*.

Similarly, the accusative is used to express an object predicate (i.e. a word or phrase referring to the same person, thing, etc., as the object):

Τον θεωρώ *φίλο μου*.
I consider him *a friend of mine*.

Second, the accusative is used for the object of most prepositions (for more on prepositions see Chapter 8):

2   **Ο Γιάννης ήρθε από** *την Αθήνα*.
    John came from *Athens*.

3   **Χάρισα το βιβλίο στον** *Γιάννη*.
    I gave the book to *John*.

The accusative has a variety of other uses. Noun phrases in the accusative may be used adverbially, especially in expressions of measurement in time or space. Such uses of noun phrases in the accusative include the following:

- Duration (time)

    4   **Δούλεψα** *όλη μέρα*.
        I worked *all day*.

- Distance (space or time)

    5   **Έτρεξα** *τρία χιλιόμετρα*.
        I ran *three kilometres*.

    6   **Κράτησε** *ένα χρόνο*.
        It lasted *a/one year*.

- Point in time

    7   **τη νύχτα**
        during the night

    8   **την Κυριακή το απόγευμα**
        on Sunday afternoon

    9   **την άλλη μέρα**
        the next day

> The use of the accusative

10 τον Αύγουστο
    in August

11 την πρώτη Φεβρουαρίου
    on the first of February (see also section 5.5)

12 την άνοιξη
    in spring

13 το Πάσχα
    at Easter

14 το 2004 (το δύο χιλιάδες τέσσερα)
    in 2004

15 τρεις φορές
    three times

- Rate (time or weight)

    16 τρεις φορές *την ώρα*
        three times *an hour*

    17 χίλια δολάρια *τον τόνο*
        a thousand dollars *a tonne*

- Dimensions

    18a ένα ξύλο *δέκα πόντους* μακρύ
         a stick *ten centimetres* long

      b ένα ξύλο *δέκα πόντους* μήκος
         a stick *ten centimetres* [in] length

These examples are two alternative ways of saying the same thing.

- Degree of separation (space or time)

    19 Μένω *δυο δρόμους* παρακάτω.
        I live *two streets* further down.

    20 Η αδελφή μου είναι *ένα χρόνο* μεγαλύτερη/πιο μεγάλη από μένα.
        My sister is *one year* older than me.

- Goal or aim

    21 Πήγα *περίπατο.*
        I went *for a walk.*

- In exclamations (whether or not the speaker is addressing the person described):

    22 την καημένη! (fem. sg.)
        poor thing!

- Location at or motion to

    In colloquial usage the accusative of a place name (used without the article) may express location at or motion to the place:

    23 Θα είμαι [στην] *Κόρινθο* (cf. nom. η Κόρινθος).
        I'll be in *Corinth.*

    24 Πας [στους] *Αμπελοκήπους;* (cf. nom. οι Αμπελόκηποι)
        Are you going to *Ambelokipi?*

    In these examples the word in square brackets is inserted in less colloquial usage.

3.52 The use of the genitive

A noun phrase in the genitive may be governed by a verb, or it may depend on a noun. When a noun phrase in the genitive is governed by a verb, it most commonly acts as the indirect object (see 3.52.1). When it depends on a noun, a noun phrase in the genitive most commonly indicates the person or thing that possesses the noun on which it depends, though it may indicate various other, more abstract, relations instead. Broadly speaking, the genitive depending on a noun is equivalent to the English possessive case ('the girl's') or to the noun preceded by 'of' ('of the girl').

3.52.1 The genitive governed by a verb

When it is governed by a verb, the genitive form of a weak personal pronoun or a noun phrase normally indicates that the pronoun or (more rarely) the noun phrase is the indirect object of the verb, i.e. the person to whom an action is done. In examples 1–3 the indirect object denotes the person or thing to which something is given or said:

> **The use of the genitive**

1   *Μου χάρισε ένα κολιέ.*
    (S)he gave *me* a necklace.

2   *Της είπα τα νέα.*
    I told *her* the news.

3   *Είπα της Μαρίας τα νέα.*
    I told *Mary* the news.

When the indirect object is a noun phrase rather than a pronoun, it is more usually expressed by **σε** + accusative (see section 8.2).

In example 4 the indirect object denotes the person for whom the action is done:

4   *Σου έχω φράουλες σήμερα.*
    I've got strawberries *for you* today.

In example 5 the indirect object may be interpreted as the person from whom something is removed:

5   *Του πήραν τα παπούτσια.*
    They took the shoes *from him* OR They took *his* shoes.

In examples 6–7 the indirect object indicates the person affected by the action of the verb:

6   *Του έπεσε το μαντίλι.*
    He dropped *his* handkerchief (lit. *'to/from him* fell the handkerchief').

7   *Μου έσπασε ένα δόντι.*
    One of *my* teeth has broken (δόντι is the subject) OR (S)he/it broke one of *my* teeth (δόντι is the direct object) (lit. *'to me* broke (3rd sg.) a tooth').

The genitive is also used to indicate the object (usually a weak pronoun) of certain verbs that do not take direct objects, such as **αρέσω** 'I please', **πάω** 'I suit', and **φαίνομαι** 'I seem':

8   *Δεν μου αρέσει αυτό το κρασί.*
    I don't like this wine (lit. 'This wine doesn't please *me*').

9   *Σου πάει αυτό το φόρεμα.*
    This dress suits *you* (sg.).

10 *Εύκολο μου φαίνεται.*
    It looks easy *to me*.

3.52.2 The genitive depending on a noun

- Possessive genitive

When a noun phrase or a weak pronoun is in the genitive it may indicate that the person or thing which it denotes is the possessor of the person or thing denoted by the noun on which it depends:

11a το σπίτι *του Κώστα*
    Kostas's house

  b το σπίτι *του*
    his house

12a τα κλαδιά *των δέντρων*
    the branches *of the trees*

  b τα κλαδιά *τους*
    their branches

For the use of the article in this construction see section 3.54.

- Subjective and objective genitive

A noun phrase or pronoun in the genitive depending on an abstract noun may indicate a more abstract relationship:

13 η δημιουργία *του Παύλου*
   Paul's creation

14 η δημιουργία *της κατάστασης αυτής*
   the creation *of this situation*

In example 13 the noun phrase **του Παύλου** is an example of the subjective genitive, because Paul is the person who creates (i.e. the subject of the creative process), while in example 14 the noun phrase **της κατάστασης αυτής** is an example of the objective genitive, since the situation is what is created (i.e. the object of the creative process).

- Other uses of the genitive

A noun phrase in the genitive may be used in a wide variety of ways, including the following:

15 η Μάχη *του Μαραθώνα*
   the Battle *of Marathon* (place)

16 οι Έλληνες *του εικοστού πρώτου αιώνα*
the Greeks *of the twenty-first century* (time)

17 η πίκρα *του χωρισμού*
the sorrow *of parting* (cause)

18 ένα ποτήρι *της μπίρας*
a *beer*-glass (i.e. a glass for beer: purpose)

19 ένας καθηγητής *φιλολογίας*
a *literature* teacher/professor (specification)

20 οδός ***Κοραή***
Korais Street (street name)

21 σοκολάτα *πολυτελείας*
luxury chocolate (quality)

22 άνθρωποι *τέτοιου είδους*
people *of such a kind* (quality)

23 ένα παιδί *τεσσάρων χρονών*
a *four-year-old* child (measurement)

24 μια σειρά *πέντε διαλέξεων*
a series *of five lectures* (content)

25 στιγμές *ευτυχίας*
moments *of happiness* (content)

The use of the genitive

3.52.3 The genitive depending on a numeral, adjective or pronoun

A noun phrase or pronoun in the genitive may depend on a numeral, adjective or pronoun.

Numerals and certain adjectives and pronouns may be followed by a weak personal pronoun in the genitive which specifies more narrowly the scope of the word on which it depends. (If the item that depends on any of these words is a noun phrase rather than a weak pronoun, this noun phrase has to be in the accusative preceded by **από**: see section 8.2, example 6.)

26 οι τρεις *σας*
the three *of you*

27 κανένας *τους*
none/any *of them*

28 ο καθένας *μας*
    each *of us*

29 όλοι *μας*
    all *of us*

The intensive pronoun **μόνος** 'alone' may be followed by a weak personal pronoun in the genitive, the whole phrase meaning 'by oneself', in the sense of either 'without company' or 'without help': **μόνη μου** 'by myself (fem.)' (see section 4.9).

3.52.4 Other uses of the genitive

The genitive of the weak personal pronoun may be used after the comparative or superlative form of an adjective, e.g. **μεγαλύτερός μου** 'bigger/older (masc. sg. nom.) than me'. In practice, however, the comparative is more usually followed by **από** + accusative, e.g. **μεγαλύτερος από μένα** (see section 10.22).

The weak pronoun in the genitive may depend on certain exclamatory words in greetings, wishes, and other exclamations (for more on greetings and wishes see section 12.3). Here again, the pronoun specifies the person to or for whom the wish is made:

30 Καλημέρα *σας*!
    Good day *to you* (pl.)!

31 Μπράβο *της*!
    Good for *her*!

32 Περαστικά *του*!
    I hope he gets well soon! (lit. '[may it be] passing *to him*')

33 Γεια *σου* (sg.) or Γεια *σας* (pl.)!
    Hello/Goodbye!

In colloquial usage there are certain fixed expressions consisting of noun phrases in the genitive, which have a metaphorical adverbial or adjectival use. Here are a few examples:

34 Δεν βρήκα φόρεμα *της προκοπής*.
    I didn't find a dress [that was] *any good*.

35 Έγινε *της κακομοίρας* or *της τρελής*.
    There was *a terrible commotion*.

36 Η κοντή φούστα είναι *της μόδας*.
    Short skirts are *in fashion*.

Certain prepositions whose use is chiefly confined to formal contexts govern the genitive (see section 8.2).

A noun phrase in the genitive may sometimes depend on a noun that has been omitted:

37 Πήγα *στου Γιάννη*.
    I went to John's [house].

38 Αυτό το σπίτι μοιάζει με *του Γιάννη*.
    This house is like John's [house].

3.53 The use of the vocative

The vocative indicates that the person or thing denoted by the noun phrase is being addressed:

39 Έλα, *Στέφανε*!
    Come on, Stephen!

40 Δολοφόνε!
    Murderer!

A word in the vocative may, in familiar usage, be preceded by the exclamatory words **μωρέ**, **ρε** or **βρε**, which are uninflected for case, number, and gender (see section 12.1).

3.54 The use of the definite article

The definite article in Greek is used in a broadly similar way as in English, i.e. to show that the noun that it modifies denotes a specific item; compare example 1a, which uses the definite article, with 1b, which uses the indefinite article:

1a *ο* σκύλος
    the dog

b   *ένας* σκύλος
    a dog

In addition to the uses of the definite article that Greek has in common with English, the Greek definite article is used in the following circumstances:

3
The noun and the noun phrase

- with proper names referring to specific persons or places:

  2 *η Μαρία*
     Mary

  3 *ο κύριος Παπαδόπουλος*
     Mr Papadopoulos

  4 *η Θεσσαλονίκη*
     Thessaloniki

When proper names are used in the vocative to address someone, the article is not used (**Μαρία!** 'Mary!', **Κύριε Παπαδόπουλε!** 'Mr Papadopoulos!').

- with nouns modified by the possessive pronoun when the noun refers to a specific item; with the definite article the possessive is the equivalent of 'my', etc. (5a), whereas without the definite article it corresponds to 'of mine', etc. (5b–c):

  5a *ο φίλος μου*
      my friend

   b *ένας φίλος μου*
      a friend *of mine*

   c *κάτι φίλοι μου*
      some friends *of mine*

- with nouns accompanied by a demonstrative ('this', 'that'):

  6 *αυτό το σπίτι*
     this house

- with nouns accompanied by the quantifiers **όλος** 'all' and **ολόκληρος** 'whole' (the latter can be used without the article, as in 8b):

  7 *όλος ο κόσμος*
     everyone (lit. 'all the world')
  8a *ολόκληρο το χωριό*
     the whole village
   b *ολόκληρα χρόνια*
     (for) years on end (lit. 'whole years')

- with abstract nouns when they are viewed as denoting a definite entity:

   > The use of the definite article

   9   *Ο φόβος είναι ένστικτο.*
       Fear is an instinct.

- with nouns denoting substances:

   10 *Ο γρανίτης είναι πολύ σκληρός.*
       Granite is very hard.

- with plural nouns (11–12) and adjectives (13) denoting whole classes of items:

   11 *Οι άντρες αγαπάνε το ποδόσφαιρο.*
       Men love football.

   12 *Αγαπάω τα πουλιά.*
       I love birds.

   13 *Οι νέοι ακούνε συνέχεια μουσική.*
       Young people listen to music all the time.

Example 11 also illustrates the use of the definite article with various other kinds of noun (here **ποδόσφαιρο**) where English does not use it.

- with days of the week, months, years, seasons and festivals, where the whole phrase either denotes the item itself (14a–18a) or (in the accusative) refers to the occasion on which something happens (14b–18b):

   14a Προτιμώ *το Σάββατο*.
        I prefer Saturday (cf. *ένα Σάββατο* 'one Saturday').

   b   *Το Σάββατο* θα πάμε εκδρομή.
        On Saturday we'll go for an outing.

   15a Δεν μου αρέσει *ο Φεβρουάριος*.
        I don't like February.

   b   *Τον Φεβρουάριο* βρέχει πολύ.
        It rains a lot *in* February.

   16a *Το 2001* δεν ήταν καλή χρονιά.
        2001 wasn't a good year.

b *Το 2001 πήγαμε στην Αγγλία.*
We went to England *in* 2001.

17a *Ο περασμένος χειμώνας ήταν πολύ βαρύς.*
Last winter was very harsh.

b *Τον χειμώνα κάνουμε σκι.*
In winter/*In the* winter we go skiing.

18a *Αγαπώ το ελληνικό Πάσχα.*
I love Greek Easter.

b *Το Πάσχα πήγαμε στην Κρήτη.*
We went to Crete *at* Easter.

- with dates and times of day:

19 στις τέσσερις
on the fourth [of the month]; at four (o'clock)

- in expressions of rate (in the accusative):

20 ενάμισι εκατομμύριο *τον* μήνα
one and a half million *a/per* month

21 εκατό χιλιόμετρα *την* ώρα
a hundred kilometres *an/per* hour

- in the neuter, to turn any word or phrase into a noun phrase or noun clause, e.g. to make a noun out of another part of speech (22); when talking about a word (23); or to introduce a complement clause, especially when it precedes the main clause (24–25):

22 Αυτός ποτέ δεν σκέφτεται *το αύριο*.
He never thinks about tomorrow (**αύριο** is normally an adverb).

23 Πώς γράφεται *το* «υγεία»;
How is [the word] '*υγεία*' spelt (lit. 'written')?

24 *Το ότι δεν γύρισε ακόμα* είναι κακό σημάδι.
[The fact] that (s)he hasn't come back yet is a bad sign.

25 *Το να λες τέτοια πράγματα* είναι δύσκολο.
To say (2nd sg.) such things is difficult.

Finally, unlike in English, the definite article is normally repeated before the second and subsequent nouns of a co-ordinated sequence if the first one is itself accompanied by the definite article:

26 τα αγόρια και τα κορίτσια
    the boys and girls

For the forms of the definite article see section 3.6.

3.55 The use of the indefinite article

The basic function of **ένας, μια, ένα** is to denote the number 'one'. It is also used as a pronoun with a similar meaning to **κάποιος** 'someone':

1 Ήρθε *ένας* και σε ζητούσε.
   Someone came asking for you (lit. 'and you (acc. sg.) was-asking-for (3rd sg.)').

This means that it is not always used exactly like the English indefinite article 'a, an', though in many contexts it corresponds exactly to English:

2 Τον δάγκωσε *ένας* σκύλος.
   A dog bit him.

3 Είδα *μια* φίλη σου.
   I saw *a* (female) friend of yours (sg.).

For the forms of the indefinite article see section 3.7.

3.56 Absence of article

In many contexts Greek does not use an article at all where English uses the indefinite article, or 'any' or 'some'. Among these uses are the following:

- with a predicate (e.g. after the verbs **είμαι** 'I am' and **γίνομαι** 'I become': see also section 6.1):

    1 Είναι φιλόλογος.
       (S)he's *a* literature teacher.

    2 Έγινε φιλόλογος.
       (S)he became *a* literature teacher.

- after **σαν** 'like' (see also section 10.22.2):

    3 Έτρεμε σαν πουλί.
       (S)he was trembling like *a* bird.

3
The noun and the noun phrase

- with the object of a verb, where the speaker does not wish to stress that the object is specific or definite; this happens especially in fixed expressions (4–6) and in interrogative, negative and conditional sentences (7–11):

    4   Φοράει σακάκι.
        (S)he's wearing *a* jacket (the speaker is not making a contrast between one particular jacket and another, but between wearing a jacket and not wearing a jacket).

    5   Επιτέλους βρήκα ρολόι.
        At last I've found *a* watch (the speaker is not stressing that (s)he's now found a particular watch, but simply that (s)he's found a watch, whereas previously (s)he hadn't found one).

    6   Κάνω τηλεφώνημα.
        I'm making *a* phone call.

    7   Έχεις κινητό;
        Have you got *a* mobile?

    8   Δεν έχω κινητό.
        I haven't got *a* mobile.

    9   Αν είχα κινητό θα τον έπαιρνα.
        If I had *a* mobile I would call him.

    10 Έχεις αδέλφια;
        Have you *any* brothers and sisters?

    11 Δεν έχω αδέλφια.
        I don't have *any*/I have *no* brothers and sisters.

- with the subject, when that subject is indefinite, especially in interrogative (12), negative (13) and conditional (14) sentences:

    12 Υπάρχει γυναίκα που να μην το ξέρει;
        Is there *a* woman who doesn't know it?

    13 Δεν υπάρχει γυναίκα που να μην το ξέρει.
        There isn't *a* woman who doesn't know it.

    14 Αν με ρωτούσε γυναίκα, θα την έστελνα στη συνάδελφό μου.
        If *a* woman asked me, I would send her to my (female) colleague.

No article is used at all in noun phrases denoting an unspecified amount of a substance (15–16) or an unspecified number of items (17), where English uses 'some':

15 Θέλω κρασί.
I want *some* wine.

16 Χύθηκε κρασί στο τραπεζομάντιλο.
Some wine has spilled on the tablecloth.

17 Αγόρασα παπούτσια.
I bought *some* shoes.

3.57 The use of adjectives

Almost all adjectives inflect for gender, number and case. For the forms of adjectives see sections 3.32–3.47.

The chief function of the adjective is to modify a noun. An adjective may modify the noun in either attributive or predicative use.

In attributive use an adjective modifies the noun in the same phrase; it must agree with its noun in gender, number and case (for agreement within the noun phrase see section 3.48):

1 *ένας μαύρος σκύλος* (masc. nom. sg.)
a *black* dog

2 *μια μαύρη γάτα* (fem. nom./acc. sg.)
a *black* cat

The adjective normally comes immediately before the noun. It may, however, appear after the noun for special emphasis. In such cases, if the noun is preceded by the definite article, the article must be repeated before the adjective, as in example 4:

3 *ένας σκύλος μαύρος*
a **black** dog (as opposed to a dog of a different colour)

4 *η γάτα η μαύρη*
the **black** cat (as opposed to the cat(s) of a different colour)

In predicative use the adjective refers to the subject or direct object without being in the same phrase; again, it agrees with the noun it refers to in gender, number and case (see also section 6.1):

3 The noun and the noun phrase

5   Ο σκύλος είναι *μαύρος* (the adjective μαύρος is a predicate of the subject σκύλος).
    The dog is *black*.

6   Αυτή η γάτα είναι *μαύρη*.
    This cat is *black*.

7   Ο Γιάννης παντρεύτηκε *μικρός* (masc. nom. sg.).
    John married *young*.

8   Το άσπρο κρασί πίνεται *παγωμένο* (neuter nom. sg.).
    White wine is drunk *chilled*.

9   Έβαψα τον τοίχο *άσπρο* (masc. acc. sg.: the adjective άσπρο is a predicate of the direct object τοίχο).
    I painted the wall *white*.

In predicative use an adjective may refer to a pronoun (10) or to an item that is not explicitly mentioned (11):

10 Τον έβαψα *άσπρο* (άσπρο is an object predicate).
    I painted him/it *white*.

11 Είναι *έξυπνη* (έξυπνη is a subject predicate).
    She/it's *clever*.

Example 10 may refer either to a man or to an item that is denoted in Greek by a masculine noun, such as τοίχος 'wall'. Example 11 may refer either to a woman or to an item that is denoted in Greek by a feminine noun, such as γάτα 'cat' or ιδέα 'idea'.

The passive perfect participle is used like an adjective in both attributive and predicative use (for its formation see section 6.16). Example 8 above, using παγωμένος 'chilled, frozen' (from παγώνω 'I chill, freeze'), shows the passive perfect participle in predicative use. An example of its attributive use is μια παγωμένη μπίρα 'a chilled beer'.

In noun phrases specifying a person's nationality, Greek uses the noun where English uses the adjective:

12a ο *άγγλος* (masc. noun) πρωθυπουργός
  b η *αγγλίδα* (fem. noun) πρωθυπουργός
    the *British* prime minister

13a Είμαι *Άγγλος* (masc. noun).
  b Είμαι *Αγγλίδα* (fem. noun).
    I'm *British*.

Compare the following phrases in which the adjective is used to denote non-humans (λαός doesn't strictly denote human individuals, but the concept of 'people'):

14   ο *αγγλικός* (masc. adj.) λαός
     the English people

15   η *αγγλική* (fem. adj.) κουζίνα
     English cooking

16   το *αγγλικό* (neuter adj.) χιούμορ
     English humour

As we saw in section 3.54, example 13 (**οι νέοι** 'young people'), Greek adjectives can be used as nouns. Unlike in English, the adjective used in this way can be singular:

17   ο νέος
     the young [man]

In addition, a number of Greek adjectives are used to refer to specific items in phrases where the noun may be omitted. Here are some examples; the noun that can be optionally omitted is given here in square brackets:

18   το δημοτικό [σχολείο]
     (the) primary school

19   η δημοτική [γλώσσα]
     the demotic language (i.e. spoken Greek)

20   η ελληνική [γλώσσα]
     Greek (i.e. the Greek language)

21   η Φιλοσοφική [Σχολή]
     the Arts Faculty (of a university)

22   ο τελικός [αγώνας]
     the final (in sport)

23   το τετραγωνικό [μέτρο]
     square metre

24   το κυπριακό [ζήτημα]
     the Cyprus question

25   ο εμφύλιος [πόλεμος]
     the civil war

26   η λαϊκή [αγορά OR γλώσσα]
     street market OR slang

The use of adjectives

27 η πρώτη [παράσταση OR ταχύτητα]
    first performance OR first gear

Adjectives may be modified by adverbs:

28 πολύ καλός
    very good

29 πιο καλός
    better (lit. 'more good')

30 λίγο καλύτερος
    a bit better

31 *καθαρά* οικονομικός
    purely economic

They may also be modified by weak pronouns in the genitive to indicate possession (32); the adjective **γνωστός** 'known' is regularly accompanied by a genitive weak pronoun to indicate the person that the relevant item is known to (33):

32 το παλιό *μας* σπίτι
    our old house (= our previous house; cf. το παλιό σπίτι *μας*
    'our house which is old')

33 μια γνωστή *μου* καθηγήτρια
    a (female) professor who is an acquaintance *of mine* (lit. 'a known *to-me* professor (fem.)')

As in English, adjectives in Greek may take complements. These may be prepositional phrases (34), or clauses introduced by **να** (35) or **ότι** (36):

34 Είναι *δυνατή στα μαθηματικά*.
    She's good (lit. 'strong') *at maths*.

35 Είναι *ικανός να κάνει αυτή τη δουλειά*;
    Is he *capable of doing this job*?

36 Δεν είναι *σίγουρο ότι θα έρθουν*.
    It's not *certain (that) they'll come*.

Chapter 4

Pronouns and determiners

Pronouns are words that stand instead of nounphrases. They perform the syntactic functions of nounphrases as subjects, objects, etc. English examples include 'he', 'she', 'someone', 'anything', 'who?'. Determiners are words that modify nouns. We use this term in this book to refer to words other than articles, adjectives and numerals. Determiners in English include 'some', 'any', and 'which' (e.g. in the phrase 'which book?'). In Greek, most pronouns, apart from personal pronouns, can also be used as determiners. For a table of pronouns and determiners (apart from personal pronouns) see Appendix 1.

4.1 Personal pronouns: weak (clitic) forms

Personal pronouns are used to refer to the three grammatical persons: first (sg. 'I, me'; pl. 'we, us'), second ('you') and third (sg. 'he, him, she, her, it'; pl. 'they, them').

There are two distinct types of personal pronoun in Greek: emphatic and weak. In this section we present the weak forms; the emphatic pronouns are presented in section 4.2.

Weak pronouns are used only in close connection with verbs, nouns, adverbs and certain other words. They consist of one syllable and they are not stressed. They are sometimes known as clitic pronouns, which means that they are always pronounced together with the word they depend on (see also section 1.8). There are no weak forms for the nominative case of the first and second person, because the verb form always indicates the person of the subject; if a subject pronoun has to be present because the subject is emphasized, then an emphatic pronoun is used, as in section 4.2, example 1.

4 Pronouns and determiners

Weak personal pronouns

First person: 'me, us'   Second person: 'you'

	Sg.	Pl.		Sg.	Pl.
Acc.	με	μας	Acc.	σε	σας
Gen.	μου	μας	Gen.	σου	σας

Third person: 'him, her, it, them'

	Sg.			Pl.		
	M	F	N	M	F	N
Nom.	τος	τη	το	τοι	τες	τα
Acc.	τον	τη(ν)	το	τους	τις/τες	τα
Gen.	του	της	του	τους	τους	τους

1. The nominative forms of the weak pronoun are only used in exclamatory and interrogative constructions after να 'there!' and πού 'ν' 'where is/are', e.g. να τη! 'there she is!', πού 'ν' τα; 'where are they?'.

2. Τις/τες: these two forms, τις is the obligatory form used before the verb, while either can be used after the gerund and after imperatives (for more on word order see below).

Weak pronouns are used far more frequently than emphatic pronouns. A weak personal pronoun may:

- act as the direct object (in the accusative) or indirect object (in the genitive) of a verb;
- act as a possessive pronoun (in the genitive) after a noun;
- be used as a subjective or objective genitive after a noun (see also section 3.52.2);
- (in the genitive) follow an adjective, numeral, pronoun or quantifier;
- (in the genitive) depend on an adverb.

A weak pronoun may be used as the direct or indirect object of a verb. When it is a direct object, it appears in the accusative case; when it is an indirect object it is in the genitive. Nothing can separate a weak object pronoun from the verb. Weak pronouns as objects appear immediately before the verb (1–2), except with imperative forms and with the gerund (3–4):

> | Personal pronouns: weak (clitic) forms

1 *Σε είδα.*
I saw *you* (sg.).

2 *Δεν θα τους δεις.*
You (sg.) won't see *them* (masc.).

3 *Κοίταξέ με!*
Look (sg.) at *me*!

4 *Ξεφυλλίζοντάς το* (neut. sg.), *καταλαβαίνουμε ότι πρόκειται για αξιόλογο βιβλίο.*
Flicking through *it*, we realize it's a noteworthy book.

For an explanation of the second stress on the verb forms in examples 3 and 4 see section 1.8. For the use of weak pronouns referring to an object noun phrase see section 10.20.

Two weak object pronouns can be used together, one for the indirect object, the other for the direct object. In such cases the indirect object comes before the direct object (5–6: see also section 6.1), though after imperatives or a gerund the order is flexible (7):

5 *Σου το είπα.*
I told you (lit. '*To-you it* I-said').

6 *Μη μου τα δείξεις.*
Don't show *them to me*.

7 *Πες του το* (less commonly *Πες το του*).
Tell him (lit. 'Say *to-him it*' or 'Say *it to-him*').

In colloquial usage, the genitive singular form **σου** may be reduced to **σ'** before a third-person pronoun: example 5 above would become *Σ' το είπα* (sometimes written *Στο είπα*).

The genitive of the weak pronoun is regularly used as a possessive pronoun ('my', 'your', 'their', etc.; for the emphatic possessive see section 4.4). In this use, it normally comes immediately after the noun, which is normally preceded by the definite article (but see section 3.54):

6 *ο αδελφός της*
her brother

7 *τα λεφτά τους*
their money

When used as a possessive pronoun, the weak pronoun may be placed after an adjective or the quantifier **όλος** instead of after the noun:

8   το καινούριο *μας* σπίτι
    our new house

9   με όλη *μου* τη δύναμη
    with all *my* strength

The genitive of the weak pronoun may be used after the comparative form of an adjective to express the second term of a comparison (10), or after the relative superlative form of an adjective to indicate the group of items among which the other term is supreme (11):

10 Η Άννα είναι μεγαλύτερή *του* (alternatively μεγαλύτερη απ' αυτόν).
    Anna is bigger/older *than him*.

11 Η Άννα είναι η μεγαλύτερή *μας* (alternatively η μεγαλύτερη από όλους μας).
    Anna is the biggest/oldest *of us*.

The genitive of the weak pronoun can also be used after numerals (12), certain types of pronoun (13–16: compare sections 4.6 and 4.9) or the quantifier όλος (16) to specify the person (first, second or third) denoted by the other term:

12 οι δύο *μας*
    the two *of us*

13 μόνη *της*
    on *her* own

14 ο καθένας *τους*
    each one *of them*

15 κανένας *μας*
    none *of us*

16 όλοι *σας*
    all *of you*

Finally, weak pronouns in the genitive are used after certain adverbs (mostly adverbs of place: see section 8.3):

17 δίπλα *μας*
    next *to us*

18 μέσα *της*
    inside *her/it* (fem.)

4.2 Personal pronouns: emphatic forms

The emphatic pronouns inflect for number and case; in addition, the third-person forms inflect for gender too.

Emphatic personal pronouns

First person: 'I, we'

	Sg.	Pl.
Nom.	εγώ	εμείς
Acc.	εμένα	εμάς
Gen.	εμένα	εμάς

Second person: 'you'

	Sg.	Pl.
Nom.	εσύ	εσείς
Acc.	εσένα	εσάς
Gen.	εσένα	εσάς

Third person: 'he, she, they'

	Sg.			Pl.		
	M	F	N	M	F	N
Nom.	αυτός	αυτή	αυτό	αυτοί	αυτές	αυτά
Acc.	αυτό(ν)	αυτή(ν)	αυτό	αυτούς	αυτές	αυτά
Gen.	αυτού	αυτής	αυτού	αυτών	αυτών	αυτών

1. The accusative forms of the first- and second-person pronouns lose their initial vowel when preceded by the prepositions από, για, e.g. για μένα 'for me'. The initial vowel of the nominative forms of the first- and second-person pronouns is often dropped in rapid speech when preceded by other words ending in a vowel; here the omission of the vowel is normally indicated by an apostrophe, e.g. Ξέρω 'γώ; 'How should I know?'

2. The third-person pronoun is also used as the demonstrative 'this' (see section 4.3). It declines like adjectives in -ος, -η, -ο (see section 3.33), except that a final ν is often added to the forms of the masculine and feminine accusative singular. Other demonstratives can also be used as third-person pronouns and are declined in the same way: τούτος, -η, -ο 'this one', εκείνος, -η, -ο 'that one'.

3. There are alternative colloquial forms of the genitive of the third-person pronoun: masculine and neuter singular αυτουνού, feminine singular αυτηνής, plural αυτωνών (all genders). There is also a colloquial version of the masculine accusative plural: αυτουνούς.

4 Pronouns and determiners

Emphatic pronouns are used to distinguish one person from another. They may function as the subject (1–2) or object (3–4) of a verb, or as the object of a preposition (5–6), or simply on their own (7):

1 *Εσύ το είπες!*
   You (sg.) said it! ('It was you that said it')

2 *Εγώ δεν θέλω να πάω.*
   (As for me,) **I** don't want to go.

3 *Εσάς είδαμε!*
   We saw **you** (pl.)! ('It was you we saw') (direct object)

4 *Εμένα δώσ' το!*
   Give it to **me**! (indirect object)

5 *Το έκανα γι' αυτόν.*
   I did it for **him**.

6 *ένας από μας*
   one of *us*

7 *– Ποιος το θέλει; – Εγώ!*
   'Who wants it?' '*Me*!' ('*I* do')

Emphatic pronouns may also be used to accompany noun phrases:

8 *εμείς οι Έλληνες* (masc. nom.)
   we Greeks

4.3 Demonstrative pronouns and determiners

There are three demonstratives: **αυτός**, **τούτος** and **εκείνος**. They all decline like adjectives in -ος, -η, -ο (see section 3.33). They may be used either as emphatic third-person pronouns ('he', 'she', 'it': see section 4.2) or as true demonstratives ('this', 'that') functioning as pronouns or as determiners modifying a noun (which must be preceded by the definite article). Demonstratives are used to point to something, as in examples 1–3 below.

Of the three, **τούτος** is the least commonly used; it refers to something close to the speaker ('this'). **Αυτός** also refers to something near the speaker ('this'), while **εκείνος**, which is less frequently used, refers to something distant from the speaker ('that'). Example 1 shows **αυτός** and **εκείνος** being used as demonstrative pronouns:

1 *Θέλω αυτό, όχι εκείνο* (neut. sg.).
   I want *this* [one] (neut.), not *that* [one].

When one of these words is used as a determiner (i.e. with a noun), the noun must be immediately preceded by the definite article, and the determiner must appear outside the combination of article + noun. When the noun denotes something that is present at the time of speaking, the normal order is determiner + article + noun:

Demonstrative pronouns and determiners

2   Μου αρέσει *αυτή η ομπρέλα*.
    I like *this* umbrella.

3   *Εκείνο το παιδί* όλο παίζει.
    That child is always playing.

In written language a determiner may be used to refer to something that has been previously mentioned. In this case it normally follows the noun rather than precedes it:

4   Θυμάμαι το πρώτο μας σπίτι. *Το σπίτι αυτό* βρισκόταν στο κέντρο της πόλης.
    I remember our first house. *This house* was in the centre of town.

Finally, the demonstratives **αυτός** and **εκείνος** may be used with a relative clause:

5   *Αυτός που* ήρθε χθες ήταν περίεργος άνθρωπος.
    The one who came yesterday was a strange man.

6   *Εκείνοι που* λένε τέτοια πράγματα θα έπρεπε να τιμωρηθούν.
    Those who/People who say such things ought to be punished.

The qualitative demonstrative **τέτοιος** 'such, of such a kind, like this/that, this/that sort of' declines like adjectives in **-ος, -α, -ο** (see section 3.34) and functions as a pronoun (7–8) or determiner (9):

7   Δεν είχαμε *τέτοιους* στα νιάτα μου.
    We didn't have *such people/that sort of people/people like that* in my youth.

8   Θέλω ένα *τέτοιο*.
    I want one *like that/one of those*.

9   Δεν έχουμε *τέτοια* πράγματα.
    We don't have *such* things/*that sort of* thing/things *like that*.

It is also commonly used in the phrase **κάτι τέτοιο** 'something like that'.

The quantitative demonstrative **τόσος** 'so much/many' declines like adjectives in **-ος, -η, -ο** (section 3.33). It may be used as a pronoun (10) or a determiner (11):

10 Ήρθαν *τόσοι σήμερα!*
   So many [people] came today!

11 Μη βάζεις *τόση ζάχαρη!*
   Don't put in *so much* sugar!

'So much/many' can also be expressed by the adverb **τόσο** followed by the appropriate form of **πολύς**; alternatively, both **τόσος** and **πολύς** can be declined:

12 *τόσο/τόσα πολλά σπίτια*
   so many houses

4.4 Possessive pronouns and determiners

The weak pronoun in the genitive is used as a non-emphatic possessive pronoun (see section 4.1). The emphatic possessive **δικός** (**μου** etc.) is both a pronoun and a determiner (i.e. it may be used on its own, or together with a noun). Like the other emphatic pronouns, it is used to distinguish between persons or generally to give emphasis ('*my* house', as opposed to yours etc., or else 'my *own* house', or simply 'mine'). These forms are a combination of **δικός** with the genitive of the weak personal pronoun. **Δικός**, which must agree with the gender, number and case of the item possessed, is normally declined like adjectives in **-ος, -η, -ο** (see section 3.33), but there is an alternative set of feminine forms in colloquial use (**δικιά** etc.), which declines like adjectives in **-ος, -ια, -ο** (see section 3.35). **Δικός** (**μου** etc.) may be preceded by the definite article or not, according to whether it is used in a definite phrase or an indefinite phrase.

(ο, η, το) δικός, -ή, -ό μου	my, mine, my own
(ο, η, το) δικός, -ή, -ό σου	your, yours, your own (where the possessor is a single person)
(ο, η, το) δικός, -ή, -ό του	his, his own ('its' etc., where the possessor is non-human)
(ο, η, το) δικός, -ή, -ό της	her, hers, her own ('its' etc., where the possessor is non-human)

(o, η, το) δικός, -ή, -ό μας	our, ours, our own
(o, η, το) δικός, -ή, -ό σας	your, yours, your own (addressed to more than one person, or to a single person in the polite plural form)
(o, η, το) δικός, -ή, -ό τους	their, theirs, their own

Like adjectives, the emphatic possessive can be used attributively (1–2) or predicatively (3–4) (see also section 3.57), or as the object of a preposition (5). Note the use of the definite article in the definite phrases in examples 1, 3 and 5, and its omission in the indefinite phrases in 2 and 4:

1 *Το δικό μας σπίτι είναι παλιό.*
   Our house is old.

2 *Δεν έχει δικό της σπίτι.*
   She hasn't got a house *of her own* (lit. '*her own* house').

3 *Το τελευταίο σπίτι είναι το δικό μας.*
   The last house is *ours* (i.e. it's the one where we live).

4 *Το τελευταίο σπίτι είναι δικό μας.*
   The last house is *ours* (i.e. it belongs to us).

5 *Πάμε στο σπίτι σου ή στο δικό μου;*
   Shall we go to your house or *mine*?

4.5 Interrogative pronouns and determiners

Interrogative pronouns and determiners ('who?', 'which?', 'what?', 'how much?') belong to the category known as question words. (Other question words correspond to 'why?', 'when?', 'where?'. For the use of question words in direct and indirect questions see sections 10.6 and 10.10.)

There are three interrogative pronouns and determiners: **ποιος** 'who?', 'which?', **τι** 'what?' and **πόσος** 'how much?'. **Τι** is indeclinable and may modify nouns of any gender, number or case. **Πόσος** declines like adjectives in -ος, -η, -ο (see section 3.33). **Ποιος** declines like adjectives in -ος, -α, -ο, except that the accusative form of the masculine (and sometimes the feminine singular) adds an -ν and extended versions of the genitive singular and plural and the masculine accusative plural forms may be used:

ποιος who?, which?

Singular

	M	F	N
Nom.	ποιος	ποια	ποιο
Acc.	ποιον	ποια(ν)	ποιο
Gen.	ποιου/ποιανού	ποιας/ποιανής	ποιου/ποιανού

Plural

	M	F	N
Nom.	ποιοι	ποιες	ποια
Acc.	ποιους/ποιανούς	ποιες	ποια
Gen.	ποιων/ποιανών	ποιων/ποιανών	ποιων/ποιανών

In place of the genitive singular forms, τίνος 'whose?' is often used for the masculine and neuter, but not for the feminine. There is a genitive plural τίνων (all genders).

4.6 Indefinite pronouns and determiners

Indefinite pronouns and determiners can be divided into two kinds: specific ('someone', 'something') and non-specific ('anyone', 'anything,' 'no one', 'nothing').

The specific pronouns and determiners are **κάποιος** (declined like adjectives in -ος, -α, -ο, as in section 3.34, but with masculine accusative singular **κάποιον** when used as a pronoun, i.e. without a noun), and indeclinable **κάτι**:

1 *Κάποιος έρχεται.*
   Someone's coming.

2 *Είδα κάποιον να έρχεται.*
   I saw someone coming.

3 *Κάτι λείπει.*
   Something's missing.

As a determiner, **κάποιος** may be used with a noun in any number, gender or case. **Κάτι** may be used as a determiner with plural nouns of any gender and in any grammatical case to mean 'some':

4   *κάποια δασκάλα*
    some (female) teacher *or other*

5   *κάποια έργα*
    some plays/films (*or other*)

6   *κάτι φίλοι μου*
    some friends of mine

Κάτι can be accompanied by a number of determiners, e.g. **κάτι άλλο** 'something else', **κάτι τέτοιο** 'something like that', **κάτι δικό μου** 'something of my own'; it may also be accompanied by an adjective, in which case the definite article is normally used, e.g. **κάτι το ωραίο** 'something nice'.

The non-specific pronouns and determiners are **κανείς/κανένας** 'any(one), no (one)' and the indeclinable **τίποτα** or **τίποτε** 'any(thing), no(thing)'. The declension of **κανείς/κανένας** resembles that of the indefinite article **ένας** (see section 3.7) and only has singular forms:

	M	F	N
Nom.	κανείς/κανένας	καμιά/καμία	κανένα
Acc.	κανένα(ν)	καμιά(ν)/καμία(ν)	κανένα
Gen.	κανενός	καμιάς/καμίας	κανενός

1. The feminine forms with stressed -ι- (καμία etc.) are more emphatic.
2. The final -ν may be added to the masculine and feminine accusative singular forms when they are followed by a word beginning with a vowel or voiceless plosive. In addition, **κανέναν** is the normal form of the masculine accusative singular when used as a pronoun (i.e. without a noun).
3. In colloquial speech, the neuter **κανένα** may be shortened to **κάνα**, but only when used as a determiner, i.e. modifying a noun, or in the compound **καναδυό** (see p. 99).

The non-specific pronouns and determiners (like the non-specific adverbs: see the end of section 7.2) are normally used in interrogative or negative clauses, or in other clauses that do not make a statement. Examples of interrogative use:

Indefinite pronouns and determiners

7 Εμφανίστηκε *κανένας*;
   Did *anyone* show up?

8 Είπες *τίποτα*;
   Did you say *anything*?

When they are used negatively with a verb, the verb must be accompanied by the appropriate negative particle **δεν** or **μην**:

9 *Κανένας* δεν εμφανίστηκε.
   Nobody showed up.

10 Μη στείλεις *κανέναν* εδώ.
   Don't send *anyone* here.

11 Δεν είπα *τίποτα*.
   I didn't say *anything*.

12 Προτιμώ να μην πεις *τίποτα*.
   I prefer you to say *nothing*.

These words are also used without a verb in a negative sense:

13 – Ποιος ήρθε σήμερα; – *Κανένας*.
   'Who came today?' '*Nobody*'.

14 – Τι θέλεις; – *Τίποτα*.
   'What do you want?' '*Nothing*'.

In addition, these words are used in subjunctive (15), conditional (16) and imperative (17) clauses:

15 Ίσως να σε δει *κανένας* δάσκαλος.
   Perhaps a teacher will see you.

16 Αν σε δει *κανένας* δάσκαλος, θα σε αναφέρει.
   If a teacher sees you, he'll report you.

17 Για ρώτα *κανένα* δάσκαλο.
   Ask a teacher.

The use of these words as determiners (i.e. modifying nouns) is illustrated in examples 15–17 above and 18 below.

When used in positive declarative sentences, these items have a vague sense of 'approximately one':

18 Περιμέναμε *καμιά* ώρα.
   We waited *about an* hour.

The indefinite non-specific determiner **κανένας** is used in the expression **καμιά φορά** 'occasionally' (not 'never'), while **καμιά** is also used with approximative numerals (see section 5.4), e.g. **καμιά δωδεκαριά** 'about a dozen'. The indeclinable colloquial compound **καναδυό** (short for **κανένα δυο**) means 'one or two, a couple (of)'.

The form **κανείς** has two distinct functions. First, it may be used as a slightly more formal alternative of **κανένας**. Second, it is used in rather formal styles to denote the indefinite subject of a verb in a non-negative clause, where it corresponds to the English 'one'; in this use it normally comes immediately after the verb:

> Εύκολα βλέπει *κανείς* τα φριχτά αποτελέσματα του πολέμου.
> *One* easily sees (i.e. 'it's easy to see') the frightful results of war.

The more colloquial alternative would be to use the second person singular of the verb in the same indefinite sense.

Τίποτα, like **κάτι**, can be accompanied by a number of determiners, or by an adjective, e.g. **τίποτ' άλλο** 'anything else; nothing else', **τίποτα τέτοιο** 'anything like that; nothing like that', **τίποτα το ωραίο** 'anything nice; nothing nice'.

4.7 Relative and correlative pronouns and determiners

Relative pronouns and determiners ('who', 'which', 'that') are used to introduce relative clauses. (For relative clauses see section 10.9.)

The basic equivalent of the English relative pronoun is the indeclinable relative particle **που**. This does not agree in gender and number with the noun modified by the relative clause (in 'the man who came', the phrase 'the man' is modified by the relative pronoun 'who'). Unlike the English relative (e.g. 'who' and 'which'), the Greek relative does not change according to whether the modified noun denotes a human or a non-human.

1 Ο άνθρωπος *που* ήρθε είναι ο αδελφός μου.
   The man *who* came is my brother.

2 Ο άνθρωπος *που* είδες είναι ο αδελφός μου.
   The man (*whom*) you saw is my brother.

3 Το δέντρο *που* φυτρώνει στην αυλή μου είναι πορτοκαλιά.
   The tree *that/which* is growing in my back yard is an orange.

4   Το δέντρο *που* είδες είναι πορτοκαλιά.
    The tree (*that*) you saw is an orange.

In examples 2 and 4 note that a Greek relative clause must begin with the relative pronoun or particle; the pronoun cannot be omitted, whereas in English it can be omitted when it acts as the direct or indirect object of the relative clause.

It is possible to use **που** to introduce any relative clause. However, there is a more complicated alternative: the relative pronoun phrase **ο οποίος**. This consists of the definite article followed by the word **οποίος**, and both items must be inflected not only for gender and number to agree with the modified noun, but also for case to suit their syntactical function within the relative clause (i.e. whether the relative pronoun phrase is the subject, direct object, etc.). Οποίος declines like adjectives in -ος, -α, -ο (see section 3.34). For examples of use see section 10.9.

Apart from **που** and **ο οποίος**, there are the following correlative pronouns and determiners, which are used in free relative clauses (i.e. relative clauses that do not modify a noun):

- **όποιος, -α, -ο** 'whoever', which declines like adjectives in section 3.34 (this must not be confused with the relative **ο οποίος**, which is always used with the article and is always stressed on the last but one syllable)
- **οποιοσδήποτε**, fem. **οποιαδήποτε**, neut. **οποιοδήποτε** 'whoever' (stronger than **όποιος**)
- **ό,τι** (indeclinable) 'that which, what, whatever' (distinguished from the complementizer **ότι** by the comma after the first letter; also distinguish this from **τι** 'what' used in interrogative sentences)
- **οτιδήποτε** (indeclinable) 'whatever' (stronger than **ό,τι**)
- **όσος, -η, -ο** (declined like adjectives in section 3.33) 'as much as, as many as, however much; (pl.) those which, however many'
- **οσοσδήποτε**, fem. **οσηδήποτε**, neut. **οσοδήποτε** (same meaning as **όσος**, but stronger)

These items can be used as pronouns (i.e. without nouns) or as determiners (i.e. with nouns). When used as a pronoun, the masculine singular accusative of **όποιος** is **όποιον**, with final -ν. For examples of their use see section 10.9.2.

4.8 The universal pronouns *καθένας* and *καθετί* and the distributive determiner *κάθε*

Καθένας and **καθετί** normally function as pronouns, although they are occasionally used as determiners. **Καθένας** 'every one, each one' is inflected in a broadly similar way to the numeral and indefinite article **ένας** (section 3.7) and the indefinite pronoun and determiner **κανένας** (section 4.6):

	M	F	N
Nom.	καθένας	καθεμιά/καθεμία	καθένα
Acc.	καθένα	καθεμιά/καθεμία	καθένα
Gen.	καθενός	καθεμιάς/καθεμίας	καθενός

Καθετί 'each thing' is indeclinable. Each of these pronouns may optionally be preceded by the definite article:

1 Το ξέρει *ο καθένας* μας.
   Each one of us knows it.

2 Παραπονιέται με *το καθετί*.
   (S)he complains about *every single thing*.

Κάθε 'each, every' is an indeclinable determiner used with singular nouns only. It too may optionally be preceded by the definite article:

3 Προσέχει (την) *κάθε* λέξη.
   (S)he takes care over *every* word.

For **κάθε** in expressions of time see section 7.1.

4.9 Other pronouns and determiners

The intensive pronouns and determiners **ίδιος** 'same' and **μόνος** 'only, alone' decline like adjectives in -ος, -α, -ο (section 3.34) and -ος, -η, -ο (section 3.33) respectively.

Ίδιος has two chief uses, in both of which it is preceded by the definite article. As a pronoun, **ο ίδιος** means either 'the same' or '(my)self' according to the context:

4 Pronouns and determiners

1   *Τα ίδια είναι.*
    They're *the same (things)* (neuter).

2   Θέλω να μιλήσω με *την ίδια*.
    I want to speak to *her in person* (lit. *herself*).

As a determiner, when it immediately precedes the noun it accompanies, **ο ίδιος** means 'the same':

3   Έχουμε *το ίδιο πρόβλημα*.
    We have *the same* problem.

When the definite article is repeated before the noun it accompanies, or when it follows an emphatic pronoun, **ο ίδιος** means 'myself', 'yourself', etc.:

4   Θέλω να μιλήσω με *την ίδια* τη Μαρία/τη Μαρία *την ίδια*.
    I want to speak to Mary *herself*.

5   Εσύ *ο ίδιος* το είπες.
    You *yourself* said it.

Ίδιος is also used without the definite article to mean 'identical, alike':

6   Όλες οι καρέκλες είναι *ίδιες*.
    All (the) chairs are *alike*.

Μόνος, with or without a noun, typically means 'only':

7   Ήταν ο *μόνος* φοιτητής που ήρθε.
    He was the *only* student (masc.) who came.

8   Ήταν ο *μόνος* που ήρθε.
    He was the *only* [one] who came.

Used with a weak pronoun in the genitive, **μόνος** means 'by myself', in the sense of either 'without company' or 'without help':

9   Μένει *μόνη της*.
    She lives *on her own*.

10 *Μόνη της* το έκανε.
    She did it *by herself*.

The contrastive pronoun and determiner **άλλος** 'other, next' (sometimes 'previous') declines like adjectives in -ος, -η, -ο with the following alternative emphatic forms for the genitive: masculine and neuter singular **αλλουνού**, feminine singular **αλληνής**, plural (all genders) **αλλωνών**.

11 τα *άλλα* παιδιά
    the *other* children

12   την *άλλη* φορά
     the *next*/previous) time

'Άλλος may be used more than once in a single sentence in the sense of 'some . . . others . . .':

13   *Άλλοι ήρθαν, άλλοι όχι.*
     Some came, *others* didn't (lit. 'others not').

After the pronouns and determiners κάποιος, κανένας, ποιος and όποιος, άλλος is the equivalent of 'else': κάποιος άλλος 'someone else', κανένας άλλος 'nobody else', ποιος άλλος 'who else', όποιος άλλος 'whoever else'.

When used with a numeral, άλλος may either precede or follow the numeral, but with different meanings:

14a *άλλο ένα* μπουκάλι
     one more bottle (i.e. an extra one)

  b *ένα άλλο* μπουκάλι
     a different bottle

Άλλος τόσος has the sense of 'as much again' (i.e. twice as much):

15   Αν είχαμε *άλλα τόσα* λεφτά θα μπορούσαμε να αγοράσουμε το σπίτι.
     If we had *twice as much* money, we would be able to buy the house.

For the use of the reciprocal expression ο ένας τον άλλο 'each other', see section 10.24.

4.10   Quantifiers

A quantifier is a word that expresses quantity without expressing number. The quantifiers όλος 'all' and ολόκληρος '(the) whole' decline like adjectives in -ος, -η, -ο (section 3.33). Like the demonstratives αυτός, τούτος and εκείνος (see section 4.3), when used with a noun όλος (always) and ολόκληρος (often) are accompanied by the definite article, in which case they always appear outside the article + noun combination:

1   *όλος* ο κόσμος
     all the world/everyone

2   Έφαγε την πίτα *ολόκληρη*.
     (S)he/it ate the *whole* pie.

The plural of **όλος** also functions as a pronoun, meaning 'all of them', or (typically in the masculine) 'everyone', or (in the neuter) 'everything':

3   Ήρθαν *όλοι* (masc. pl.).
    Everyone came/They *all* came.

4   Τα κατάλαβα *όλα*.
    I understood *everything*/I understood it *all*.

Other quantifiers include the following:

- **πολύς** 'much, a lot of; too much; (pl.) many; too many'; comparative **περισσότερος** 'more' (note that Greek does not normally distinguish between 'much/many' and 'too much/too many')
- **αρκετός** 'quite a lot of'
- **κάμποσος** (less commonly **καμπόσος**) 'quite a few'
- **μπόλικος** 'plenty of'
- **μερικοί** (plural only) 'some'
- **λίγος** '(a) little, (pl.) (a) few'; comparative **λιγότερος** 'less; (pl.) fewer'
- **ελάχιστος** 'very little; (pl.) very few'
- **ο υπόλοιπος** 'the rest of' (always with definite article)
- **ένα σωρό** 'a whole load of'

The expression **ένα σωρό** (originally a noun phrase in the accusative meaning 'a pile') is used in colloquial speech and is indeclinable:

5   Ήρθαν *ένα σωρό* Ιταλοί.
    A whole load of Italians came.

All the other quantifiers inflect for gender, number and case. They decline like adjectives in **-ος, -η, -ο** except **πολύς**, for which see section 3.38. The following examples illustrate the use of **υπόλοιπος**:

6   *το υπόλοιπο* αλεύρι (nom./acc.)
    the rest of the flour

7   *οι υπόλοιπες* μαθήτριες (nom.)
    the rest of the schoolgirls

Some quantifiers have corresponding adverbs: **πολύ** 'very' (used with the positive forms of adjectives), 'much' (used with comparative forms of adjectives), 'a lot' (comparative **περισσότερο** 'more'); **αρκετά** 'quite (a bit)'; **λίγο** 'a little, a bit' (comparative **λιγότερο** 'less'); **ελάχιστα** 'very little, hardly' (used with adjectives) (see section 7.1: adverbs of quantity).

Chapter 5

Numerals

5.1 Table of cardinal and ordinal numerals

The table on pp. 106–7 gives the forms of the cardinal and ordinal numerals from 1 to 1,000,000,000 (a billion). The cardinal numerals are the basic forms ('one', 'two', 'three', etc.). The ordinal numerals indicate position in a series ('first', 'second', 'third', etc.). Several of the cardinal numerals are declined for gender and case. In the table those forms which decline are printed in italics, in their nominative masculine forms. The details of their declensional patterns are given in section 5.2. The ordinal numerals are all declined like adjectives in **-ος, -η, -ο** (see section 3.33). 'Zero' or 'nought' is the neuter noun **μηδέν** (see section 3.29).

When counting, we use the declinable numbers in their neuter forms: **ένα, δύο, τρία, τέσσερα**, etc. For the use of the full stop and comma in Greek cardinal numerals and decimals see section 2.4.

Another system of numerals, which employs either the capitals or the lower-case letters of the Greek alphabet, is sometimes used for certain special purposes. We shall limit ourselves to the capital letters, which, when followed by an acute accent, are used as ordinal numerals rather in the way Roman numerals are used in English. According to this alphabetic system, the numbers from one to ten are: **Α'** =1, **Β'** = 2, **Γ'** = 3, **Δ'** = 4, **Ε'** = 5, **ϛ'** = 6, **Ζ'** = 7, **Η'** = 8, **Θ'** = 9, **Ι'** = 10. (Note the special case of **ϛ'**, often written as **ΣΤ'** (and pronounced **στίγμα**), for the numeral 6.) From eleven to nineteen, **Ι** is combined with the relevant number, e.g. **ΙΔ'** = 14; 20 is **Κ'**. Numbers of this kind are often used for chapters or volumes of books, acts or scenes of a play, centuries, and the names of kings, queens, emperors, patriarchs and popes. Some examples:

5 Numerals

	Cardinal numerals	Ordinal numerals
1	*ένας*	πρώτος
2	*δύο/δυο*	δεύτερος
3	*τρεις*	τρίτος
4	*τέσσερις*	τέταρτος
5	*πέντε*	πέμπτος
6	*έξι*	έκτος
7	*επτά/εφτά*	έβδομος
8	*οκτώ/οχτώ*	όγδοος
9	*εννέα/εννιά*	ένατος
10	*δέκα*	δέκατος
11	*ένδεκα/έντεκα*	ενδέκατος
12	*δώδεκα*	δωδέκατος
13	*δεκατρείς*	δέκατος τρίτος
14	*δεκατέσσερις*	δέκατος τέταρτος
15	*δεκαπέντε*	δέκατος πέμπτος
16	*δεκαέξι/δεκάξι*	δέκατος έκτος
17	*δεκαεπτά/δεκαεφτά*	δέκατος έβδομος
18	*δεκαοκτώ/δεκαοχτώ*	δέκατος όγδοος
19	*δεκαεννέα/ δεκαεννιά*	δέκατος ένατος
20	*είκοσι*	εικοστός
21	*είκοσι ένας*	εικοστός πρώτος
22	*είκοσι δύο*	εικοστός δεύτερος
30	*τριάντα*	τριακοστός
40	*σαράντα*	τεσσαρακοστός
50	*πενήντα*	πεντηκοστός
60	*εξήντα*	εξηκοστός
70	*εβδομήντα*	εβδομηκοστός
80	*ογδόντα*	ογδοηκοστός
90	*ενενήντα*	ενενηκοστός
100	*εκατόν/εκατό*	εκατοστός
101	*εκατόν ένας*	εκατοστός πρώτος
200	*διακόσιοι*	διακοσιοστός

Table of cardinal and ordinal numerals

300	τριακόσιοι/ τρακόσιοι	τριακοσιοστός
400	τετρακόσιοι	τετρακοσιοστός
500	πεντακόσιοι	πεντακοσιοστός
600	εξακόσιοι	εξακοσιοστός
700	επτακόσιοι/ εφτακόσιοι	επτακοσιοστός
800	οκτακόσιοι/ οχτακόσιοι	οκτακοσιοστός
900	εννιακόσιοι/ εννεακόσιοι	εννεακοσιοστός
1.000	χίλιοι	χιλιοστός
2.000	δύο χιλιάδες	δισχιλιοστός
3.000	τρεις χιλιάδες	τρισχιλιοστός
10.000	δέκα χιλιάδες	δεκακισχιλιοστός
1.000.000	ένα εκατομμύριο	εκατομμυριοστός
1.000.000.000	ένα δισεκατομμύριο	δισεκατομμυριοστός

1. For some numerals there are alternative forms. These are shown in the table separated by an oblique line (/). The form given first is the more common, or the more stylistically neutral. But it is often largely a matter of personal preference. For the numeral 'two', δύο (pronounced as two syllables) is more emphatic than δυο (one syllable) and is also the form used in counting; otherwise, δυο is the form normally used in speech.

2. The cardinal numerals up to twenty consist of one word. From twenty-one onwards, the units, tens, hundreds etc. are written as separate words, e.g. τέσσερις χιλιάδες πεντακόσια ενενήντα εννέα 'four thousand five hundred and ninety-nine'.

1 Τόμος ΣΤ' (= Τόμος έκτος)
Volume 6

2 Πράξη Γ' (= Πράξη τρίτη)
Act 3 (or III)

3 στον ΙΘ' αιώνα (= στον δέκατο ένατο αιώνα)
in the 19th century

4 η Βασίλισσα Ελισάβετ Β' (= η Βασίλισσα Ελισάβετ η δεύτερη)
Queen Elizabeth II

5 ο Μιχαήλ Η' (= ο Μιχαήλ ο όγδοος)
Michael VIII

5.2 The declined forms of cardinal numerals

The cardinal numerals 'one', 'three' and 'four', when used alone or in a number ending in any of these digits (except for 'eleven' – ένδεκα/έντεκα – which is indeclinable), are declined as follows:

ένας one

	M	F	N
Nominative	ένας	μία/μια	ένα
Accusative	ένα(ν)	μία(ν)/μια(ν)	ένα
Genitive	ενός	μιας	ενός

These forms are almost identical to the indefinite article (see section 3.7). The feminine forms **μία** and **μίαν**, pronounced as two syllables, are more emphatic and stress the singularity of the noun referred to. We can contrast *μία άποψη* 'one point of view' with *μια άποψη* 'a point of view'.

τρεις three

	M	F	N
Nom./Acc	τρεις	τρεις	τρία
Gen.	τριών	τριών	τριών

The numeral 'thirteen' (δεκατρείς) is declined in the same way, as are all numbers ending in 3: είκοσι τρεις, τριάντα τρεις, etc.

τέσσερις four

	M	F	N
Nom./Acc.	τέσσερις	τέσσερις	τέσσερα
Gen.	τεσσάρων	τεσσάρων	τεσσάρων

Similarly the numeral 'fourteen' (δεκατέσσερις) and all numbers ending in 4.

The adjective **μισός** 'half' often combines with cardinal numerals, with some special forms according to the gender and case of the noun which it modifies, e.g. masculine **ενάμισης χρόνος** 'one and a half years', feminine **μιάμιση ώρα** 'one and half hours', genitive **μιάμισης ώρας** 'of one and half hours', neuter **ενάμισι λίτρο** 'one and a half litres'. Note the forms **τρεισήμισι** (masculine and feminine), **τριάμισι** (neuter) and **τεσσερισήμισι** (masculine and feminine), **τεσσαράμισι** (neuter) for 'three and a half' and 'four and a half' respectively. The forms **δυόμισι, πεντέμισι, εξήμισι, εφτάμισι, οχτώμισι** etc. are indeclinable. These forms are also used for the half-hours when telling the time: see section 5.5, example 6.

The forms of the other cardinal numerals which decline are as follows:

- **διακόσιοι, διακόσιες, διακόσια** 'two hundred' and all the hundreds follow the plural declension of adjectives in **-ος** (see section 3.34). The genitive often undergoes a shift of stress to the penultimate syllable, e.g. **τριακοσίων μέτρων** 'of three hundred metres';
- **χίλιοι, χίλιες, χίλια** 'a thousand' is also an adjective and follows the same declension, with possible shift of stress in the genitive, as for the hundreds;
- the thousands from 2,000 onwards consist of the cardinal numerals 'two', 'three', 'four', etc. with the feminine plural noun **χιλιάδες** 'thousands', with which they must agree (rather than with any noun to which the number refers), e.g. **είκοσι τρεις χιλιάδες** 'twenty-three thousand'. There is a genitive case **χιλιάδων**, e.g. **δεκατεσσάρων χιλιάδων** 'of fourteen thousand';
- **εκατομμύριο** 'million' and **δισεκατομμύριο** 'billion' are neuter nouns, declined like the nouns in section 3.21. Examples: **ένα εκατομμύριο** 'a/one million'; **σαράντα τρία εκατομμύρια** 'forty-three million'; **ένα ποσό των είκοσι ενός εκατομμυρίων ευρώ** 'a sum of twenty-one million euros'.

5.3 Multiplicative numerals

Multiplicative numerals express the idea of 'single', double', 'treble' etc. They end in **-πλός** and are declined like adjectives in **-ος, -η, -ο** (section 3.33). The commonest such forms are: **απλός** 'single' (or 'simple'), **διπλός** 'double', **τριπλός** 'treble' (or 'triple'), **τετραπλός** 'quadruple'. Similarly **πολλαπλός** 'multiple'.

5.4 Collective numerals

Collective numerals express the idea of 'group of two', 'group of three', etc. They are feminine nouns formed with one of two suffixes: either **-άδα** (inclusive numerals for a definite number) or **-αριά** (approximative numerals for an approximate number). The latter are usually preceded by the indefinite determiner **καμιά**. Examples of inclusive numerals are: **δυάδα** 'group of two, duo', **τριάδα** 'group of three, trio, Trinity', **τετράδα** 'group of four', **δεκάδα** 'group of ten'. Examples of approximative numerals are: **καμιά πενταριά** 'about five', **καμιά δωδεκαριά** 'about a dozen', **καμιά εικοσαριά** 'twenty or so'.

5.5 Numerals in expressions of time, space and quantity

In this section we give examples of the uses of numerals in various kinds of expression.

Dates are expressed with the feminine accusative singular of the ordinal numeral for the first day of the month, and for other days by **στις** with the feminine accusative plural of the cardinal numeral:

1   την πρώτη Απριλίου
    on the first of April

2a στις είκοσι τέσσερις Σεπτεμβρίου
 b στις είκοσι τέσσερις του Σεπτέμβρη
    on the twenty-fourth of September

The definite article is normally used with the more colloquial names of the months, as in example 2b.

Dates in years are expressed with either **το** or **στα**:

3   το 2004/στα 2004
    in 2004

Times of day are expressed by **στη** (for 'one') or **στις** (for other numbers) with the feminine accusative of the cardinal numeral; 'o'clock' can be expressed by **η ώρα**:

4   στις τρεις η ώρα
    at three o'clock

The following examples show how minutes and fractions of the hour are expressed:

5   στις οχτώ και δέκα (λεπτά)
    at ten (minutes) past eight

> Numerals in expressions of time, space and quantity

6 στις πέντε και μισή/στις πεντέμισι (see section 5.2)
   at half past five

7 στη μία και τέταρτο
   at a quarter past one

8 Είναι δώδεκα παρά είκοσι.
   It's twenty to twelve.

For the use of the accusative to express duration or point in time see section 3.51.

Ages are expressed by the genitive:

9 *Πόσω(ν) χρονών είσαι; –Δεκαεννέα*
   'How old are you?' 'Nineteen.'

10 Είμαι *είκοσι ενός χρονών*.
   I am twenty-one years old.

11 ένα μωρό *τεσσάρων μηνών*
   a four-month-old baby

Expressions of height, depth, size and distance use the accusative (see also section 3.51):

12a ένα κτήριο *δεκαπέντε μέτρα* ψηλό
  b ένα κτήριο *δεκαπέντε μέτρα* ύψος
    a building fifteen metres high

13 μια λακκούβα *είκοσι πόντους* βάθος
   a pothole twenty centimetres deep

14 ένα σίδερο *δύο μέτρα* μήκος με *πέντε εκατοστά* φάρδος
   an iron bar two metres long by five centimetres wide

15 Το χωριό μου είναι *έξι χιλιόμετρα* μακριά.
   My village is six kilometres away.

In expressions of quantity the term of measurement and the things measured are in the same case ('in apposition'):

16 Ήταν εκεί *δυο χιλιάδες άνθρωποι*.
   There were two thousand people there.

17 Αγόρασα *τρία κιλά ντομάτες*.
   I bought three kilos of tomatoes.

18 Ο καθένας ήπιε *δυο λίτρα νερό*.
   Each person drank two litres of water.

Chapter 6
The verb and the verb phrase

6.1 Introduction to the verb phrase

6.1.1 Constituents of the verb phrase

A verb is a word which expresses the ways in which the subject of the sentence acts, the state in which it is, a change it undergoes, etc. Before dealing with the forms of the verb itself, we shall consider the ways in which the verb phrase functions in the sentence.

The verb phrase consists of either a verb alone (1), or a verb combined with a number of other elements such as objects (2–5), subject and object predicates (6), adverbial modifiers (7), etc. The Greek verb may also be preceded by particles expressing mood, tense, or negation (9–10) and weak object pronouns (10–11).

Here are some examples of verb phrases in Greek:

    1 Ο Νίκος *έφυγε*.
       Nick *left*.

    2 Ο Νίκος *έφερε τον Γιάννη*.
       Nick *brought John*.

    3 Ο Νίκος *έδωσε το βιβλίο στον Γιάννη*.
       Nick *gave the book to John*.

    4 Ο Νίκος *έδωσε της Μαρίας ένα ωραίο δαχτυλίδι*.
       Nick *gave Mary a beautiful ring*.

    5 Ο Νίκος *θα μιλήσει στον Γιάννη*.
       Nick *will speak to John*.

    6 Ο Νίκος *έγινε υπουργός*.
       Nick *became a minister*.

7   Ο Νίκος *έφυγε χθες*.
    Nick *left yesterday*.

8   Ο Νίκος *έβαλε το βιβλίο στην τσάντα του*.
    Nick *put the book in his bag*.

9   Ο Νίκος *θα φύγει χωρίς τη Μαρία*.
    Nick *will leave without Mary*.

10 Ο Νίκος *δεν θα σου δώσει τα λεφτά*.
    Nick *won't give you the money*.

11 Ο Νίκος *μου είπε ότι δεν θα φύγει αύριο*.
    Nick *told me that he won't leave tomorrow*.

Verbs are intransitive when they do not require an object, as in example 1, transitive when they take one or more objects. The object which is directly affected by the action of the verb is the direct object (2). It is usually in the accusative case. The object which is indirectly affected by the action of the verb is referred to as the indirect object and is expressed by either a prepositional phrase (3, 5) or the genitive case (4).

The same verb may appear both as transitive and intransitive with or without change in meaning, as in examples 12–15:

12 Ο Γιάννης *διαβάζει την εφημερίδα*.
    John *is reading the newspaper*.

13 Ο Γιάννης *διαβάζει* πολύ.
    John *reads* a lot.

14 Η Ελένη *γελάει* συνέχεια.
    Helen *is* always *laughing*.

15 Η Ελένη *γέλασε τον Νίκο*.
    Helen *fooled Nick*.

6.1.2 Objects and predicates

The direct object is expressed by either a full noun phrase typically in the accusative case (16a), or an emphatic pronoun in the accusative (16b), or a weak pronoun in the accusative (16c) or a combination of the two (16d). The weak pronoun is placed immediately before the verb form unless it is a gerund or an imperative:

16a Ο Βασίλης *κάλεσε την 'Αννα*.
     Basil invited *Anna*.

  b Ο Βασίλης *κάλεσε εμένα*.
     Basil invited *me*.

c Ο Βασίλης *με* κάλεσε.
Basil invited *me*.

d Ο Βασίλης *την* κάλεσε *την Άννα*.
Basil *did* invite *Anna*.

A verb may also have two objects, one direct and one indirect. The indirect object may be expressed in the genitive case and it may consist of either a full noun phrase (17a), or a weak pronoun (17b), or a combination of these (17c). Both object noun phrases may combine with weak pronouns (17d). In addition, the weak pronouns may completely replace the noun phrases (17e):

17a Η Λένα *χάρισε ένα ρολόι του Βασίλη*.
Lena gave Basil a watch.

b Η Λένα *του χάρισε ένα ρολόι*.
Lena gave *him* a watch.

c Η Λένα *του χάρισε του Βασίλη ένα ωραίο ρολόι*.
Lena gave Basil a beautiful watch.

d Η Λένα *του το χάρισε του Βασίλη το ρολόι*.
Lena gave Basil the watch.

e Η Λένα *του το χάρισε*.
Lena gave *it* to *him*.

There are some differences between objects expressed with full noun phrases and those expressed by weak pronouns. The full noun phrases may occur in either order so that the direct object may either precede the indirect object (17a) (though this order is becoming less usual than the reverse), or follow it (17c–d). The combinations of weak pronouns, on the other hand, are more restricted. The indirect object in the genitive must always precede the direct object in the accusative (17d). Furthermore, not all combinations of person are possible. The permitted sequences consist of combinations of any member of column A with any member of column B:

A	B
μου	τον
σου	την
του	το
της	τους
μας	τις
σας	τα
τους	

There are some verbs which take two objects, such as **διδάσκω** 'I teach', **κερνώ** 'I treat to', whose direct and indirect objects are both in the accusative case:

> Introduction to the verb phrase

18 Κέρασε *τον Γιάννη* ένα παγωτό.
    Treat *John* to an ice-cream.

The indirect object is most usually expressed by a prepositional phrase introduced by **σε**:

19 Ο Μιχάλης έστειλε μήνυμα *στη Χρυσούλα*.
    Michael sent a message *to Chrysoula*.

A few verbs may combine with a single object either in a prepositional phrase or in the genitive:

20a Η Αγγέλα θα μιλήσει *στον Γιάννη*.
     Angela will speak *to John*.

 b   Η Αγγέλα θα (*του*) μιλήσει *του Γιάννη*.
     Angela will speak *to John*.

A genitive weak pronoun, which is not an indirect object, may accompany a transitive or an intransitive verb, as in examples 21–23. These genitive weak pronouns express the psychological involvement of the person referred to by the pronoun with the effect of the action denoted by the verb:

21 *Του* χαλάσανε τα σχέδια.
    They spoiled *his* plans.

22 Θα *μου* σιδερώσεις το πουκάμισο;
    Will you iron my shirt *for me*?

23 Μη *μου* στενοχωρηθείς.
    Please don't get upset.

Just as in English, the verb phrase may contain a number of adverbial modifications expressing place, time, manner, cause, purpose, etc. These consist of either prepositional phrases or adverbial phrases or adverbial clauses, as in the following examples:

24 Συναντήθηκαν *στην Αθήνα* (place).
    They met *in Athens*.

25 Ήρθε *πολύ αργά* (time).
    (S)he came *very late*.

26 Του μίλησε *πολύ άσχημα* (manner).
    (S)he spoke to him *very rudely*.

27 Το έκανε *από πείσμα* (cause).
    (S)he did it *out of stubbornness*.

28 Διαβάζει πολύ *για να πάρει καλό βαθμό* (purpose).
    (S)he's studying a lot *in order to get good marks*.

Some intransitive verbs, known as linking verbs, are followed by either a noun phrase or an adjectival phrase in the nominative, which functions as the predicate of the subject. If the subject predicate is an adjectival phrase it agrees with the subject not only in case but also in number and gender (29); if the subject predicate is a noun phrase it agrees with the subject in case only (30):

29 Η αδελφή του είναι/έγινε *πολύ νευρικιά*.
    His sister is/has become *very neurotic*.

30 Ο Νίκος είναι/έγινε *η σωτηρία της*.
    Nick is/has become *her salvation*.

Some transitive verbs may, in addition to the direct object, take an object predicate in the form of either an adjective phrase (31) or a noun phrase (32). An object predicate agrees with the object to which it refers in case (i.e. the accusative), and if it is an adjectival phrase it must also agree in number and gender (31):

31 Θεωρούν τη Βάσω *πολύ έξυπνη*.
    They consider Vasso *very intelligent*.

32 Διόρισαν τη Βάσω *Υπουργό Παιδείας*.
    They appointed Vasso *Minister of Education*.

6.2 Preliminary notes on the verb system

Greek is a highly inflected language. Each verb is formed by the combination of a stem and an inflectional ending. The stem, which may be simple (γραφ- 'write') or derived (γιατρ-ευ- 'cure'), carries the essential meaning of the verb, while the inflectional ending expresses a complex system of grammatical categories, namely:

- Person: first, second, third
- Number: singular, plural

- Tense: past, non-past
- Voice: active, passive
- Aspect: perfective, imperfective
- Mood: imperative, non-imperative.

The inflected verb may be modified by the particles **να, ας, θα**, which precede the verb form and mark further divisions of mood (indicative/subjunctive) and the tense opposition (future/non-future). The only invariant, non-finite, verb forms are (a) the gerund, ending in **-οντας/-ώντας** (*παίζοντας και γελώντας* 'playing and laughing'), and (b) the non-finite verb form which follows the auxiliary **έχω** 'I have' to form the perfect tenses (*έχω μετανιώσει* 'I have changed my mind').

6.3 Person and number

The inflectional endings of a finite verb mark three persons (first, second and third: see also section 4.1) and two numbers (singular and plural). (For impersonal verbs see sections 6.6 and 10.25.) The person and number of the verb normally agree with the person and number of the subject, as in the following sentences:

1   *Εγώ* (1st sg.) *θα πληρώσω* (1st sg.) *τον λογαριασμό*.
    I will *pay* the bill.

2   *Εσείς* (2nd pl.) *να του μιλήσετε* (2nd pl.).
    You should *speak* to him.

In general, the plural of the subject pronoun and the verb refers to more than one individual, but in Greek, as in some other European languages, the second person plural may also be used to refer to only one individual in a polite and respectful manner ('plural of politeness'; see section 12.1), as above, where **εσείς** 'you' may refer to one or more persons.

Because the Greek verbal ending clearly shows variation in person and number, a subject pronoun becomes redundant and, for this reason, in many sentences no explicit subject is stated:

3   *Ελπίζω να σε βλέπουμε συχνά*.
    I hope that *we* will see you often.

4   *Ξέρεις πότε θα φτάσει;*
    Do you know when *(s)he* will arrive?

The subject pronoun is present in the sentence only if it is associated with special emphasis:

5   *Εμείς πάντως δεν ξέρουμε τίποτα.*
    We, however, know nothing.

6   *Εσύ πρέπει να του μιλήσεις.*
    You should speak to him.

7   *Αυτός είναι το πρόβλημα.*
    He's the problem.

The second person singular and third person plural can be used with general indefinite reference:

8   *Εδώ φωνάζεις* (2nd sg.) *και κανείς δεν σε ακούει.*
    Here *you shout* and nobody can hear you.

9   *Πού τρώνε* (3rd pl.) *φτηνά εδώ;*
    Where *can one eat* cheaply here?

6.4 Tense, aspect, voice and mood

Tense is the verbal category that indicates the time at which something happens. In main indicative clauses (see section 10.2) the point of time of the verb is defined in relation to the time of speaking. In other kinds of clause other factors are also relevant, such as the mood, the presence of particles and, for verbs in subordinate clauses, the tense of the main verb. The verb forms in Greek differentiate only between past and non-past. The future is formed with the particle **θα**, and the perfect and pluperfect are formed with the auxiliary verb **έχω** 'I have'.

Aspect is the verbal category that indicates whether the action, process, etc. denoted by the verb is viewed either (a) as occurring repeatedly or being in progress (imperfective aspect), or (b) in its totality as a single completed event (perfective aspect), or (c) as an event completed in the past whose completion is relevant to some other point in time (perfect aspect). The combinations of the two categories tense and aspect produce the verb forms which are often referred to as the tenses of the verb. For the use of the tenses see section 6.5.

Voice is the grammatical category that in general (and more clearly in cases of action verbs) indicates whether the subject is the initiator of the action (active voice), e.g. **ενοχλώ [κάποιον]** 'I annoy [someone]' or the entity that undergoes (is affected by) this action (passive voice), e.g. **ενοχλούμαι** 'I am annoyed'. In such situations the object of the active verb corresponds to the subject of the passive verb, while the subject of the active verb corresponds to a prepositional phrase which may be present or understood:

1 Η Ελένη (subject) *ενοχλεί πολύ* τον Μάρκο (object).
   Helen *annoys* Mark very much.

2 Ο Μάρκος (subject) *ενοχλείται πολύ από την Ελένη* (agent).
   Mark *is* very much *annoyed by Helen*.

Not all verbs have both active and passive voices. Furthermore, the correlation between active and passive voice endings and the meaning conveyed does not always hold. There are verbs with active endings which do not indicate action, e.g. πεινώ 'I am hungry', and verbs with passive endings which may indicate action and may take an object, e.g. περιποιούμαι [κάποιον] 'I look after [someone]'.

Mood is the verbal category that typically, in main clauses, indicates the attitude of the speaker towards what is conveyed by the verb. The verb forms in themselves differentiate only between the imperative mood (3), where the speaker orders, requests, etc. the hearer to do something, and the non-imperative moods. (For the use of the imperative see section 10.4.) The non-imperative forms may be either in the indicative mood (4–5) or the subjunctive mood (6–8). The indicative mood is characterized by the absence of the particles **να** and **ας** and by the fact that its negative particle is **δεν**. It is used when the speaker simply states or describes a situation. The subjunctive has the same verb form as the indicative but it is accompanied by the particles **να** or **ας** (with a few marginal exceptions) and the negative particle is **μην** (see also section 9.3). The subjunctive is used to express wishing, hoping, expecting, planning, etc.:

3 *Γράψε* το γράμμα! (imperative)
   Write the letter!

4 Η Ειρήνη *αγόρασε* καινούριο αυτοκίνητο (indicative).
   Irene *bought* a new car.

5 Η Μαίρη *δεν κατάλαβε καλά* (indicative).
   Mary *didn't understand* properly.

6 *Να καλέσουμε* και τον Γιάννη; (subjunctive)
   Should we invite John too?

7 Όχι, *να μην τον καλέσουμε* (subjunctive).
   No, *let's not invite him*.

8 *Ας φύγει* (subjunctive).
   Let him/her/it go.

Tense, aspect, voice and mood

6.5 The use of the tenses and other verb forms

Here we shall describe the use and the function of the verb forms (often referred to as tenses) derived from the combination of the categories of tense and aspect (see section 6.4). The particle **θα** may combine with any of these forms to produce a variety of future tenses and conditionals.

The various combinations of perfective/imperfective aspect and past/non-past give the first four simple forms below, while the combination of perfect aspect and past/non-past gives the two perfect tenses (names of forms are given in bold):

Aspect:	Imperfective	Perfective	Perfect
Tense:			
Non-past	δέν-ω	δέσ-ω	έχω δέσει
	'I tie,	(no English	'I have tied'
	I am tying'	equivalent)	
	present	**dependent**	**perfect**
Past	έ-δεν-α	έ-δεσ-α	είχα δέσει
	'I was tying,	'I tied'	'I had tied'
	I used to tie'		
	imperfect	**simple past**	**pluperfect**

6.5.1 Present (imperfective non-past)

The present expresses either a single event that is in progress (continuous) or a habitually repeated one:

1. **Η Κατερίνα** *ποτίζει* (repeated) **τα τριαντάφυλλα κάθε πρωί.**
   Katerina *waters* the roses *every morning*.

2. **Αυτή τη στιγμή είναι στον κήπο και** *ποτίζει* (continuous) **τα τριαντάφυλλα.**
   Right now she's in the garden *watering* the roses.

3. **Κοιμάται** (continuous) **τώρα γιατί δουλεύει τη νύχτα** (repeated).
   (S)he's asleep now because *(s)he works* nights.

4   Μην του μιλάς γιατί *δουλεύει* (continuous).
    Don't speak to him because *he's working*.

> The use of the tenses and other verb forms

The present may also be used occasionally to describe vividly an action that took place in the past. This is known as the 'historic present':

5   Χθες πρωί πρωί *χτυπάει* η πόρτα, *ανοίγω* και *βλέπω* τη Μαρία έξαλλη.
    First thing yesterday morning *there's a knock* at the door, *I open* [it] and *see* Mary furious.

The present is also used in live sports commentaries:

6   Ο Μπέκαμ *τρέχει, βρίσκει* την μπάλα, *σουτάρει* και *βάζει* γκολ.
    Beckham *runs, gets* the ball, *shoots* and *scores*.

The present may also describe future events to convey immediacy:

7   Μη στενοχωριέσαι, του το *δίνω εγώ αύριο*.
    Don't worry, *I'll give* it to him *tomorrow*.

The present may also be used to refer to an action or situation that began in the past and continues in the present, where English uses the perfect:

8   *Παίρνω* αυτό το φάρμακο *από το 1999*.
    I've been taking this medicine *since 1999*.

6.5.2 Imperfect (imperfective past)

The imperfect presents an action, process, etc. as occurring habitually (9) or continuously (10) in the past:

9   Πέρυσι *έτρεχα* κάθε πρωί για μισή ώρα και *ένιωθα* πολύ καλά.
    Last year *I ran* for half an hour *each morning* and *I felt* very well.

10 *Έτρεχε* προς την παραλία *όταν* τον είδα.
    He *was running* towards the shore *when* I saw him.

6.5.3 Simple past (perfective past)

The simple past presents an action as having been completed at some point in the past:

11 *Διάβασα* το άρθρο σου χθες και *εντυπωσιάστηκα*.
    I read your article yesterday and *I was impressed*.

12 Ο Γιάννης *κουράστηκε να επιμένει*.
    John *got tired* of insisting.

13 *Αγόρασες* τελικά αυτοκίνητο;
    Did you buy a car in the end?

6.5.4 Dependent (perfective non-past)

The dependent cannot be used on its own. It is used in combination with the future particle **θα** to form the perfective future (**θα γράψω** 'I will write') and with the particles **να** or **ας** to form the perfective subjunctive (**να/ας δέσω** 'that I tie, to tie, let me tie'). It may also occur after certain conjunctions such as **αν** (**αν φύγεις** 'if you leave') and **όταν** (**όταν φύγεις** 'when you leave'); it is obligatory after **πριν** (**πριν φύγεις** 'before you leave').

14 Ο Γιάννης *θα* μας *τηλεφωνήσει* στις οχτώ.
    John *will phone* us at eight o'clock.

15 Θέλει *να* του *τηλεφωνήσεις* στις οχτώ.
    He wants you *to phone* him at eight o'clock.

6.5.5 Perfect

The perfect is formed with the present tense of the auxiliary verb **έχω** followed by the non-finite verb form consisting of the perfective verb stem plus the suffix **-ει**, e.g. **έχω γράψει** ' I have written'. It is used when the completed action in the past has present relevance and is often interchangeable with the simple past:

16 *Έχω πιει/ήπια* τρεις καφέδες από το πρωί.
    I've drunk three coffees since the morning.

17 *Έχω βαρεθεί/βαρέθηκα* να περιμένω.
    I've got tired of waiting.

6.5.6 Pluperfect

This tense is formed with the past tense of the auxiliary verb **έχω** followed by the non-finite form, e.g. **είχα γράψει** 'I had written'. It is used to express an action completed in the past with consequences relevant to another past situation, either explicitly stated or understood:

18 Τον *είχαμε* ήδη *συναντήσει* τον Γιώργο όταν σε είδαμε.
    We'd already met George when we saw you.

19 Στις εννέα το πρωί *είχανε* κιόλας *αναχωρήσει*.
At nine o'clock in the morning *they had* already *left*.

6.5.7 Future

The future consists of the future particle **θα** followed either by the imperfective non-past (present tense) to form the imperfective future, which presents the action as habitual or continuous, e.g. **θα δένω** 'I will tie repeatedly' or 'I will be tying continuously', or by the dependent to form the perfective future, e.g. **θα δέσω** 'I will tie', which presents the action as completed.

The imperfective future is used to indicate that the action of the verb will be taking place repeatedly or continuously in the future:

20 *Κάθε Τετάρτη θα τρώμε* στου Μήτσου την ταβέρνα.
Every Wednesday *we'll eat* at Mitsos's taverna.

21 'Οταν φτάσεις *θα δουλεύει*.
When you get there *(s)he'll be working*.

The perfective future is used to indicate that the action of the verb will be completed at a particular point in time in the future:

22 *Θα συναντήσω* τη Μαίρη *αύριο το απόγευμα*.
I'll meet Mary *tomorrow afternoon*.

6.5.8 Conditional

This is formed by the future particle **θα** followed by the imperfect. It expresses suppositions or counterfactual conditions (for more on conditional clauses see section 10.13):

23 Αν είχα αυτοκίνητο, *θα πήγαινα* να τον δω.
If I had a car *I would go* and see him.

24 Αν ήξερα ότι ήσουνα εδώ θα σε καλούσα.
Had I known you were here *I would have invited you*.

6.5.9 Future perfect

This consists of the future particle **θα** followed by the perfect. It expresses an action that will have been completed at a particular point in time in the future and will be relevant to that point in time:

25 Μέχρι το καλοκαίρι *θα έχει τελειώσει* το βιβλίο που γράφει.
By the summer *(s)he'll have finished* the book (s)he's writing.

26 Ελπίζω ότι *θα έχει βρει* το ποσό που χρειάζεται.
I hope that *(s)he'll have found* the amount (s)he needs.

6.5.10 Perfect conditional

This consists of the future particle **θα** followed by the pluperfect. It describes an action that could have happened but failed to do so. It is used in the main clause of counterfactual conditions (see section 10.13).

27 Αν τον είχες γνωρίσει *θα τον είχες συμπαθήσει* κι εσύ.
If you had met him *you too would have liked him.*

28 Αν είχανε λεφτά *θα τον είχανε στείλει* στην Αγγλία.
If they had money *they would have sent him* to England.

6.5.11 The gerund

This is an uninflected verb form used adverbially. Its subject is normally identical with the subject of the clause in which it occurs. Occasionally, the subject of the gerund may be different from that of the clause (32). The gerund expresses manner (29), simultaneity of time (30) and occasionally cause (31).

29 Ο αδελφός της Ρίτας ήρθε *τρέχοντας* να της πει τα νέα.
Rita's brother *came running* to tell her the news.

30 *Μπαίνοντας* τους άκουσα να μιλούν ψιθυριστά.
As I came in I heard them whispering.

31 *Αναγνωρίζοντας* την αξία του θα του δώσουν προαγωγή.
Because they recognize his importance they will give him a promotion.

32 *Φεύγοντας ο Γιώργος,* η Ελένη άρχισε να κλαίει.
As George left, Helen started to cry.

6.6 Defective, impersonal and deponent verbs

Before we set out the basic verb forms, we must note that some verbs do not possess the full range of forms for each person, number, tense, aspect and voice. Different verbs lack different parts of the system.

Defective verbs have no perfective forms and exist only in the imperfective aspect (see section 6.4). Examples of defective verbs are: **ανήκω** 'I belong', **γειτονεύω** 'I am in the neighbourhood (of)', **είμαι** 'I am' (see section 6.7), **ευθύνομαι** 'I am responsible', **έχω** 'I have' (see section 6.18), **μάχομαι** 'I fight', **ξέρω** 'I know', **οφείλω** 'I owe, am obliged', **περιμένω** 'I wait (for)', **τρέμω** 'I tremble', **χρωστώ** 'I owe'.

Impersonal verbs have only third-person singular forms. The two most common verbs of this kind are **πρέπει** 'it is necessary (that)' and **πρόκειται** 'be about to'. Both verbs are normally followed by **να** and a verb in the present or dependent:

1 Πρέπει να γυρίσεις μέχρι το μεσημέρι.
   You must return by midday.

2 Έπρεπε να δουλεύω κάθε μέρα.
   I had to work every day.

3 Δεν πρόκειται να φύγουμε σήμερα.
   We're not going to leave today.

For impersonal uses of other verbs see section 10.25.

Deponent verbs have only passive forms. It is important to note that these verbs are active in meaning, but their endings are those of the passive voice. Examples: **αισθάνομαι** 'I feel', **αρνούμαι** 'I refuse', **δέχομαι** 'I receive, accept', **εργάζομαι** 'I work', **μιμούμαι** 'I imitate', **ντρέπομαι** 'I am ashamed', **φαίνομαι** 'I appear, seem', **φοβάμαι** 'I fear'. A few other verbs are semi-deponent: they have passive forms for the present and imperfect, but active forms for other tenses. The main ones are: **γίνομαι** 'I become, happen', **έρχομαι** 'I come', **κάθομαι** 'I sit'. For their other tenses see the table of irregular verbs (section 6.25).

The basic forms

Sections 6.7–6.13 give the basic forms of the verbs: the present, imperfect, simple past, dependent, imperfective and perfective imperatives (active and passive in each case) and the gerund. From these basic forms certain other forms are created; these are detailed in sections 6.17–6.20.

6.7 The verb 'to be'

The verb 'to be' ('I am', 'you are', etc.) is irregular, i.e. the pattern of personal endings is not the same as for any other verb, so it needs to be learnt separately. There are only two sets of tense forms: present and past (imperfect).

		Present		Imperfect	
Sg.	1	είμαι	I am	ήμουν(α)	I was
	2	είσαι	you are	ήσουν(α)	you were
	3	είναι	(s)he/it is	ήταν(ε)	(s)he/it was
Pl.	1	είμαστε	we are	ήμαστε/ ήμασταν	we were
	2	είστε/ είσαστε	you are	ήσαστε/ ήσασταν	you were
	3	είναι	they are	ήταν(ε)	they were

1. The forms of the imperfect with the additional vowel at the end (ήμουνα, ήσουνα, ήτανε) are less formal alternatives.
2. The difference between the other alternative forms (shown separated by /) is largely a matter of personal choice.

Note the different spellings of the initial vowel in the present (εί-) and imperfect (ή-).

6.8 First-conjugation verbs

Greek verbs are divided into two main categories:

(1) those that, in their active present tense, have the stress on the last syllable of the stem, e.g. γράφω 'I write', διαβάζω 'I read' (and, in fact, the majority of Greek verbs);

(2) those that have a first person singular of the active present stressed on the last vowel, e.g. αγαπώ 'I love', τηλεφωνώ 'I telephone'.

We refer to verbs as belonging to the first or second conjugation, according to this fundamental distinction. In this section the basic forms of first-conjugation verbs will be given. Those of second-conjugation verbs will be given in sections 6.9–6.11. For each tense or mood we give an approximate English meaning. For information about the use of the tenses and other verb forms see section 6.5.

First-conjugation verbs

χάνω I lose

Present		Active	Passive
Sg.	1	χάνω I lose	χάνομαι I get lost, lose myself
	2	χάνεις	χάνεσαι
	3	χάνει	χάνεται
Pl.	1	χάνουμε	χανόμαστε
	2	χάνετε	χάνεστε/ χανόσαστε
	3	χάνουν(ε)	χάνονται

1. The stress remains on the same syllable, except for the passive 1st person plural, and the alternative form of the passive 2nd person plural, where it moves forward by one syllable.
2. The active 3rd person plural form with -ε is frequent in the spoken language, but less often used in more formal contexts.
3. In the passive 2nd person plural the form in -εστε is more formal, while that in -όσαστε is more colloquial.

Imperfect		Active	Passive
Sg.	1	έχανα I was losing, used to lose	χανόμουν(α) I was getting lost, losing myself
	2	έχανες	χανόσουν(α)
	3	έχανε	χανόταν(ε)

6 The verb and the verb phrase

Pl.	1	χάναμε	χανόμασταν
	2	χάνατε	χανόσασταν
	3	έχαναν/χάνανε	χάνονταν/ χανόντουσαν/ χανόντανε

1. In the active imperfect, verbs with a one-syllable stem beginning with a consonant have a syllabic augment ε- in the singular and in the 3rd person plural, and this augment carries the stress (see section 6.21 for more details). The 3rd person plural form with -ε (and no augment) is more colloquial. Verbs with stems of more than one syllable have no augment, e.g. διάβαζα 'I was reading', from διαβάζω.

2. In the passive imperfect the stress moves forward one syllable, except for the 3rd person plural in -ονταν. The alternative singular forms with -α (1st and 2nd persons) or -ε (3rd person) are colloquial. The two alternative endings for the 3rd person plural, -όντουσαν and -όντανε, are also colloquial.

Simple past

		Active	Passive
Sg.	1	έχασα I lost	χάθηκα I was lost, lost myself
	2	έχασες	χάθηκες
	3	έχασε	χάθηκε
Pl.	1	χάσαμε	χαθήκαμε
	2	χάσατε	χαθήκατε
	3	έχασαν/χάσανε	χάθηκαν/χαθήκανε

1. The simple past tenses, active and passive, are based on the relevant perfective stems, and it is necessary to know what these stems are for each verb. (For the formation of the perfective stems of first-conjugation verbs see section 6.14.) The verb χάνω has an active perfective stem χασ- and passive χαθ-. The active forms have the same endings as the active imperfect, added to the perfective stem. The syllabic augment ε- is required for verbs with one-syllable stems, in the singular and in the 3rd person plural, just as in the imperfect.

2. The passive simple past is formed by adding an extra syllable -ηκ- and the past personal endings to the passive perfective stem: χάθ-ηκ-α. The endings are the same as the corresponding ones for the active simple past. The stress falls on the third syllable from the end in all forms. The 3rd person plural in -ανε is less formal.

First-conjugation verbs

Dependent

		Active	Passive
Sg.	1	χάσω (no English equivalent)	χαθώ (no English equivalent)
	2	χάσεις	χαθείς
	3	χάσει	χαθεί
Pl.	1	χάσουμε	χαθούμε
	2	χάσετε	χαθείτε
	3	χάσουν(ε)	χαθούν(ε)

1. The active and passive dependent forms are based on the same stem as the active and passive simple past tenses respectively. The active endings are the same as those of the active present tense. The stress falls on the last syllable of the stem. The passive endings are the same, except for the vowel -ει- in the 2nd person plural. But there is a very important difference: the stress falls on the first (or only) syllable of these endings, rather than on the stem.
2. The 3rd person plural in both active and passive has a less formal alternative ending in -ε.

Imperfective imperative

Active
Sg. χάνε lose!
Pl. χάνετε

The imperative has only 2nd person forms, singular and plural. The endings -ε and -ετε are attached to the imperfective (present) stem. The plural form is identical to the 2nd person plural of the active present tense. In verbs of more than two syllables the stress of the singular form goes back to the third syllable from the end, e.g. διάβαζε 'read!' There is no passive imperfective imperative.

For the use of the imperative forms and alternative ways of expressing commands see section 10.4.

Perfective imperative

	Active	Passive
Sg.	χάσε lose!	χάσου get lost! lose yourself!
Pl.	χάστε	χαθείτε

1. The perfective imperative is formed from the perfective stem. The singular forms add **-ε** for the active and **-ου** for the passive. In verbs of more than two syllables the stress of the active form is on the third syllable from the end: contrast ετοίμασε 'prepare (something)!' with ετοιμάσου 'get yourself ready!' Note that the passive singular imperative uses the active perfective stem.

2. The active plural ending is **-τε** when the last consonant of the stem is λ, ρ, σ, ξ or ψ. After other consonants the ending is **-ετε**, e.g. πλύνετε 'wash!' (from πλένω). Sometimes verbs with perfective stems ending in ν have the shorter ending in colloquial use, e.g. κάντε 'do!' The plural of the passive perfective imperative is the same as the 2nd person plural of the dependent.

3. Active singular imperatives with a stem ending in λ, ρ, σ, ξ or ψ often drop the final vowel when followed by a 3rd-person weak pronoun or an object with the definite article. Examples: γράψ' το 'write it!', φέρ' τα βιβλία 'bring the books!'.

4. Some verbs form their active perfective imperative irregularly. See the table of irregular verbs in section 6.25.

Gerund

χάνοντας   losing

The gerund is formed by adding the ending **-οντας** to the imperfective stem. It is active in meaning. For the use of the gerund see section 6.5.11.

6.9 Second-conjugation verbs (type A)

Verbs of the second conjugation are divided into two types, according to the vowel which predominates in the endings of the active present tense. Those of the first type (A) are characterized by the **α** vowel in the endings of this tense. Type B is dealt with in section 6.10.

Verbs of type A include the following: **αγαπώ** 'I love', **απαντώ** 'I answer', **βαστώ** 'I bear', **βουτώ** 'I dive', **γελώ** 'I laugh', **γεννώ** 'I give birth (to), bear', **γλεντώ** 'I celebrate', **διψώ** 'I am thirsty', **κολλώ** 'I stick', **κρατώ** 'I hold',

κρεμώ 'I hang', **κυβερνώ** 'I govern', **μελετώ** 'I study', **μετρώ** 'I count', **μιλώ** 'I speak', **νικώ** 'I conquer', **ξενυχτώ** 'I stay up at night', **ξεχνώ** 'I forget', **ξυπνώ** 'I (a)wake', **πατώ** 'I step, tread', **πεινώ** 'I am hungry', **περνώ** 'I pass', **περπατώ** 'I walk', **πετώ** 'I fly, throw', **πηδώ** 'I jump', **πουλώ** 'I sell', **προτιμώ** 'I prefer', **ρωτώ** 'I ask', **σταματώ** 'I stop', **τραβώ** 'I pull', **φυσώ** 'I blow', **χαιρετώ** 'I greet', **χαλώ** 'I break, spoil', **χτυπώ** 'I hit'. Some other verbs that can follow type A are listed in section 6.10.

Second-conjugation verbs (type A)

αγαπώ I love

Present

		Active	Passive
Sg.	1	αγαπώ/αγαπάω I love	αγαπιέμαι I am loved
	2	αγαπάς	αγαπιέσαι
	3	αγαπάει/αγαπά	αγαπιέται
Pl.	1	αγαπάμε/αγαπούμε	αγαπιόμαστε
	2	αγαπάτε	αγαπιέστε/ αγαπιόσαστε
	3	αγαπούν(ε)/αγαπάνε	αγαπιούνται

1. The stress always falls on the endings. The passive present has a non-syllabic -ι- (see section 1.2) between the stem αγαπ- and the personal endings.
2. Where alternative forms exist, the active endings -άω, -άει, -άμε and -άνε and the passive 2nd person plural in -όσαστε are regarded as less formal.

Imperfect

		Active	Passive
Sg.	1	αγαπούσα I used to love	αγαπιόμουν(α) I used to be loved
	2	αγαπούσες	αγαπιόσουν(α)
	3	αγαπούσε	αγαπιόταν(ε)

6
The verb and the verb phrase

Pl.	1	αγαπούσαμε	αγαπιόμασταν
	2	αγαπούσατε	αγαπιόσασταν
	3	αγαπούσαν(ε)	αγαπιόνταν(ε)/ αγαπιόντουσαν/ αγαπιούνταν(ε)

1. The active forms consist of the stem, an extra syllable **-ούσ-**, which always carries the stress, and the personal endings of the active past tenses. Verbs of type B form their active imperfect in exactly the same way.

2. An alternative way of forming the active imperfect of type A verbs is also in use, mainly in central and southern Greece. Here the extra syllable is **-αγ-**, and the stress falls on the third syllable from the end: *αγάπαγα, αγάπαγες, αγάπαγε, αγαπάγαμε, αγαπάγατε, αγάπαγαν/αγαπάγανε*. These alternative forms are not normally used in formal contexts.

3. The passive forms are similar to those of the passive imperfect of first-conjugation verbs, but have a non-syllabic **-ι-** inserted between the stem and the ending.

Simple past

		Active	Passive
Sg.	1	αγάπησα I loved	αγαπήθηκα I was loved
	2	αγάπησες	αγαπήθηκες
	3	αγάπησε	αγαπήθηκε
Pl.	1	αγαπήσαμε	αγαπηθήκαμε
	2	αγαπήσατε	αγαπηθήκατε
	3	αγάπησαν/ αγαπήσανε	αγαπήθηκαν/ αγαπηθήκανε

Verbs of the second conjugation normally form their perfective stems by adding the syllable **-ησ-** for the active and **-ηθ-** for the passive. (For important exceptions to this way of forming the perfective stems see section 6.15.) To form the active simple past, the past endings are added directly to the active perfective stem. As in first-conjugation verbs, the passive simple past has the additional syllable **-ηκ-** before the endings. In all these forms the stress falls on the third syllable from the end.

Exceptionally, two verbs in this category have a syllabic augment in the 1st, 2nd and 3rd persons ingular and the 3rd person plural of the active simple past: **δρω** 'I act' has the simple past **έδρασα**, and **σπάω** (an alternative to **σπάζω**) 'I break' has **έσπασα**. Apart from these special cases, second-conjugation verbs do not have an augment.

Second-conjugation verbs (type A)

Dependent

		Active	Passive
Sg.	1	αγαπήσω (no English equivalent)	αγαπηθώ (no English equivalent)
	2	αγαπήσεις	αγαπηθείς
	3	αγαπήσει	αγαπηθεί
Pl.	1	αγαπήσουμε	αγαπηθούμε
	2	αγαπήσετε	αγαπηθείτε
	3	αγαπήσουν(ε)	αγαπηθούν(ε)

The dependent is based on the perfective stem, which usually ends in **-ησ-** for the active and **-ηθ-** for the passive. (For exceptions see section 6.15.) The endings and position of stress are the same as for first-conjugation verbs.

Imperfective imperative

	Active
Sg.	αγάπα love!
Pl.	αγαπάτε

The active imperfective imperative endings are **-α** for singular and **-άτε** for plural. Both forms are stressed on the penultimate syllable. There are no passive forms.

Perfective imperative

	Active	Passive
Sg.	αγάπησε love!	αγαπήσου be loved!
Pl.	αγαπήστε	αγαπηθείτε love one another!

The perfective imperative is formed from the perfective stems, just as for first-conjugation verbs.

6 The verb and the verb phrase

> Gerund
>
> αγαπώντας   loving
>
> The gerund of second-conjugation verbs has the ending -ώντας. The stress is on the penultimate syllable. For the use of the gerund see section 6.5.

6.10 Second-conjugation verbs (type B)

Type B verbs of the second conjugation differ from those of type A in the endings of the active present, which (apart from the first person singular) have the vowels ει or ου. There are also differences in the endings of the passive present and imperfect tenses, and in the imperfective imperative. Examples of type B verbs are: **αποτελώ** 'I constitute', **ζω** 'I live', **μπορώ** 'I can, am able', **παρακαλώ** 'I request, beg', **προσπαθώ** 'I try', **συγχωρώ** 'I forgive'.

The following verbs can follow either type A or type B: **ακολουθώ** 'I follow', **κυκλοφορώ** 'I circulate, go round', **λιποθυμώ** 'I faint', **προχωρώ** 'I proceed, go forward', **συζητώ** 'I discuss', **συμπαθώ** 'I am fond of, forgive', **τηλεφωνώ** 'I telephone', **φιλώ** 'I kiss', **χωρώ** 'I fit in, have room for'. Such verbs tend to have type B endings in more formal contexts.

θεωρώ I consider, regard

> Present
>
> | | | Active | Passive |
> | --- | --- | --- | --- |
> | Sg. | 1 | θεωρώ I consider | θεωρούμαι I am considered |
> | | 2 | θεωρείς | θεωρείσαι |
> | | 3 | θεωρεί | θεωρείται |
> | Pl. | 1 | θεωρούμε | θεωρούμαστε |
> | | 2 | θεωρείτε | θεωρείστε |
> | | 3 | θεωρούν(ε) | θεωρούνται |
>
> The endings of the passive present are rather different from those of type A verbs. The first vowel of the endings is ου for the 1st person singular and 1st and 3rd persons plural, ει for the remaining persons (compare the corresponding active forms). This vowel carries the stress.

Second-conjugation verbs (type B)

Imperfect

		Active	Passive
Sg.	1	θεωρούσα I used to consider	(θεωρούμουν) I was/used to be considered
	2	θεωρούσες	(θεωρούσουν)
	3	θεωρούσε	θεωρούνταν(ε
Pl.	1	θεωρούσαμε	(θεωρούμασταν)
	2	θεωρούσατε	(θεωρούσασταν)
	3	θεωρούσαν(ε)	θεωρούνταν(ε)

1. The active imperfect is formed in the same way as for type A verbs. (Note that type B verbs do not have the alternative formation in -αγα etc.)
2. In the passive imperfect the bracketed forms are not normally used for θεωρώ. But there are several other verbs, including deponents (see section 6.6), which do have 1st and 2nd person forms, e.g. στερώ 'I deprive', ασχολούμαι 'I am occupied', μιμούμαι 'I imitate', προσποιούμαι 'I pretend'. Such verbs may have the additional vowel -α in the 1st and 2nd persons singular, like verbs of the first conjugation.

Simple past

		Active	Passive
Sg.	1	θεώρησα I considered	θεωρήθηκα I was considered
	2	θεώρησες	θεωρήθηκες
	3	θεώρησε	θεωρήθηκε
Pl.	1	θεωρήσαμε	θεωρηθήκαμε
	2	θεωρήσατε	θεωρηθήκατε
	3	θεώρησαν/ θεωρήσανε	θεωρήθηκαν/ θεωρηθήκανε

The stems of the simple past are normally -ησ- (active) and -ηθ- (passive), but for exceptions see section 6.15. The endings are the same as those of type A verbs.

Verbs of this type do not normally have a syllabic augment, but there is one important exception: ζω 'I live' has the active simple past έζησα, with stressed augment in the singular and in the 3rd person plural έζησαν (but also ζήσανε).

6
The verb and the verb phrase

Dependent

		Active	Passive
Sg.	1	θεωρήσω (no English equivalent)	θεωρηθώ (no English equivalent)
	2	θεωρήσεις	θεωρηθείς
	3	θεωρήσει	θεωρηθεί
Pl.	1	θεωρήσουμε	θεωρηθούμε
	2	θεωρήσετε	θεωρηθείτε
	3	θεωρήσουν(ε)	θεωρηθούν(ε)

The dependent forms are based on the active and passive perfective stems, and correspond exactly to those of verbs of type A.

Imperfective imperative

	Active
Sg.	—
Pl.	θεωρείτε consider!

Type B verbs have no singular form for the imperfective imperative. The plural form is the same as the 2nd person plural of the present tense.

Perfective imperative

	Active	Passive
Sg.	θεώρησε consider!	θεωρήσου be considered! consider yourself!
Pl.	θεωρήστε	θεωρηθείτε

Gerund

θεωρώντας considering

The perfective imperative and the gerund are formed in the same way as those of type A verbs.

6.11 Second-conjugation verbs with passive only

Second-conjugation verbs with passive only

There are four verbs which are similar to second-conjugation verbs (with stress on the endings in the imperfective tenses), but do not have active forms. They can be called deponent verbs (see section 6.6); that is to say, they have passive forms, but are active in meaning. These verbs are **θυμάμαι** 'I remember', **κοιμάμαι** 'I sleep, go to sleep', **λυπάμαι** 'I regret, I am sorry' and **φοβάμαι** 'I fear, am afraid (of)'.

κοιμάμαι I sleep

		Present	Imperfect
Sg.	1	κοιμάμαι/κοιμούμαι I sleep	κοιμόμουν(α) I was sleeping, used to sleep
	2	κοιμάσαι	κοιμόσουν(α)
	3	κοιμάται	κοιμόταν(ε)
Pl.	1	κοιμόμαστε	κοιμόμασταν
	2	κοιμάστε/κοιμόσαστε	κοιμόσασταν
	3	κοιμούνται	κοιμόνταν(ε)/ κοιμόντουσαν

1. The alternative forms given for the 1st person singular and the 2nd person plural of the present tense are both widely used.
2. The imperfect endings are the same as those the passive imperfect of first-conjugation verbs, except that the 3rd person plural has only forms stressed on the ending.

		Simple past	Dependent
Sg.	1	κοιμήθηκα I slept, fell asleep etc.	κοιμηθώ (no English equivalent) etc.

The simple past and the dependent are formed in exactly the same way as the corresponding passive forms of second-conjugation verbs.

	Perfective imperative
Sg.	κοιμήσου sleep!
Pl.	κοιμηθείτε

The perfective imperative is formed in the same way as the passive perfective imperative of second-conjugation verbs.

These verbs have no imperfective imperative or gerund.

6.12 Verbs with contracted active present forms

Some verbs which have a stem ending in a vowel have 'contracted' forms in the active present tense. The endings of the active present are: -ω, -ς, -ει, -με, -τε, -νε. Note that the endings of the second person singular and the first, second and third persons plural have no vowel. The main verbs which follow this pattern are: **ακούω** 'I hear', **καίω** 'I burn', **κλαίω** 'I weep', **λέω** 'I say', **πάω** 'I go', **τρώω** 'I eat', **φταίω** 'I am to blame'. Further details will be given below for each of these verbs.

λέω I say, tell

			Present	Imperfect
Sg.		1	λέω I say	έλεγα I was saying, used to say
		2	λες	έλεγες
		3	λέει	έλεγε
Pl.		1	λέμε	λέγαμε
		2	λέτε	λέγατε
		3	λένε	έλεγαν/λέγανε

The active imperfect adds a -γ- to the stem, before the normal endings of the imperfect. Verbs which have a stem beginning with a consonant have the syllabic augment ε- in the singular and the first form of the 3rd person plural. The augment is stressed.

> | Imperfective imperative (active) |
> |---|
> | Sg. λέγε speak! |
> | Pl. λέγετε |

Verbs with contracted active present forms

> | Gerund |
> |---|
> | λέγοντας saying |
>
> The imperfective imperative and the gerund also have a -γ- before the endings.

For convenience we give some further notes on each of these verbs:

- λέω forms its passive present and imperfect from the stem λεγ-: λέγομαι, λεγόμουν(α) The simple past and the dependent are irregular: είπα, πω. For other irregularities see the table of irregular verbs (section 6.25).
- ακούω: active imperfect άκουγα; passive present ακούγομαι, imperfect ακουγόμουν(α). Imperfective imperative sg. άκου, pl. ακούτε. Simple past άκουσα, dependent ακούσω.
- καίω: active imperfect έκαιγα; passive present καίγομαι, imperfect καιγόμουν(α). Imperfective imperative not normally used. Simple past έκαψα, dependent κάψω.
- κλαίω: active imperfect έκλαιγα. Simple past έκλαψα, dependent κλάψω. The passive of this verb is rarely used.
- πάω: this form functions both as an alternative present to πηγαίνω, and as the dependent of the same verb. The other imperfective forms (including the gerund) are based on the stem πηγαιν-. Simple past πήγα. There are no passive forms.
- τρώω: active imperfect έτρωγα; passive present τρώγομαι, imperfect τρωγόμουν(α). Imperfective imperative sg. τρώγε, pl. τρώτε. Simple past έφαγα, dependent φάω, which is conjugated in the same way as the present of λέω.
- φταίω: active imperfect έφταιγα. Simple past έφταιξα, dependent φταίξω. This verb has no imperative and no passive forms.

6.13 Verbs with irregular form of active dependent

The active dependents of the 'regular' verbs examined in sections 6.8–6.10 are stressed on the last syllable of the stem, e.g. **χάσω, χάσεις** etc. from **χάνω** 'I lose'. There are some common verbs which have an irregular dependent form consisting of a single syllable in the first person singular, e.g. **βρω** from **βρίσκω** 'I find'. These dependent forms are stressed on the endings, which are slightly different from those of regular verbs. In fact the endings are the same as those of the *passive* dependent forms of regular verbs (compare **χαθώ, χαθείς**, etc.).

Sg.	1	βρω
	2	βρεις
	3	βρει
Pl.	1	βρούμε
	2	βρείτε
	3	βρουν/βρούνε

The singular forms and the 3rd person plural form **βρουν** are monosyllables and are therefore written without an accent.

The following table lists verbs which have dependent forms of this kind. The active simple past forms are also given, as they are also formed irregularly:

Present		Simple past	Dependent
βγαίνω	I go out	βγήκα	βγω
βλέπω	I see	είδα	δω
βρίσκω	I find	βρήκα	βρω
λέω	I say	είπα	πω
μπαίνω	I go in	μπήκα	μπω
πίνω	I drink	ήπια	πιω

Special mention must be made of the dependent of έρχομαι. There are two forms: έρθω is conjugated regularly (as in section 6.8); the form 'ρθώ, which can follow the particles να and θα (subjunctive and perfective future respectively), loses its initial vowel and is stressed on the endings, like the dependent forms given above: (να/θα) 'ρθώ, (να/θα) 'ρθείς, etc.

Perfective stems of first-conjugation verbs

Other irregular forms of these verbs, such as the perfective imperative, are given in the table of irregular verbs (section 6.25).

The formation of active and passive perfective stems

The perfective stems are used to form the simple past, the dependent and the perfective imperative, active and passive, for each verb. In the following two sections, we give the most common ways of forming these stems for first- and second-conjugation verbs. The passive perfect participle, which is formed from the passive perfective stem, will be examined in section 6.16.

6.14 Perfective stems of first-conjugation verbs

The formation of the perfective stems of first-conjugation verbs depends on the ending of the imperfective stem. In the examples below, verbs which have no passive perfective forms are marked with a dagger (†).

6.14.1 Imperfective stems ending in a vowel:

(a) active perfective -σ-, passive perfective -στ- (or, more formally, -σθ-), e.g. ακούω 'I hear', άκουσα, ακούστηκα. Examples: αποκλείω 'I exclude', ελκύω 'I pull'. Similarly the deponent verb συγκρούομαι 'I collide'.

(b) active perfective -σ-, passive perfective -θ-, e.g. ιδρύω 'I establish', ίδρυσα, ιδρύθηκα. Examples: αναλύω 'I analyse', απολύω 'I dismiss', †δύω 'I go down, set [of the sun]', επενδύω 'I invest', †ισχύω 'I am valid', συνδέω 'I connect'.

(c) when the imperfective stem ends in -ε-, the active perfective stem ends in -ευσ-, passive perfective in -ευστ-, e.g. εμπνέω 'I inspire', ενέπνευσα, εμπνεύστηκα. (For the internal augment in the active simple past see section 6.23.) Examples: †καταρρέω 'I collapse' (simple past κατέρρευσα), †πλέω 'I float, sail', †πνέω 'I breathe'.

141

6.14.2 Imperfective stems ending in a labial consonant or cluster containing a labial:

(d) imperfective stem in -β-, -π-, -πτ-, -φ- or -φτ-, active perfective -ψ-, passive perfective -φτ- (or, more formally, -φθ-), e.g. γράφω 'I write', έγραψα, γράφτηκα. Examples: αλείφω 'I smear', ανάβω 'I light', αποκαλύπτω 'I discover', απορρίπτω 'I reject', †αστράφτω 'I flash', βάφω 'I dye', βλάπτω (or βλάφτω) 'I harm', γλείφω 'I lick', εγκαταλείπω 'I abandon', θάβω 'I bury', κλέβω 'I steal' (see also the table of irregular verbs), κρύβω 'I hide', †λάμπω 'I shine', †λείπω 'I am missing', παραλείπω 'I omit', προβλέπω 'I foresee', ράβω 'I sew', σκάβω 'I dig', †σκοντάφτω 'I stumble', †σκύβω 'I stoop', στρίβω 'I twist, turn', τρίβω 'I rub', υπογράφω 'I sign'. Similarly the deponent verbs επισκέπτομαι 'I visit', σκέφτομαι (or σκέπτομαι) 'I think'.

(e) when the imperfective stem ends in -αυ- or -ευ-, active perfective -αψ-/-εψ-, passive perfective -αυτ-/-ευτ-, e.g. γιατρεύω 'I cure', γιάτρεψα, γιατρεύτηκα. Examples: αγριεύω 'I make angry, become angry', ανακατεύω 'I mix, stir', †βασιλεύω 'I set [of the sun]', βολεύω 'I arrange, fix', †γυρεύω 'I ask for, seek', δουλεύω 'I work', δυσκολεύω 'I make difficult', †ζηλεύω 'I envy', ζωηρεύω 'I enliven', καβαλικεύω 'I ride', †καλυτερεύω 'I improve', †κινδυνεύω 'I am in danger', †κοντεύω 'I draw near', μαγειρεύω 'I cook', μαζεύω 'I gather', μπερδεύω 'I confuse', ξοδεύω 'I spend', παντρεύω 'I marry', παύω 'I cease', πιστεύω 'I believe', †ταξιδεύω 'I travel', φυτεύω 'I plant', χορεύω 'I dance'. Similarly the deponent verb ονειρεύομαι 'I dream'.

(f) some verbs with imperfective stem in -αυ- or -ευ-, have active perfective -αυσ-/-ευσ-, passive perfective -αυτ-/-ευτ-, (or, more formally, -αυθ-/-ευθ-), e.g. δεσμεύω 'I bind, tie down', δέσμευσα, δεσμεύτηκα. Examples: αντιπροσωπεύω 'I represent', απαγορεύω 'I forbid', απογοητεύω 'I disappoint', απομνημονεύω 'I memorize', γενικεύω 'I generalize', διακινδυνεύω 'I risk', εκπαιδεύω 'I instruct', ερμηνεύω 'I interpret', θεραπεύω 'I treat, cure', †μεταναστεύω 'I migrate', μνημονεύω 'I mention', προμηθεύω 'I supply', προστατεύω 'I protect', †σκοπεύω 'I aim', υπαγορεύω 'I dictate'. Similarly the deponent verbs αστειεύομαι 'I joke', εκμεταλλεύομαι 'I exploit', ερωτεύομαι 'I fall in love (with)', υποπτεύομαι 'I suspect'.

> **6.14.3** *Imperfective stems ending in a velar consonant or cluster containing a velar:*

Perfective stems of first-conjugation verbs

(g) imperfective stem in -γ-, -γγ-, -γχ, -κ-, -σκ-, -χ- or -χν-, active perfective -ξ-, passive perfective in -χτ- (or, more formally, -χθ-), e.g. ρίχνω 'I throw', έριξα, ρίχτηκα. Examples: ανοίγω 'I open', †αντέχω 'I endure', δείχνω 'I show', διαλέγω 'I choose', διδάσκω 'I teach', διώχνω 'I chase off, throw out' (active simple past έδιωξα), ελέγχω 'I control, check', †λήγω 'I expire', μπλέκω 'I entangle', πλέκω 'I weave', προσέχω 'I pay attention (to), take care', σπρώχνω 'I push', σφίγγω 'I squeeze', †τρέχω 'I run', τυλίγω 'I wind, wrap', φτιάχνω 'I make, fix' (active simple past έφτιαξα), ψάχνω 'I search (for)'. Similarly the deponent verbs δέχομαι 'I receive', πετάγομαι 'I jump up'.

> **6.14.4** *Imperfective stems ending in a dental consonant:*

(h) imperfective stem in -δ- or -θ-, active perfective -σ-, passive perfective -στ-, e.g. πείθω 'I persuade', έπεισα, πείστηκα. Examples: διαψεύδω 'I contradict', †νιώθω 'I feel' (active simple past ένιωσα), πλάθω 'I shape, mould', †σπεύδω 'I hasten'.

> **6.14.5** *Imperfective stems ending in -σσ- or -ττ-:*

(j) active perfective -ξ-, passive perfective -χτ- (or, more formally, -χθ-), e.g. κηρύσσω 'I proclaim', κήρυξα, κηρύχτηκα. Examples: αναπτύσσω 'I develop', ανταλλάσσω 'I exchange', επιφυλάσσω 'I keep in reserve', πλήττω 'I hit, get bored', συντάσσω 'I draw up, compile'. Similarly the deponent verbs εξελίσσομαι 'I develop', υπαινίσσομαι 'I hint at'.

> **6.14.6** *Imperfective stems ending in -ζ-:*

(k) active perfective -σ-, passive perfective -στ- (or, more formally, -σθ-), e.g. εξετάζω 'I examine', εξέτασα, εξετάστηκα. Examples: †αδειάζω 'I empty' (active simple past άδειασα), αναγκάζω 'I compel', γνωρίζω 'I know, get to know', δανείζω 'I lend', διαβάζω 'I read', ζαλίζω 'I make dizzy', κουράζω 'I tire'. Similarly the deponent verbs αγωνίζομαι 'I struggle', εργάζομαι 'I work', φαντάζομαι 'I imagine', χρειάζομαι 'I need'. The great majority of verbs ending in -άζω or -ίζω form their perfective stems in this way. Some common exceptions are given in the next paragraph.

(l) active perfective -ξ-, passive perfective -χτ- (or, more formally, -χθ-), e.g. πειράζω 'I annoy', πείραξα, πειράχτηκα. Examples: αγγίζω 'I touch', αλλάζω 'I change', †βουλιάζω 'I sink', κοιτάζω 'I look at', κράζω 'I call', †νυστάζω 'I am sleepy', παίζω 'I play', στηρίζω 'I support', σφάζω 'I slaughter', τινάζω 'I shake', †τρίζω 'I creak', †τρομάζω 'I scare, take fright', †φωνάζω 'I call, shout'.

6.14.7 Imperfective stems ending in -ν- (after a vowel):

(m) active perfective -σ-, passive perfective -θ-, e.g. δένω 'I tie', έδεσα, δέθηκα. Examples: απλώνω 'I spread', γδύνω 'I undress', λύνω 'I undo', ντύνω 'I dress', σηκώνω 'I lift', χάνω 'I lose', χύνω 'I pour', ψήνω 'I roast', and all verbs ending in -ώνω, except ζώνω (see next paragraph).

(n) active perfective -σ-, passive perfective -στ-, e.g. κλείνω 'I close', έκλεισα, κλείστηκα. Examples: ζώνω 'I encircle', ξύνω 'I scratch', πιάνω 'I catch' (active simple past έπιασα), σβήνω 'I extinguish', †φτάνω 'I arrive', †φτύνω 'I spit'.

(o) active perfective -ν-, passive perfective -θ-, e.g. κρίνω 'I judge', έκρινα, κρίθηκα. Examples: διακρίνω 'I distinguish', †κλίνω 'I incline'. Similarly the deponent verb ανταποκρίνομαι 'I correspond'.

(p) active perfective -ν-, passive perfective -νθ-, e.g. μολύνω 'I pollute', μόλυνα, μολύνθηκα. Examples: απευθύνω 'I address', αποθαρρύνω 'I discourage', απομακρύνω 'I remove', διευθύνω 'I manage', ενθαρρύνω 'I encourage', μεγεθύνω 'I enlarge, magnify', οξύνω 'I sharpen, aggravate'. Similarly the deponent verbs αισθάνομαι 'I feel', αμύνομαι 'I defend myself'.

Verbs with present ending in -αίνω need to be divided into six types:

(q) active perfective -αν-, passive perfective -ανθ-, e.g. θερμαίνω 'I warm', θέρμανα, θερμάνθηκα. Examples: †ανασαίνω 'I breathe', απολυμαίνω 'I disinfect', επισημαίνω 'I point out', ευφραίνω 'I gladden', †πεθαίνω 'I die', †συμπεραίνω 'I conclude', υγραίνω 'I moisten', υφαίνω 'I weave'. Similarly the deponent verb κυμαίνομαι 'I fluctuate'.

(r) active perfective -αν-, passive perfective -αθ-, e.g. τρελαίνω 'I madden', τρέλανα, τρελάθηκα. Examples: βουβαίνω 'I strike dumb', γλυκαίνω 'I sweeten', ζεσταίνω 'I warm', κουφαίνω 'I deafen', μαραίνω 'I wither', ξεραίνω 'I dry', πικραίνω 'I make bitter'. Similarly the deponent verb σιχαίνομαι 'I detest'.

(s) active perfective -υν-, no passive perfective forms, e.g. †βαραίνω 'I weigh down (on)', βάρυνα. Examples: †ακριβαίνω 'I raise the price of, become dearer', †ασχημαίνω 'I make ugly, become ugly', †βαθαίνω 'I deepen', †ελαφραίνω 'I lighten', †κονταίνω 'I shorten', †μακραίνω 'I lengthen', †παχαίνω 'I fatten, become fat', †πληθαίνω 'I increase', †σκληραίνω 'I harden', †φτωχαίνω 'I make poor, become poor', †χοντραίνω 'I get fat'.

(t) active perfective drops the syllable -αιν-, normally no passive perfective forms, e.g. †παθαίνω 'I suffer', έπαθα. Examples: †αποτυχαίνω 'I fail' (simple past απέτυχα), †καταλαβαίνω 'I understand', †λαχαίνω 'I come across, happen', μαθαίνω 'I learn' (see table of irregular verbs), †πετυχαίνω 'I succeed', †πηγαίνω 'I go' (see table of irregular verbs), †προλαβαίνω 'I have time to do, catch', †τυχαίνω 'I chance'.

(u) active perfective -ασ-, no passive perfective forms, e.g. †χορταίνω 'I satisfy, become satisfied', χόρτασα. Examples: †προφταίνω 'I do something in time', †σωπαίνω 'I fall silent'.

(v) active perfective -ησ-, passive perfective -ηθ-, e.g. αυξαίνω 'I increase', αύξησα, αυξήθηκα. Examples: †αμαρταίνω (or αμαρτάνω) 'I sin', ανασταίνω 'I resurrect', †αρρωσταίνω 'I fall ill', †βλασταίνω (or βλαστάνω) 'I sprout'.

6.14.8 *Imperfective stems ending in -αρ- or -ιρ-:*

(w) active perfective -αρισ-/-ιρισ- or -αρ-/-ιρ- (see below), passive perfective -αριστ-/-ιριστ-, e.g. σοκάρω 'I shock', σοκάρισα or σόκαρα, σοκαρίστηκα. Examples: γαρνίρω 'I garnish', λουστράρω 'I shine', †μπαρκάρω 'I embark', μπλοκάρω 'I block', πακετάρω 'I pack up', †παρκάρω 'I park', †πασάρω 'I pass (on)', †ποζάρω 'I pose', προβάρω 'I try on, try out', σερβίρω 'I serve', τρακάρω 'I crash', τσεκάρω 'I check, tick', †φλερτάρω 'I flirt', †φρενάρω 'I brake'. The active perfective forms with the extra syllable -ισ- are only found for the singular and the third person plural of the simple past. They are not found in the dependent. So the simple past of παρκάρω has the following possible forms: παρκάρισα/πάρκαρα, παρκάρισες/πάρκαρες, παρκάρισε/πάρκαρε, παρκάραμε, παρκάρατε, παρκάρισαν/πάρκαραν/παρκάρανε. The dependent is παρκάρω etc.

Important note: the above lists include only the more common verbs. Further examples are given in the *Comprehensive Grammar*, pp. 147–55. For verbs not included in the lists it is advisable to consult a good dictionary.

6.15 Perfective stems of second-conjugation verbs

Most verbs of the second conjugation, both type A and type B, form their perfective stems by adding -ησ- (active) and -ηθ- (passive) to the imperfective stem. For example: γεννώ 'I give birth to', active simple past γέννησα, passive simple past γεννήθηκα. (See sections 6.9 and 6.10 for the full forms.) Exceptions to this pattern are given below. For each verb we indicate whether it follows type A or type B in the forms based on the imperfective stem. Verbs which have no passive perfective forms are marked with a dagger (†).

(a) active perfective -ασ-, passive perfective -αστ-, e.g. κρεμώ (A) 'I hang', κρέμασα, κρεμάστηκα. Examples: (αντ)ανακλώ (A) 'I reflect', αποσπώ (A) 'I detach, send on secondment', γελώ (A) 'I laugh, deceive', †διψώ (A) 'I am thirsty', †δρω (A) 'I act' (active simple past έδρασα), ξεγελώ (A) 'I fool', †ξεσπώ (A) 'I break out', †πεινώ (A) 'I am hungry', †σπάω (A) 'I break' (active simple past έσπασα), †σχολώ (A) 'I stop working', χαλώ (A) 'I spoil', †χαμογελώ (A) 'I smile'. Similarly the deponent verb καταριέμαι (A) 'I curse'.

(b) active perfective -εσ-, passive perfecive -εστ-, e.g. αποτελώ 'I constitute', αποτέλεσα, αποτελέστηκα. Examples: αρκώ (B) 'I suffice, limit', †διαρκώ (B) 'I last', †διατελώ 'I remain, am', καλώ (B) 'I call', †καρτερώ (A/B) 'I wait', †μπορώ (A) 'I can', συντελώ 'I contribute', †χωρώ (A/B) 'I contain, fit (into)'.

(c) active perfective -εσ-, passive perfective -εθ-, e.g. επαινώ 'I praise', επαίνεσα, επαινέθηκα. Examples: αφαιρώ (B) 'I remove', †βαρώ (A) 'I beat, sound', διαιρώ (B) 'I divide', εξαιρώ (B) 'I except', καταφρονώ (B) 'I despise', †πονώ (A/B) 'I pain, hurt', στενοχωρώ (B) 'I distress' (also -ησ-, -ηθ-), φορώ (A) 'I put on, wear'. Similarly the deponent verbs βαριέμαι (A) 'I am bored, fed up', παραπονιέμαι (A) 'I complain'.

(d) active perfective -αξ-, passive perfective -αχτ-, e.g. πετώ (A) 'I throw, fly', πέταξα, πετάχτηκα. Examples: βαστώ (A) 'I bear', κοιτώ (A) (alternative to κοιτάζω) 'I look at'.

(e) active perfective -ηξ-, passive perfective -ηχτ-, e.g. τραβώ (A) 'I pull', τράβηξα, τραβήχτηκα. Examples: †βογκώ (A) 'I groan', βουτώ (A) 'I dive', †βροντώ (A) 'I thunder' (active perfective also -ησ-), ζουλώ (A) 'I squeeze', πηδώ (A) 'I jump' (active perfective also -ησ-), ρουφώ (A) 'I suck', σκουντώ (A) 'I prod', †φυσώ (A) 'I blow', †χυμώ (A) 'I rush'.

(f) verbs with imperfective stem ending in a consonant + -ν- have active perfective -ασ-, passive perfective -αστ-, e.g. ξεχνώ (A) 'I forget', ξέχασα, ξεχάστηκα. Examples: †γερνώ (A) 'I grow old', κερνώ (A) 'I treat [e.g. to a drink]', ξεπερνώ (A) 'I exceed', †ξερνώ (A) 'I vomit', περνώ (A) 'I pass'.

6.16 The passive perfect participle

All passive perfect participles end in **-μένος** and are fully inflected for number, gender and case, like the adjectives in section 3.33. They are formed from verbs, although not all verbs have this form. In particular, intransitive verbs (which cannot have a direct object) do not normally have a passive perfect participle. (Some exceptions are given below.) The starting point for the formation of these participles is the passive perfective stem. Some participles have a consonant before the ending **-μένος,-** while others do not. Below we give the most common patterns for the formation of the passive perfect participle from the passive perfective stem, with examples of each kind:

(a) *-στ-/-σθ-/-νθ-* → *-σμένος*: **αναγκασμένος** 'compelled', **εμπνευσμένος** 'inspired', **καλεσμένος** 'invited', **κουρασμένος** 'tired', **μολυσμένος** 'polluted', **ξεπερασμένος** 'superseded', **ξεχασμένος** 'forgotten', **ορισμένος** 'fixed, certain (unspecified)', **σβησμένος** 'extinguished', **σερβιρισμένος** 'served', **χαλασμένος** 'spoilt, broken'.

(b) *-θ-* (after a vowel, *λ* or *ρ*) → *-μένος*: **αγαπημένος** 'loved', **αυξημένος** 'increased', **γεννημένος** 'born', **δεμένος** 'tied', **κολλημένος** 'stuck', **ντυμένος** 'dressed', **ολοκληρωμένος** 'completed', **παρμένος** 'taken', **πικραμένος** 'embittered', **σταλμένος** 'sent', **στενοχωρημένος** 'upset', **χαμένος** 'lost', **ψημένος** 'roasted'.

(c) *-φτ-/-φθ-* → *-μμένος*: **αναμμένος** 'lit', **γραμμένος** 'written', **εγκαταλειμμένος** 'abandoned', **θαμμένος** 'buried'.

(d) *-χτ-/-χθ-* → *-γμένος*: **αναπτυγμένος** 'developed', **ανοιγμένος** 'opened', **εκλεγμένος** 'elected', **προσεγμένος** 'cared for', **στηριγμένος** 'supported', **τραβηγμένος** 'pulled'. In some verbs the *-γ-* is sometimes omitted, e.g. **πετα(γ)μένος** 'thrown'.

Note also:

- Verbs in **-εύω** have a passive perfect participle in either **-ευμένος** or **-εμένος**. The first form is found with verbs that are used in more formal contexts; the second is informal. Examples: **απογοητευμένος** 'disappointed', **γενικευμένος** 'generalized', **δεσμευμένος** 'tied down, obligated', **μπερδεμένος** 'confused', **παντρεμένος** 'married'.

- Verbs in **-αίνω** present many irregularities in the way they form their passive perfect participle (if they have one). Here we must restrict ourselves to a few examples: **αποτυχημένος** 'failed, unsuccessful' (from **αποτυχαίνω**), **ζεσταμένος** 'warmed' (**ζεσταίνω**), **μαθημένος** 'learnt' (**μαθαίνω**), **πεθαμένος** 'dead' (**πεθαίνω**), **υφασμένος** 'woven' (**υφαίνω**), **χορτασμένος** 'satiated, full up' (**χορταίνω**). For other forms the use of a good dictionary is recommended.

- Some verbs which do not have finite passive forms *do* have passive perfect participles. Examples: **ακουμπισμένος** 'leaning' (from **ακουμπώ**), **αρρωστημένος** 'ill' (**αρρωσταίνω**), **διψασμένος** 'thirsty' (**διψώ**), **δυστυχισμένος** 'unhappy' (**δυστυχώ**), **ευτυχισμένος** 'happy' (**ευτυχώ**), **θυμωμένος** 'angry' (**θυμώνω**), **κλαμμένος** 'in tears' (**κλαίω**), **λιποθυμισμένος** 'fainted, unconscious' (**λιποθυμώ**), **πεινασμένος** 'hungry' (**πεινώ**), **ταξιδεμένος** 'much-travelled' (**ταξιδεύω**), **χορτασμένος** 'satiated, full up'.

- Some passive perfect participles of learned origin have an extra syllable prefixed to the verb stem (and following any prepositional prefix). This phenomenon is known as reduplication. Examples of such forms in frequent use are: **αποδεδειγμένος** 'proven' (**αποδεικνύω**), **διατεθειμένος** 'disposed' (**διαθέτω**), **δεδομένος** 'given' (**δίνω**), **εκτεταμένος** 'extended' (**εκτείνω**), **πεπεισμένος** 'persuaded, convinced' (**πείθω**), **συγκεκριμένος** 'specific' (**συγκρίνω**), **συνδεδεμένος** 'connected' (**συνδέω**), **υπογεγραμμένος** 'undersigned' (**υπογράφω**), **τετελεσμένος** 'accomplished' (**τελώ**), **τετριμμένος** 'trite' (**τρίβω**).

For verbs which form their passive perfect participle irregularly, see the table of irregular verbs (section 6.25).

6.16.1 Use of the passive perfect participle

The passive perfect participle functions as an adjective, agreeing in gender, number and case with the noun it modifies:

1 *χαμένα λόγια*
   wasted (lit. 'lost') words

It can be modified by adverbs:

2 Ύστερα από αυτά που έγιναν, η Αλίκη ήταν *εντελώς απογοητευμένη*.
   After what happened, Alice was completely disillusioned.

3 Το συνέδριο ήταν *πολύ καλά οργανωμένο*.
   The conference was very well organized.

Like other adjectives (see the end of section 3.57), it can be used with complements in the form of prepositional phrases:

4 *Δυναμωμένοι από τις εμπειρίες τους*, συνέχισαν τον αγώνα.
   Strengthened by their experiences, they continued the struggle.

5 Βρήκαμε τον Κώστα ήδη *ντυμένο για το γάμο*.
   We found Kostas already dressed for the wedding.

The formation of other tenses and verb forms

6.17 The perfective and imperfective futures

Most verbs have two future tenses, the perfective and the imperfective, which differ according to aspect (see section 6.4 and, for the use of the tenses, section 6.5). The perfective future refers to an action or event which will take place and be completed at a future point in time. It consists of the particle θα and the dependent form of the verb, as in the following examples:

θα γράψω	I shall write, I'm going to write
θα βγούμε	we'll go out
θα μιλήσουν	they will speak, they're going to speak
θα σηκωθεί	(s)he/it will get up
θα τρελαθούμε	we shall go mad

Any weak pronouns must be placed immediately before the verb, e.g. **θα μου το δώσεις** 'you will give me it'. Verbs which do not have perfective forms have no perfective future (see section 6.6).

The imperfective future, which denotes a repeated, habitual or continuous event in the future, is formed with the particle θα and the present tense form of the verb, e.g.

θα είμαστε	we shall be
θα θυμάμαι	I'll remember
θα αλληλογραφούμε	we shall correspond [by letter]

6.18 The perfect tenses and the auxiliary verb *έχω*

As in English, the three perfect tenses in Greek – perfect, pluperfect and future perfect – are formed with the auxiliary verb 'to have'. We give first the basic forms of **έχω** 'I have'. The present tense has the same endings as first-conjugation verbs. The past (imperfect) tense has a different vowel **ει-** for the first syllable, but the endings are the same as those of other active imperfects.

		Present	Past
Singular	1	έχω I have	είχα I had
	2	έχεις	είχες
	3	έχει	είχε
Plural	1	έχουμε	είχαμε
	2	έχετε	είχατε
	3	έχουν(ε)	είχαν(ε)

The perfect tense consists of the present tense of **έχω** followed by a special verb form called the non-finite. The non-finite is in fact identical to the third person singular of the dependent and exists in both active and passive voices; for instance **χάσει** and **χαθεί** are, respectively, the active and passive non-finite forms of **χάνω** 'I lose'. Note that the active non-finite has the stress on the penultimate syllable, while the passive non-finite has the stress on the final syllable. Thus the active perfect of **χάνω** is **έχω χάσει** 'I have lost', **έχεις χάσει** 'you have lost', etc. and the passive perfect is **έχω χαθεί** 'I have been lost' (or 'I have lost myself'), **έχεις χαθεί** 'you have been lost', etc. The verbs given in section 6.13, which have an irregular form for the active dependent, have a one-syllable non-finite form, e.g. **έχω βρει** 'I have found', **έχουμε δει** 'we have seen'.

Verbs of the second conjugation form their non-finite and perfect in the same way as first-conjugation ones, e.g. **έχω αγαπήσει** 'I have loved', **έχω αγαπηθεί** 'I have been loved'. Deponent verbs have only a passive form of the perfect (but with active meaning), e.g. **έχω εργαστεί** 'I have worked', **έχω κοιμηθεί** 'I have slept', **έχω σκεφτεί** 'I have thought'. Any weak pronouns must be placed before the appropriate form of **έχω** but after the negative particle, e.g. **δεν μας έχει μιλήσει** '(s)he hasn't spoken to us'.

The pluperfect (or past perfect) tense consists of the past of **έχω** followed by the non-finite form: **είχα χάσει** 'I had lost', **είχα χαθεί** 'I had been lost' (or 'I had lost myself').

The future perfect consists of the particle **θα** followed by the perfect, e.g. **θα έχω φτάσει** 'I shall have arrived', **θα έχω σηκωθεί** 'I shall have got up'. Any weak pronouns must be placed immediately before the relevant part of **έχω**, e.g. **θα σου το έχουν στείλει** 'they will have sent you it'.

The three perfect tenses exist only for verbs which have corresponding (active and/or passive) perfective forms. The use of the perfect tenses is discussed in section 6.5.

6.19 The conditional and perfect conditional

The conditional is formed with the particle **θα** and the imperfect tense, e.g. **θα ήμουν(α)** 'I would be', **θα έχανα** 'I would lose', **θα γινόμουν(α)** 'I would become', **θα φοβόμουν(α)** 'I would be afraid [of]'. Any weak pronouns must be placed between **θα** and the verb form, e.g. **θα σας το έδινα** 'I would give you it'.

There is also a perfect conditional, which is formed with **θα** and the pluperfect tense, e.g. **θα είχα έρθει** 'I would have come', **θα είχα χαθεί** 'I would have got lost', **θα είχα κοιμηθεί** 'I would have fallen asleep'.

For the uses of the conditional and the perfect conditional see section 10.13. The various uses of the particle **θα** are summarized in section 9.3.

6.20 The subjunctive forms

Unlike many other languages, Greek does not have separate subjunctive forms as such. Instead a subjunctive clause or sentence is indicated by the use of the particles **να** or **ας** before the verb, and a different negative particle **μην** (instead of **δεν**). The verb may be in any tense. For further information on the subjunctive mood see section 6.4, and for various uses of the subjunctive sections 9.3, 10.3 and 10.4.

6 The verb and the verb phrase

Augment

6.21 Syllabic augment

Syllabic augment is the vowel **ε-** prefixed to the stem of the verb in a past tense, e.g. **έ-γραψα** 'I wrote'. The augment is required when the verb has a one-syllable stem beginning with a consonant, and a one-syllable ending. Since the stress of past-tense forms normally falls on the third syllable from the end, the augment carries the stress. It follows that when the ending of the verb has more than one syllable, no augment is needed. The augment is obligatory only in the active imperfect and simple past of first-conjugation verbs, and then only in the first, second and third persons singular, and the third person plural when the ending is **-αν**. For the relevant forms of **χάνω** see section 6.8. (For the small number of second-conjugation verbs that have syllabic augment in the simple past, see sections 6.9 and 6.10.)

There are some irregular verbs with a one-syllable perfective stem which do not have the augment in the simple past. They are: **βγήκα** 'I went out' (from **βγαίνω**), **βρήκα** 'I found' (from **βρίσκω**), **μπήκα** 'I went in' (from **μπαίνω**), **πήγα** 'I went' (from **πηγαίνω**) and **πήρα** 'I took' (from **παίρνω**). However, the imperfects of these verbs (with the exception of **πηγαίνω**) do have the augment in the singular and the third person plural, e.g. **έβγαινε** '(s)he/it was going out', **έπαιρναν** 'they used to take'.

6.22 Vocalic augment

Syllabic augment applies to verbs that begin with a consonant. Vocalic augment, on the other hand, is relevant to verbs that begin with a vowel. It involves a change of the initial vowel in some verbs beginning with **ε-**, **α-** or **αι-**. These vowels, with vocalic augment, become **η-**. There are two words in common use which may have vocalic augment on stressed initial vowels in their active past tenses: **ελπίζω** 'I hope' sometimes has imperfect **ήλπιζα**, simple past **ήλπισα** (instead of **έλπιζα, έλπισα**), and **ελέγχω** 'I control' can have **ήλεγχα** and **ήλεγξα**. But, as with syllabic augment, it is normally only a stressed syllable that can have vocalic augment.

There are three very common verbs that have the augment **η-** in some past-tense forms (even though these are not verbs beginning with a vowel):

- **θέλω** 'I want' has imperfect **ήθελα**, but in the forms with a two-syllable ending there is no **ή-**: **θέλαμε** 'we wanted';
- **ξέρω** 'I know' has imperfect **ήξερα**, but, like **θέλω**, no extra vowel in **ξέραμε** 'we knew', etc.;
- **πίνω** 'I drink' has simple past **ήπια**, with **ή-** in all persons and numbers, but imperfect **έπινα**.

6.23 Internal augment

Verbs that have a prepositional prefix place the augment, if they have one, between the preposition and the verb stem. These prefixes are derived from Ancient Greek prepositions (many of them no longer used as independent prepositions in the present-day language). They are: **αμφι-, ανα-, αντι-, απο-, δια-, εισ-, εκ-** (**εξ-** before a vowel), **εν-** (**εμ-** before a labial consonant, **εγ-** before a velar), **επι-, κατα-, μετα-, παρα-, περι-, προ-, προσ-, συν-,** (**συμ-** before a labial consonant, **συγ-** before a velar, **συλ-** before λ), **υπερ-** and **υπο-**. Prepositions that end in a vowel drop the vowel before the augment, except for **περι-** and **προ-**. Thus, **υποβάλλω** 'I submit' has simple past **υπ-έ-βαλα**, and **εκλέγω** 'I elect' has **εξ-έ-λεξα**. When the augment would not have stress, it is normally omitted. So the first person plural of the simple past of these two verbs is **υποβάλαμε** and **εκλέξαμε**. For further examples, see the following in the table of irregular verbs (section 6.25): **αναβάλλω, ανακλώ, αναμιγνύω, ανατέλλω, αποδεικνύω, απονέμω, αποσπώ, αποτυχαίνω, διαθέτω, διακόπτω, εκπλήσσω, συμπίπτω**. In some verbs with prepositional prefixes the internal augment is never used, e.g. **προτείνω** 'I suggest', simple past **πρότεινα**.

Some verbs have two prepositional prefixes, e.g. **συμπεριλαμβάνω** 'I include'. In such cases the augment comes between the second preposition and the stem: **συμπεριέλαβα** 'I included'.

Finally, we must note some instances of internal vocalic augment, that is, a change of vowel to -η- in verbs with a prepositional prefix when the simple verb begins with a vowel. The most common example is the imperfect and simple past of **υπάρχω** 'I exist': **υπήρχα, υπήρξα**. Internal vocalic augment also occurs in **απήργησα**, simple past of **απεργώ** 'I go on strike'. It is optional in **παρήγγειλα**, simple past of **παραγγέλλω** 'I order', as an alternative to **παράγγειλα**.

6 The verb and the verb phrase

Irregular verbs

6.24 Definition of an irregular verb

Sections 6.14 and 6.15 give the basic patterns for the formation of perfective stems of first- and second-conjugation verbs. These stems are used to create the active and passive simple past, dependent and perfective imperative, the perfect passive participle and the non-finite forms used in the perfect tenses. Verbs which do not conform to one of these patterns are regarded as irregular. The table in section 6.25 gives details of the most common irregular verbs. Also included in the table are verbs of the second conjugation which do not form their perfective stem with the syllable -ησ- (for the active) and -ηθ- (passive), and verbs which have irregular passive perfect participles.

6.25 Table of irregular verbs

The table is set out as follows: the first column gives the active present tense of the verb or, in the case of deponent verbs, the passive present. Second-conjugation verbs are marked A or B according to the type of endings used in the imperfective forms (see sections 6.9 and 6.10). Impersonal verbs are given in the third person singular. For verbs with a prepositional prefix, we give only the most common examples. e.g. παραγγέλλω 'I order'. Other compounds of the same verb with a different prefix, e.g. αναγγέλλω 'I announce', απαγγέλλω 'I recite', are not listed separately, unless they present significant differences.

The second column normally gives just one basic meaning of the verb; for the full range of meanings you should consult a dictionary.

In the third column we give the first person singular of the active simple past. In the case of verbs which do not have a simple past, the imperfect is given if it is formed irregularly. For deponent verbs the simple past (which has a passive form) is given in this column. If the dependent or the perfective imperative is formed irregularly, these forms are also given. Where the simple past contains an augment (see sections 6.21–6.23), the augment must be removed to form the dependent.

The fourth column gives the first person singular of the passive simple past; the passive dependent is given if it cannot be predicted from the simple past.

The fifth column gives the passive perfect participle. A dash (—) in the fourth or fifth column indicates that no form exists.

Alternative forms are shown separated by an oblique line (/). When a whole word is bracketed, it is rarely used.

Present	Meaning	Active simple past	Passive simple past	Passive perfect participle
ακουμπώ (Α)	lean	ακούμπησα	—	ακουμπισμένος
αναβάλλω	postpone	ανέβαλα	αναβλήθηκα	αναβλημένος
ανακλώ (Α)	reflect	ανέκλασα	ανακλάστηκα	ανακλασμένος
αναμιγνύω	mix	ανέμιξα	αναμίχθηκα	ανα(με)μιγμένος
ανασταίνω	resurrect	ανάστησα	αναστήθηκα	αναστημένος
ανατέλλω	rise	ανάτειλα/ανέτειλα	—	—
ανεβαίνω	go up	ανέβηκα dep. ανέβω/ανεβώ imp. ανέβα, ανεβείτε	—	ανεβασμένος
ανέχομαι	tolerate	ανέχτηκα	—	—
αντέχω	endure	άντεξα	—	—
απαλλάσσω	exempt	απάλλαξα	απαλλάχτηκα dep. απαλλαγώ	απαλλαγμένος
απέχω	am far from	imperf. απείχα	—	—
αποδεικνύω	prove	απέδειξα	αποδείχθηκα	απο(δε)δειγμένος
απολαμβάνω	enjoy	απήλαυσα dep. απολαύσω	—	—

Present	Meaning	Active simple past	Passive simple past	Passive perfect participle
απονέμω	award	απένειμα	απονεμήθηκα	απονεμημένος
αποσπώ (Α)	detach	απέσπασα	αποσπάστηκα	αποσπασμένος
αποτελώ (Β)	constitute	αποτέλεσα	αποτελέστηκα	αποτελεσμένος
αποτυχαίνω	fail	απέτυχα dep. αποτύχω	—	αποτυχημένος
αρέσω	please	άρεσα	—	—
αρκώ (Β)	suffice	άρκεσα/ήρκεσα	αρκέστηκα	—
αυξάνω/-αίνω	increase	αύξησα	αυξήθηκα	αυξημένος
αφαιρώ (Β)	remove	αφαίρεσα	αφαιρέθηκα	αφηρημένος
αφήνω	leave	άφησα imp. άφησε/άσε, αφήστε/άστε	αφέθηκα	αφημένος
βάζω	put	έβαλα	βάλθηκα	βαλμένος
βαριέμαι	am bored	βαρέθηκα	—	—
βαρώ (Α)	strike	βάρεσα	—	—
βαστώ (Α)	bear	βάσταξα/βάστηξα	βαστάχτηκα/ βαστήχτηκα	βαστα(γ)μένος/ βαστη(γ)μένος

βγάζω	take out	έβγαλα	βγάλθηκα	βγαλμένος
βγαίνω	go out	βγήκα, dep. βγω imp. βγες/έβγα, βγείτε	—	βγαλμένος
βλέπω	see	είδα, dep. δω imp. δες, δέστε/δείτε	ειδώθηκα dep. ιδωθώ	ιδωμένος
βογκώ (Α)	groan	βόγκηξα	—	—
βόσκω	graze	βόσκησα	(βοσκήθηκα)	βοσκημένος
βούλομαι	wish	βουλήθηκα	—	—
βουτώ (Α)	dive	βούτηξα	βουτήχτηκα	βουτηγμένος
βρέχω	wet	έβρεξα	βράχηκα	βρε(γ)μένος
βρίσκω	find	βρήκα, dep. βρω imp. βρες, βρείτε	βρέθηκα	—
βροντώ (Α)	thunder	βρόντηξα/ βρόντησα	—	—
βυζαίνω	suckle	βύζαξα	βυζάχτηκα	βυζαγμένος

Present	Meaning	Active simple past	Passive simple past	Passive perfect participle
γδέρνω	skin	έγδαρα	γδάρθηκα	γδαρμένος
γελώ (Α)	laugh	γέλασα	γελάστηκα	γελασμένος
γέρνω	lean	έγειρα	—	γερμένος
γερνώ (Α)	grow old	γέρασα	—	γερασμένος
γίνομαι	become	έγινα, dep. γίνω	—	γινωμένος
δέομαι	pray	δεήθηκα	—	—
δέρνω	beat	έδειρα	δάρθηκα	δαρμένος
διαβαίνω	pass (by)	διάβηκα dep. διαβώ	—	—
διαθέτω	dispose	διέθεσα	διατέθηκα	διατεθειμένος
διακόπτω	interrupt	διέκοψα	διακόπηκα	διακεκομμένος
διαμαρτύρομαι	protest	διαμαρτυρήθηκα	—	διαμαρτυρημένος/διαμαρτυρόμενος
δίνω	give	έδωσα	δόθηκα	δοσμένος
διψώ (Α)	am thirsty	δίψασα	—	διψασμένος
δρω (Α)	act	έδρασα	—	—

εγείρω	erect	ήγειρα	εγέρθηκα	εγερμένος
εισάγω	import	εισήγαγα dep. εισαγάγω	εισάχθηκα	εισηγμένος
εκλέγω	elect	εξέλεξα dep. εκλέξω	εκλέχτηκα dep. εκλεγώ	εκλεγμένος
εκπλήσσω	surprise	εξέπληξα dep. εκπλήξω	εξεπλάγην dep. εκπλαγώ	—
εκρήγνυμαι	explode	εξερράγην dep. εκραγώ	—	—
εκτείνω	extend	εξέτεινα dep. εκτείνω	εκτάθηκα	εκτεταμένος
επαινώ (Β)	praise	επαίνεσα	επαινέθηκα	επαινεμένος
επεμβαίνω	intervene	επενέβηκα/ επενέβην dep. επέμβω	—	—
εξάγω	export	εξήγαγα dep. εξαγάγω	εξάχθηκα	εξηγμένος
εξαιρώ (Β)	except	εξαίρεσα/εξήρεσα dep. εξαιρέσω	εξαιρέθηκα	εξαιρεμένος
έρχομαι	come	ήρθα/ήλθα dep. έρθω/έλθω imp. έλα, ελάτε	—	—

Present	Meaning	Active simple past	Passive simple past	Passive perfect participle
εύχομαι	wish	ευχήθηκα	—	—
εφευρίσκω	invent	εφηύρα/εφεύρα dep. εφεύρω	εφευρέθηκα	—
έχω	have	imperf. είχα	—	—
ζουλώ (Α)	squeeze	ζούληξα	ζουλήχτηκα	ζουλημγμένος
ζω (Β)	live	έζησα	—	—
θαρρώ (Β)	believe	θάρρεψα	—	—
θέλω	want	θέλησα imperf. ήθελα	—	ηθελημένος
θέτω	place	έθεσα	τέθηκα	—
θίγω	touch	έθιξα	θίχτηκα/εθίγην	θιγμένος
θρέφω (cf. τρέφω)	nourish	έθρεψα	θρέφτηκα	θρεμμένος
καθιστώ (Α) pass. καθίσταμαι	render	κατέστησα	κατέστην dep. καταστώ	κατεστημένος

κάθομαι	sit	κάθισα/έκατσα imp. κάθισε/κάτσε κάθιστε	—	καθισμένος
καίω	burn	έκαψα	κάηκα	καμένος
καλώ (B)	call	κάλεσα	καλέστηκα	καλεσμένος
κάνω	make	έκανα/έκαμα	—	καμωμένος
καρτερό (A/B)	wait patiently	καρτέρεσα	—	—
καταπίνω	swallow	κατάπια	—	—
καταριέμαι (A)	curse	καταράστηκα	—	καταραμένος
καταφρονώ (B)	scorn	καταφρόνεσα	καταφρονέθηκα	καταφρονεμένος
κατεβαίνω	go down	dep. κατέβω/κατεβώ imp. κατέβα κατεβείτε κατέβηκα	—	κατεβασμένος
κερδίζω	earn	κέρδισα	κερδήθηκα	κερδισμένος
κερνώ (A)	treat	κέρασα	κεράστηκα	κερασμένος
κλαίω	weep	έκλαψα	κλαύτηκα	κλαμένος
κλέβω	steal	έκλεψα	κλάπηκα (steal)/ κλέφτηκα (elope)	κλεμμένος
κόβω	cut	έκοψα	κόπηκα	κομμένος

Present	Meaning	Active simple past	Passive simple past	Passive perfect participle
κοιτάζω/ κοιτώ (Α)	look	κοίταξα	κοιτάχτηκα	κοιταγμένος
κρεμώ (Α) pass. κρέμομαι	hang	κρέμασα	κρεμάστηκα	κρεμασμένος
κυλώ (Α)	roll	κύλησα	κυλίστηκα	κυλισμένος
λαμβάνω/ λαβαίνω	receive	έλαβα	—	—
λέ(γ)ω	say	είπα, dep. πω imp. πες, πέστε/πείτε	λέχθηκα/ ειπώθηκα	ειπωμένος
μαθαίνω	learn	έμαθα	μαθεύτηκα	μαθευμένος
μεθώ (Α)	get drunk	μέθυσα	—	μεθυσμένος
μένω	stay	έμεινα	—	—
μπαίνω	enter	μπήκα, dep. μπω imp. μπες/έμπα, μπείτε	—	μπασμένος

μπορώ (Β)	am able	μπόρεσα	—	—
ντρέπομαι	am ashamed	ντράπηκα	—	ντροπιασμένος
ξερνώ (Α)	vomit	ξέρασα	—	ξερασμένος
ξέρω	know	imperf. ήξερα	—	—
ξεχνώ (Α)	forget	ξέχασα	ξεχάστηκα	ξεχασμένος
παθαίνω	suffer	έπαθα	—	παθημένος
παίρνω	take	πήρα, dep. πάρω imp. πάρε, πάρτε	πάρθηκα	παρμένος
παραγγέλλω	order	παράγγειλα/ παρήγγειλα	παραγγέλθηκα	παραγγελμένος
παραδίδω/ παραδίνω	deliver	παρέδοσα	παραδόθηκα	παραδο(σ)μένος
παραπονιέμαι (Α)	complain	παραπονέθηκα imperf. παρείχα dep. παράσχω	—	παραπονεμένος
παρέχω	provide	παρασχέθηκα	—	—

Present	Meaning	Active simple past	Passive simple past	Passive perfect participle
πάσχω	suffer	έπαθα	—	—
πεινώ (Α)	am hungry	πείνασα	—	πεινασμένος
περνώ (Α)	pass	πέρασα	περάστηκα	περασμένος
πετυχαίνω	succeed	πέτυχα	—	πετυχημένος
πετώ (Α)	throw	πέταξα	πετάχτηκα	πετα(γ)μένος
πέφτω	fall	έπεσα	—	πεσμένος
πηγαίνω/πάω	go	πήγα, dep. πάω imp. πήγαινε, πηγαίνετε	—	—
πηδώ (Α)	jump	πήδηξα/πήδησα	πηδήχτηκα	πηδημένος
πίνω	drink	ήπια, dep. πιω imp. πιες, πέστε/πιείτε	πιώθηκα	πιωμένος
πλάττω/πλάσσω	mould	έπλασα	πλάστηκα	πλασμένος
πλένω	wash	έπλυνα	πλύθηκα	πλυμένος
πλήττω	am bored	έπληξα	—	—

πνίγω	strangle, drown	έπνιξα	πνιγμένος
πονώ (Α)	hurt	πόνεσα	πονεμένος
πρήζω	swell	έπρηξα	πρησμένος
προβαίνω	appear	πρόβαλα	—
προβάλλω	project	προέβαλα	προ(βε)βλημένος
προβλέπω	foresee	πρόβλεψα/ προέβλεψα	—
προσκαλώ	invite	προσκάλεσα	προσκεκλημένος
προτείνω	suggest	πρότεινα	—
ρουφώ (Α)	suck	ρούφηξα	ρουφηγμένος
σέβομαι	respect	σεβάστηκα	—
σέρνω	drag	έσυρα	συρμένος
σκουντώ (Α)	prod	σκούντηξα/ σκούντησα	σκουντηγμένος
σπάζω/σπάω (Α)	break	έσπασα	σπασμένος
σπέρνω	sow	έσπειρα	σπαρμένος
στέκομαι/στέκω	stand	στάθηκα	—

πνίγηκα		
—		
πρήστηκα		
—		
προβλήθηκα		
προβλέφθηκα		
προσκλήθηκα		
προτάθηκα		
ρουφήχτηκα		
—		
σύρθηκα		
σκουντήχτηκα		
—		
σπάρθηκα		
—		

Present	Meaning	Active simple past	Passive simple past	Passive perfect participle
στέλνω	send	έστειλα	στάλθηκα	σταλμένος
στενοχωρώ (Α/Β)	distress	στενοχώρεσα/ στενοχώρησα	στενοχωρέθηκα/ στενοχωρήθηκα	στενοχωρημένος
στρέφω	turn	έστρεψα	στράφηκα	στραμμένος
συγχαίρω	congratulate	συγχάρηκα	—	—
συμβαίνει	happens	συνέβη dep. συμβεί	—	—
συμμετέχω	participate	imperf. συμμετείχα dep. συμμετάσχω	—	—
συμπίπτω	coincide	συνέπεσα	—	—
σφάλλω	am mistaken	έσφαλα	—	εσφαλμένος
σχολώ (Α)	stop work	σχόλασα	—	σχολασμένος
σώζω	save	έσωσα	σώθηκα	σωσμένος
σωπαίνω	am silent	σώπασα imp. σώπα/σώπασε, σωπάτε/σωπάστε	—	—

τελώ (B)	perform	τέλεσα	τελέστηκα	(τε)τελεσμένος
τραβώ (A)	pull	τράβηξα	τραβήχτηκα	τραβηγμένος
τρέπω	turn	έτρεψα	τράπηκα	—
τρέφω	nourish	έθρεψα	τράφηκα	θρεμμένος
τρώω	eat	έφαγα, dep. φάω imp. φά(γ)ε, φάτε	φαγώθηκα	φαγωμένος
υπάρχω	exist	υπήρξα dep. υπάρξω	—	—
υπόσχομαι	promise	υποσχέθηκα	—	(υποσχημένος)
υφίσταμαι	exist, undergo	υπέστην dep. υποστώ	—	—
φαίνομαι	appear	φάνηκα	—	—
φέρνω	bring	έφερα	φέρθηκα	φερμένος
φεύγω	leave	έφυγα	—	—
φθείρω	corrupt	έφθειρα	φθάρ(θ)ηκα	φθαρμένος
φορώ (A/B)	wear	φόρεσα	φορέθηκα	φορεμένος
φταίω	am to blame	έφταιξα	—	—
φυλά(γ)ω	guard	φύλαξα	φυλάχτηκα	φυλαγμένος
φυσώ (A)	blow	φύσηξα	—	—

Present	Meaning	Active simple past	Passive simple past	Passive perfect participle
χαίρομαι/χαίρω	am glad	χάρηκα	—	—
χαλώ (Α)	spoil	χάλασα	—	χαλασμένος
χορταίνω	am satiated	χόρτασα	—	χορτασμένος
χυμώ (Α)	swoop	χύμηξα	—	—
χωρώ (Α/Β)	fit in	χώρεσα	—	—
ψάλλω/ψέλνω	chant	έψαλα	ψάλθηκα	ψαλμένος

In the above table there are a few forms for the active or passive simple past which end in -ην. These forms are derived from the learned language and are used mainly in formal contexts. The forms for each person, taking κατέστην 'I was rendered, made' (from καθιστώ) as our example, are as follows:

Sg.	1	κατέστην	Pl.	1	—
	2	κατέστης		2	—
	3	κατέστη		3	κατέστησαν

(The 1st and 2nd persons plural are not normally used.) Compare συνέβη 'it happened' (simple past of συμβαίνει), which is often used in newspapers.

Chapter 7

The adverb and the adverbial phrase

An adverb is typically used to indicate the manner, time or place of an action ('badly', 'yesterday', 'here'). An adverbial phrase may consist of a single adverb, or else an adverb modified by another adverb ('very badly', 'right here'). An adverbial is any adverb or any phrase or clause that functions as an adverb. Prepositional phrases (e.g. 'to London') function adverbially, but we will deal with them separately in Chapter 8. A variety of subordinate clauses function adverbially; these are dealt with in sections 10.13–10.19. For the sake of simplicity we will normally use the term 'adverb' to refer to any adverb, adverbial phrase or adverbial. A table showing some of the most basic adverbs is given in Appendix 1.

7.1 Types of adverb: manner, place, time, quantity, etc.

Adverbs are most commonly used to specify:

- manner

  Το έκανες *ωραία*.
  You did it *beautifully*.

- place

  'Ελα *δω*!
  Come *here*!

- time

  'Ελα *σήμερα*!
  Come *today*!

- quantity

  Ευχαριστώ *πολύ*.
  Thank you [*very*] *much*.

169

7 The adverb and the adverbial phrase

Most adverbs of manner are formed from adjectives, like **ωραία** 'beautifully' (i.e. 'in a beautiful way'), from **ωραίος** 'beautiful' (see sections 7.3–7.5). The other most common adverbs of manner are:

πώς	how (interrogative)
όπως	however (correlative: see section 10.9)
έτσι	thus; in this/that way; like this/that
κάπως	in some way
αλλιώς	otherwise; differently, in another way
καθόλου	(not) at all
οπωσδήποτε	in some way or other; by all means; certainly
κάπου	somehow or other
μόνο	only
μαζί	together
σιγά	softly (quietly); gently (slowly)

The most common adverbs of place are the following:

πού	where (interrogative)
όπου	where(ever) (relative and correlative)
εδώ	here
εκεί	there
κάπου	somewhere
αλλού	elsewhere, somewhere else
παντού	everywhere
πουθενά	nowhere; anywhere (in interrogative sentences)
οπουδήποτε	anywhere; wherever
πάνω	up; above; upstairs
κάτω	down; below; downstairs
μέσα	inside
έξω	outside
εμπρός, μπροστά	in front; forward(s)
πίσω	behind; back(wards)
κοντά	near
μακριά	far away
ανάμεσα	between
απέναντι	opposite
δίπλα, πλάι	nearby; next door
γύρω	around
πέρα	beyond, yonder
ψηλά	high up

χαμηλά	low down
χάμω	on the ground
δεξιά	to/on the right
αριστερά	to/on the left

> Types of adverb: manner, place, time, quantity, etc.

The most common adverbs of time are the following:

πότε	when (interrogative)
όποτε	whenever (correlative)
οπότε	at which point, whereupon (also 'in which case')
τώρα	now
τότε	then (i.e. at that time) (also 'in that case')
κάποτε	at some time; sometimes; once
άλλοτε	at another time; formerly
πάντα	always
ποτέ	never; ever (in interrogative sentences)
οποτεδήποτε	whenever; at any time
πρώτα	first
πριν	before; ago
μετά, ύστερα, έπειτα	afterwards, later; then, next
νωρίς	early
αργά	late
προχθές	the day before yesterday
χθες	yesterday
σήμερα	today
αύριο	tomorrow
μεθαύριο	the day after tomorrow
απόψε	this evening; tonight
πρόπερσι	the year before last
πέρ[υ]σι	last year
[ε]φέτος	this year
του χρόνου	next year
ήδη, κιόλας	already
αμέσως	immediately
επιτέλους	at last
μόλις	just
συχνά	often
σπάνια	rarely, seldom
τακτικά	regularly
συνήθως	usually

7 The adverb and the adverbial phrase

πάλι, ξανά	again
πια, πλέον	[any/no] more
ακόμα, ακόμη	still; yet
όλο	all the time
κάπου κάπου	from time to time
πότε πότε	occasionally
μια φορά (δυο φορές, τρεις φορές, etc.)	once (twice, three times, etc.)
καμιά φορά	from time to time

In addition, there are noun phrases introduced by the determiner **κάθε** 'each, every' and used adverbially, such as:

κάθε μέρα	every day
κάθε φορά	every time
κάθε τόσο	every so often
κάθε πόσο	how often

The chief adverbs of quantity are the following:

πόσο	how much (interrogative)
όσο	as much as (correlative)
οσοδήποτε	however much (universal correlative)
τόσο	so; so much; this/that much
κάμποσο/καμπόσο	quite a lot
κάπως	somewhat
πολύ	very; much, a lot; too [much]
περισσότερο	more (comparative: see also section 10.22)
λίγο	a little
λιγότερο	less (comparative)
ελάχιστα	very little, hardly (absolute superlative)
καθόλου	(not) at all (in negative and interrogative sentences)
τελείως, εντελώς	completely, entirely
αρκετά	quite (a lot)
σχεδόν	almost, nearly
τουλάχιστον	at least
πάνω κάτω	about, approximately
περίπου	approximately; more or less
μάλλον	rather
εξίσου	equally

πάρα   very (before πολύ: πάρα πολύ 'very much; too much')
πιο   more (before adjective or adverb to form the
          comparative and the relative superlative: see sections
          3.44–3.45 and 7.6)

For noun phrases in the accusative case in adverbial use see section 3.51.

7.2 The use of adverbs and adverbial phrases

As their name implies, most adverbs are normally used to modify a verb:

1 Μίλησε *καλά* (adverb of manner).
   (S)he spoke *well*.

2 Μίλησε *εδώ* (adverb of place).
   (S)he spoke *here*.

3 Μίλησε *χθες* (adverb of time).
   (S)he spoke *yesterday*.

4 Μίλησε *πολύ* (adverb of quantity).
   (S)he spoke *a lot*.

Some adverbs may modify an adjective or adverb. Adverbs of manner may modify a perfect passive participle:

5 *καλά* εκπαιδευμένος
   well trained

Some adverbs of time may modify an adjective or adverb:

6 *αμέσως* μετά
   immediately afterwards

Adverbs of quantity are very commonly used to modify verbs (7–11), adjectives and adverbs (12–20):

7 Μου άρεσε *πολύ*.
   I liked (him/her/it) *a lot*.

8 Μου άρεσε *περισσότερο*.
   I liked (him/her/it) *more*.

9 Φοβάμαι *λίγο*.
   I'm *a bit* frightened.

10 Μου άρεσε *λιγότερο*.
   I liked (him/her/it) *less*.

11 Μου άρεσε *αρκετά*.
I liked (him/her/it) *quite a lot*.

12 *πολύ* καλός/καλά
very good/well

13 *πολύ* καλύτερος/καλύτερα
much better

14 *τόσο* καλός/καλά
so good/well

15 *λίγο* καλύτερος/καλύτερα
a little better

16 *λιγότερο* καλός/καλά
less good/well

17 *καθόλου* καλός/καλά
not at all good/well

18 *αρκετά* καλός/καλά
quite good/well

19 *πάρα πολύ* καλός/καλά
extremely good/well

20 *πιο* καλός/καλά
better

Adverbs often modify adverbs of place. Here are some examples of combinations that are unlike English:

21 *πιο* εδώ/εκεί
on this/that side (lit. '*more* here/there')

22 *πιο* πάνω/κάτω
further up/down (lit. '*more* up/down')

23 *πιο* πριν
earlier (lit. '*more* before')

24 εδώ/εκεί πάνω/κάτω
up/down here/there (lit. 'here/there up/down')

25 εδώ/εκεί κοντά
near here/there (lit. 'here/there near')

A few adverbs of place and time may modify a noun:

> The use of adverbs and adverbial phrases

26 η *πίσω* πόρτα (place)
    the *back* door

27 η *τότε* κυβέρνηση (time)
    the *then* government

A few adverbs of quantity may modify a numeral or quantifier:

28 *σχεδόν* όλοι
    almost everybody

29 *τουλάχιστον* τέσσερις φορές
    at least four times

Some adverbs may be used on their own to form complete utterances, for example:

ναι	yes
όχι	no
μάλιστα	certainly
εντάξει	OK, all right
καλά!	good!
ωραία!	lovely! fine!

'Οχι can also be used to negate nouns, adjectives and adverbs:

30 *όχι* ο Γιάννης
    not John

31 *όχι* καλός/καλά
    not good/well

32 *όχι* εδώ
    not here

Some adverbs are used to join clauses or sentences together, for example:

όμως	however
ωστόσο	nevertheless
παρ' όλα αυτά	nevertheless
διαφορετικά	otherwise
πάντως	still, at any rate
λοιπόν	well then
άρα	therefore
επομένως	consequently
άλλωστε	besides
εξάλλου	besides

7 The adverb and the adverbial phrase

Some adverbs can either be used on their own or modify a whole sentence, for example:

ίσως	perhaps
ασφαλώς	certainly
βέβαια	of course
σίγουρα	of course
φυσικά	naturally
ευτυχώς	fortunately, luckily
δυστυχώς	unfortunately

Some adverbs (particularly τώρα, τότε, εδώ, εκεί, καλά, ωραία, ευτυχώς and μόνο) can take complement clauses introduced by που in a number of idiomatic uses, for example:

33 *τώρα που το λες*
   now *that* you mention it (lit. 'now that it you-say')

34 *τότε που ήμασταν νέοι*
   when we were young (lit. 'then that we-were young')

35 *Από δω που κάθομαι, δεν σε βλέπω.*
   From where (lit. '*here that*') I'm sitting I can't see you.

36 *Εκεί που περίμενα τον Γιάννη, ήρθε η Σοφία.*
   Whereas I was expecting John, Sophie came.

37 *Καλά που το σκέφτηκες!*
   [It's a] good [thing] you thought of it!

38 *Ευτυχώς που μου το είπες!*
   [It's] lucky you told me!

39 *Θα το αγόραζα, μόνο που είναι ακριβό.*
   I would buy it, *only* it's expensive.

A number of adverbs of place (πάνω, κάτω, μέσα, έξω, μπροστά, πίσω, κοντά, μακριά, ανάμεσα, απέναντι, δίπλα, πλάι, γύρω, πέρα) can be used as prepositions with the genitive form of the weak pronoun. The same adverbs can be combined with prepositions to make compound prepositions (see section 8.3 for their use).

The indefinite adverbs **πουθενά** 'nowhere, anywhere', **ποτέ** 'never, ever', **καθόλου** '(not) at all' are used in interrogative or negative clauses, or in other clauses that do not make a statement, or on their own, that is, in the same circumstances as non-specific indefinite pronouns and determiners (see section 4.6):

40 Θα φάμε *ποτέ*;
Will we *ever* eat?

41 *Δεν* θα φάμε *ποτέ*!
We'll *never* eat!

42 Αν το βρεις *πουθενά*, αγόρασέ το.
If you find it *anywhere*, buy it.

43 – Σ' άρεσε το έργο; – *Καθόλου*.
'Did you like the play/film?' '*Not at all*'.

The formation of adverbs from adjectives

7.3 Adverbs in -α

Many adverbs are derived directly from adjectives by a change in the ending of the word. There are two principal kinds of formation, which will be examined in this section and the following one. The difference is mainly determined by the declension pattern of the adjective in question. We shall therefore be referring to the sections in which the forms of adjectives are set out in full.

Adjectives in -ος (sections 3.33–3.35) have adverbs ending in -α, which are identical to the neuter plural (nominative and accusative) form of the corresponding adjective. Examples: άγρια 'wildly, fiercely', άσχημα 'badly', βέβαια 'certainly', γλυκά 'sweetly', ελληνικά 'in Greek', έξυπνα 'cleverly', καλά 'well', ξαφνικά 'suddenly', όμορφα 'beautifully', σπάνια 'rarely', συχνά 'often', σωστά 'correctly', τέλεια 'perfectly', χωριστά 'separately', ψηλά 'high up'. Some passive past participles also form adverbs in this way, e.g. λυπημένα 'sadly', συγκεκριμένα 'specifically'.

Adjectives in -ύς (section 3.36), in -ής with feminine -ιά (section 3.37) and those that have neuters in -ικο (section 3.40) also form adverbs which are identical to the corresponding neuter plural. Examples: βαθιά 'deep(ly)', βαριά 'heavily, gravely', δεξιά 'on the right', ζηλιάρικα 'jealously', μακριά 'far away', πεισματάρικα 'stubbornly', τεμπέλικα 'lazily'.

7.4 Adverbs in -ως

Certain other types of adjective form adverbs with the suffix -ως. They include, most importantly, adjectives in -ης with neuter -ες (section 3.39). The stress of the adverb remains on the same syllable as the masculine nominative singular of the adjective except in the case of adjectives ending in -ώδης: their adverbs have the stress on the final syllable. Examples: **ακριβώς** 'exactly', **ασφαλώς** 'surely', **διεθνώς** 'internationally', **δυστυχώς** 'unfortunately', **μανιωδώς** 'furiously', **πλήρως** 'fully', **σκανδαλωδώς** 'scandalously', **συνεπώς** 'consequently', **συνήθως** 'usually'.

A few adjectives in -ων, -ουσα, -ον (section 3.41) also have adverbs ending in -ως but formed from the stem of the neuter plural -οντ- and with stress on the penultimate syllable. Examples: **δευτερευόντως** 'secondarily', **επειγόντως** 'urgently'.

Some adjectives in -ος can also form an alternative adverb in -ως. When such adverbs are derived from adjectives stressed on the third syllable from the end, they have a shift of stress to the penultimate syllable: **σπάνιος** 'rare' → **σπανίως** 'rarely' (as a more formal alternative to **σπάνια**). Some common doublets, such as **βέβαια/βεβαίως** 'certainly', have no difference of meaning and hardly differ in usage. In other cases, however, the -ως form tends to be used in more formal contexts, or for stylistic reasons; for example, **άδικα** and **αδίκως** 'unjustly', **άσχετα** and **ασχέτως** 'irrespectively'. But sometimes there are important differences of meaning or usage between the two forms, as in the following examples:

- **καλώς** 'well, rightly', rather than **καλά**, is used in some standard expressions, such as **καλώς ήλθες** 'welcome'; **καλώς** can also mean 'lower second [degree]'
- **ευχαρίστως** 'with pleasure' but **ευχάριστα** 'pleasantly'
- **τελείως** 'completely' but **τέλεια** 'perfectly'
- **αμέσως** 'immediately' but **άμεσα** 'directly'
- **ίσως** 'perhaps' has a quite different meaning from **ίσα** 'equally'
- **απλώς** 'simply, merely' but **απλά** 'in a simple way' (though this distinction is not always made)

Some common adverbs in -ως which are derived from adjectives in -ος are: **αεροπορικώς** 'by air (mail)', **απολύτως** 'absolutely', **επανειλημμένως** 'repeatedly', **επομένως** 'consequently', **κυρίως** 'mainly'.

7.5 Other adverbs formed from adjectives

Some adverbs are formed from adjectives (or words declined like adjectives) in a different way from those described in sections 7.3 and 7.4. Certain very common adverbs are identical with the neuter *singular* (nominative and accusative) of the corresponding adjective:

- άλλος 'other' (really a contrastive pronoun/determiner; see section 4.9) has an adverbial form άλλο 'any more, any longer', which is used only in questions or in negative statements or commands, e.g. **Μην το κάνεις άλλο!** 'Don't do it any more!'; there is also an adverb **αλλιώς** 'otherwise'
- λίγος 'little' gives rise to the adverb λίγο '(a) little, to a small extent'
- μόνος 'alone, only' has the adverbial form μόνο 'only'
- πολύς 'much, many' has the adverb πολύ 'very, much, a lot' (for the forms of πολύς see section 3.38)

For the use of the adverbs of quantity λίγο and πολύ see section 7.1.

7.6 Comparison of adverbs

Like adjectives, adverbs derived from adjectives have two ways of forming the comparative degree. One way is to use πιο 'more' before the positive form of the adverb, e.g. πιο όμορφα 'more beautifully', πιο αργά 'later', πιο ψηλά 'higher', πιο σωστά 'more correctly', πιο συγκεκριμένα 'more specifically', πιο βαριά 'more heavily'. Some other adverbs of place and time (see section 7.1) can also form a comparative in the same way, e.g. πιο κάτω 'lower down, further down', πιο μέσα 'further in', πιο πέρα 'further along', πιο πίσω 'further back', πιο νωρίς 'earlier'.

Adjectives that have one-word comparative forms in -τερος can also form comparative adverbs in a similar way. The ending is -τερα, which is identical with the neuter plural (nominative and accusative) ending of the corresponding comparative adjective, e.g. αγριότερα 'more fiercely'. Similarly, such adjectives can also have an absolute superlative adverb ending in -τατα, e.g. ευκολότατα 'extremely easily'. Some further examples:

7 The adverb and the adverbial phrase

Positive adverb		Comparative	Absolute superlative
ακριβά	expensively	ακριβότερα	ακριβότατα
ακριβώς	exactly	ακριβέστερα	ακριβέστατα
αργά	slowly, late	αργότερα	—
βαθιά	deeply	βαθύτερα	βαθύτατα
γενικά	generally	γενικότερα	γενικότατα
καλά	well	καλύτερα	κάλλιστα/ άριστα
συνήθως	usually	συνηθέστερα	συνηθέστατα
φρόνιμα	prudently	φρονιμότερα	φρονιμότατα

The only adverbs of quantity (see section 7.1) that be can used in the comparative and superlative degrees are the following:

Positive adverb	Comparative	Relative superlative
λίγο (a) little	λιγότερο less	το λιγότερο/ το ελάχιστο at the least
πολύ very, much	περισσότερο/ πιο πολύ more	το πιο πολύ at the most

Note also the special form **τουλάχιστον** 'at least'.

Chapter 8

The preposition and the prepositional phrase

8.1 Introduction to prepositions and prepositional phrases

A preposition ('in', 'from', etc.) is placed immediately before a noun phrase in order to indicate the relation of this phrase to some other phrase. A phrase introduced by a preposition is known as a prepositional phrase ('in the house', 'from the river').

The chief prepositions in Greek are:

- από 'from; since; by; than'
- για 'for; about'
- μέχρι 'until, up to'
- με 'with'
- σαν 'like'
- σε 'to, into; at, in'
- χωρίς 'without'

In Greek, a noun phrase (including an emphatic personal pronoun) used after one of the basic prepositions appears in the accusative case, for example:

στην Αθήνα
to/in Athens

σ' εμένα
to me (with contrastive emphasis, i.e. not to anyone else)

However, some prepositions are used with noun phrases in the genitive case, e.g. **εναντίον** 'against', **εξαιτίας** 'because of' and **μεταξύ** 'between'; these three are the only ones that can be followed by weak personal pronouns. The uses of these and other prepositions are covered in alphabetical order

8 The preposition and the prepositional phrase

in section 8.2. Finally, there is also a group of adverbs (mostly of place) that can be used either with a weak personal pronoun in the genitive or together with one of the basic prepositions followed by a noun phrase in the accusative case; this last group is covered in section 8.3.

A few prepositions can be followed by an adverb of place or time, such as:

μέχρι εκεί
up to there

από σήμερα
from today

για τώρα
for now

8.2 The uses of individual prepositions

Here we give the chief uses of each preposition in alphabetical order.

8.2.1 Από

- 'from' in expressions of place:

  1 Είμαι *από* την Αθήνα.
     I'm *from* Athens.

  2 Έφυγα *από* την Αθήνα.
     I left Athens.

- 'from' or 'of' in expressions of cause:

  3 Θα πεθάνω *από* την πείνα.
     I'll die *of* hunger.

- 'from' or 'since' in expressions of time:

  4 Περίμενα *από* το πρωί μέχρι το βράδυ.
     I waited *from* morning till evening.

  5 Μένω στην Πάτρα *από* το 1992.
     I've been living in Patras *since* 1992.

- 'of' in partitive expressions:

  6 ένας *από* τους διαβάτες
     one *of* the passers-by

7 κανένας *από* σας
none *of* you (emphatic; cf. section 3.52.3)

- 'by' in expressions of agent:
    8 Η διαδήλωση οργανώθηκε *από* τα συνδικάτα.
    The demonstration was organized *by* the unions.

- 'made of' in expressions referring to material:
    9 ένα τραπέζι *από* μάρμαρο
    a table [made] *of* marble

- 'than' in expressions of comparison:
    10 Είμαι μεγαλύτερη *από* τη Μαρία.
    I'm older (fem.) *than* Mary (see also section 10.22).

- 'through, past, by, along' in expressions of passage (often with the verb περνώ 'I pass'):
    11 Πέρασε *από* τον διάδρομο και μπήκε στο σαλόνι.
    (S)he went *along* the hall and entered the living-room.

    12 Θα περάσω *από* το σπίτι σου.
    I'll pass *by* your house (i.e. 'I'll drop by').

    13 Η μύγα μπήκε στο σπίτι *από* το παράθυρο.
    The fly came into the house *through* the window.

In colloquial usage, **από** can be reduced to **απ'** before the definite article: *απ'* την Αθήνα '*from* Athens'.

8.2.2 Για

- 'for' in expressions of benefit:
    14 Το αγόρασα *για* σένα.
    I bought it *for* you.

- 'for' in expressions of purpose:
    15 Πάω *για* ψώνια.
    I'm going shopping (lit. 'I-go *for* shopping').

Για is also used with **να** to introduce clauses expressing purpose ('in order to/that': see section 10.17).

- 'about' in expressions of reference:

    16 Μιλούσαμε *για* τον Μιχάλη.
        We were talking *about* Michael.

8.2.3 Εναντίον

Used with the genitive of a noun phrase (17) or a weak personal pronoun (18) to mean 'against':

   17 ο πόλεμος *εναντίον* των ναρκωτικών
       the war *against* drugs

   18 Δεν έχω τίποτα *εναντίον* σου.
       I've got nothing *against* you.

8.2.4 Κατά

- Used with the accusative to mean 'about', especially in expressions of time:

    19 *κατά* τις έντεκα
        about eleven

- Used with the accusative to mean 'according to':

    20 *κατά* τη γνώμη μου
        in my opinion

- Used with the genitive to mean 'against':

    21 *κατά* της θανατικής ποινής
        against the death penalty

8.2.5 Λόγω (also, less commonly, εξαιτίας)

Λόγω is used with the genitive of a noun phrase to mean 'because of':

   22 Το ματς ματαιώθηκε *λόγω* της κακοκαιρίας.
       The match was cancelled *because of* the bad weather.

Εξαιτίας is used with the genitive of a noun phrase or weak pronoun in the same meaning:

   23 Καθυστερήσαμε *εξαιτίας* σου.
       We were late *because of* you.

8.2.6 Με

- 'with' (in the company of)

    24 Ήρθε *με* τα παιδιά της.
        She came *with* her children.

- 'with' (instrument)

    25 Έκοψε το ψωμί *με* μαχαίρι.
        (S)he cut the bread *with* a knife.

- 'by' (means of transport)

    26 Θα πάμε *με* το λεωφορείο/*με* τα πόδια.
        We'll go *by* bus/*on* foot.

- manner

    27 Τον αγαπάει *με* πάθος.
        (S)he loves him passionately (lit. '*with* passion').

- 'by' (basis of calculation)

    28 Πληρώνομαι *με* τον μήνα.
        I'm paid *by* the month.

- 'dressed in':

    29 το κορίτσι *με* τα κόκκινα
        the girl *in* red

- 'to' in expressions of periods of time:

    30 Έχουμε μάθημα έντεκα *με* δώδεκα.
        We have a lesson [from] eleven *to* twelve.

- 'despite, in spite of' (in the construction **μ' όλο**, in which **όλο** agrees with the noun in gender, number and case):

    31 *μ' όλη* τη ζέστη
        despite the heat

The construction **μ' όλο που** 'although, even though' introduces concessive clauses (see section 10.14).

8.2.7 Μετά

Used with definite noun phrases to mean 'after':

    32 *μετά* τη συναυλία
        after the concert

With emphatic pronouns and indefinite noun phrases **μετά** is normally followed by **από** (see section 8.3: Type 1).

8.2.8 Μεταξύ

Used with the genitive of noun phrases and weak personal pronouns to mean 'between, among':

33   *μεταξύ Αθήνας και Θεσσαλονίκης*
     between Athens and Thessaloniki (more commonly expressed by *ανάμεσα σε* + accusative: *ανάμεσα στην Αθήνα και τη Θεσσαλονίκη*)

34   *μεταξύ μας*
     between us; between ourselves

8.2.9 Μέχρι (also, less commonly, ως or έως)

- 'until, up to' in expressions of time; with **και** it means 'up to and including' (US: 'through'):

   35   Περίμενα *μέχρι* τις δέκα.
        I waited *till* ten [o'clock]/the tenth [of the month].

   36   Η έκθεση θα παραμείνει ανοιχτή *μέχρι και* την Κυριακή.
        The exhibition will remain open *up to and including* Sunday (US: *'through* Sunday').

- 'by' in expressions of time:

   37   Το σακάκι σας θα είναι έτοιμο *μέχρι* την Τρίτη.
        Your (pl.) jacket will be ready *by* Tuesday.

- 'as far as, up to' in expressions of place:

   38   Θα σε πάω *μέχρι* το Σύνταγμα.
        I'll take you *as far as* Syntagma.

The constructions **μέχρι να** and **μέχρι που** are used to introduce temporal clauses (see section 10.15).

8.2.10 Παρά

Used with noun phrases

- to mean 'contrary to':

   39   *παρά τη θέλησή μου*
        against my will

- often with the appropriate form of **όλος**, to mean 'despite, in spite of':

    40 *παρ' όλες τις προσπάθειές της*
        despite her efforts

- to express the number of minutes before the hour (note that the word order is the opposite of English; see also section 5.5):

    41 δέκα *παρά* είκοσι
        twenty to ten

Παρά (with the accent on the last syllable) should not be confused with the adverb **πάρα** (with accent on the first syllable), which is used in the construction **πάρα πολύ**.

Παρά is also used as a conjunction in comparative constructions ('(rather) than': see section 10.22), or in constructions such as **παρ' ότι** and **παρ' όλο που** 'although' to introduce concessive clauses (see section 10.14).

8.2.11 Προς

Used with noun phrases to mean 'towards'; with weak pronouns the construction **προς το μέρος** + genitive is used:

42 Πηγαίναμε *προς* τη Λαμία.
    We were going *towards* Lamia.

43 Γύρισε *προς το μέρος* μου.
    (S)he turned *towards* me.

With a small number of adverbs of place, **προς** is followed by the neuter plural of the definite article, **τα**:

44 *προς* τα πάνω
    upwards (lit. '*towards* the up')

45 *προς* τα πού;
    where to?, in which direction? (lit. '*towards* the where?').

8.2.12 Σαν

Used with noun phrases and emphatic personal pronouns to mean 'like' (resembling):

46 ένας άνθρωπος *σαν* το Μιχάλη
    a man *like* Michael

The uses of individual prepositions

47 Είσαι σαν (κι) εμένα.
You're *like* me.

Σαν is also used in the construction **σαν να** 'as if, as though' (see sections 10.16 and 10.22).

8.2.13 Σε

Σε is always reduced to **σ** before the definite article (and is written with it as one word); in colloquial usage it may be reduced to **σ'** before a word beginning with a vowel (**σ' όλα** 'in all things'). It is used with noun phrases and emphatic personal pronouns to mean:

- 'to' (indirect object)
  48 Το έδωσα στη Χριστίνα.
  I gave it *to* Christina.

- 'to; into' (motion)
  49 Πήγα στο Λονδίνο.
  I went *to* London.

  50 Πέρασα στο άλλο δωμάτιο.
  I went (lit. 'passed') *into* the other room.

- 'at; in' (location in space or time)
  51 Σπούδασα στα Γιάννινα.
  I studied *at/in* Yannina.

  52 στις δέκα
  at ten [o'clock *on* the tenth] OR [of the month]

- 'in' (lapse of time)
  53 σε λίγες μέρες
  in a few days

- 'on' (location)
  54 Βάλ' το στο τραπέζι.
  Put it *on* the table.

8.2.14 Χωρίς (or, less commonly, δίχως)

Used with noun phrases (55–56) and emphatic personal pronouns (57) to mean 'without':

55 Ήρθε *χωρίς* τα παιδιά της.
She came *without* her children.

56 *χωρίς* άδεια
without permission

57 Δεν θα το έκανα *χωρίς* εσένα.
I wouldn't have done it *without* you/*but for* you.

Χωρίς is also used in the construction **χωρίς να** 'without' to introduce clauses:

58 Το έκανα *χωρίς να* το θέλω.
I did it *without* wanting to (i.e. without meaning to).

8.3 Compound prepositions; adverbs used as prepositions

In addition to the one-word prepositions covered in section 8.2, Greek has a number of compound prepositions, made up of two words, that introduce noun phrases and emphatic personal pronouns. These are of two types:

- compound prepositions that can only be used with noun phrases and emphatic personal pronouns (type 1);
- compound prepositions consisting of adverb of place + preposition (type 2).

In other contexts, adverbs that form part of the second type can be used with the genitive of the weak personal pronoun instead of a preposition.

8.3.1 Type I

This type consists of a small number of basic compound prepositions:

- αντί για 'instead of'

    1 Πήγα εγώ *αντί για* το Γιώργο.
       I went *instead of* George.

Αντί is also used in the construction **αντί να** 'instead of' to introduce clauses:

2 *Αντί να* πάει ο Γιώργος, πήγα εγώ.
   Instead of George going, I went myself.

8 The preposition and the prepositional phrase

- εκτός από 'except' or 'apart from':

    3   Όλοι πήγαν *εκτός από* μένα.
        Everyone went *except* me.

    4   *Εκτός από* τους Έλληνες, πήραν μέρος και Τούρκοι.
        Apart from the Greeks, [some] Turks took part too.

Εκτός is also used in the construction **εκτός αν** (alternatively **εκτός κι αν** or **εκτός εάν**) 'unless' to introduce conditional clauses (see section 10.13).

- μετά από 'after'

    5   *μετά από* το πάρτι (από may be omitted before a noun accompanied by the definite article: see section 8.2.7).
        after the party

    6   *μετά από* μένα
        after me

Μετά is also used in the construction **μετά που** 'after' to introduce temporal clauses (see section 10.15).

- πριν από 'before'

    7   *πριν από* το πάρτι (από may be omitted before a noun accompanied by the definite article)
        before the party

    8   *πριν από* μένα
        before me

Πριν is also used as a conjunction ('before') to introduce temporal clauses (see section 10.15).

In addition, there are a number of other combinations of adverb + preposition, such as **ανάλογα με** 'according to, in proportion to', **όσο για** 'as for', **σύμφωνα με** 'according to', **σχετικά με** 'related to', **ύστερα από** 'after'.

8.3.2 Type 2

This type consists of a group of basic adverbs of place that may either (a) be accompanied by a preposition followed by a noun phrase or emphatic pronoun in the accusative, or (b) be followed by a weak personal pronoun in the genitive. When these adverbs are accompanied by prepositions, the following combinations are most common:

ανάμεσα σε	between; among
απέναντι σε/από	opposite
γύρω από/σε	around
δίπλα σε	next to
έξω από	outside (not used with weak pronoun)
κάτω από	under, below
κοντά σε	near
μαζί με	(together) with
μακριά από	a long way from; away from
μέσα	(σε) inside; (από) through; from inside (see examples below)
μπροστά από/σε	in front of
πάνω	(σε) on; (από) above (see examples below)
πίσω από	behind
πλάι σε	beside

Compound prepositions; adverbs used as prepositions

Here are some examples of these adverbs, used with and without prepositions:

9 ανάμεσα στα σπίτια
   between/among the houses

10 απέναντί μας
   opposite us

11 γύρω από το δέντρο
   around the tree

12 δίπλα σου
   next to you (sg.)

13 έξω από το σπίτι
   outside the house

14 κάτω από το τραπέζι
   under the table

15 κοντά της
   near her

16 μαζί μου
   with me

17 μακριά από την πόλη
   [far] away from the city

8 The preposition and the prepositional phrase

18 Η γάτα μας μένει συνέχεια *μέσα στο* σπίτι.
    Our cat stays *inside* the house all the time.

19 Πέρασε *μέσα από* το σπίτι.
    (S)he/it passed *through* the house.

20 μπροστά μας
    in front of us

21 Το πιάτο είναι *πάνω στο* τραπέζι.
    The plate's *on* the table.

22 Ο διακόπτης είναι *πάνω από* το τραπέζι.
    The switch is *above* the table.

23 πίσω από μένα
    behind *me* (emphatic)

24 πλάι στο σπίτι
    beside the house

Chapter 9
Conjunctions and particles

9.1 Co-ordinating conjunctions

Co-ordinating conjunctions (e.g. 'and', 'or', 'but') are used to join two phrases or two independent clauses within the same sentence. The co-ordinating conjunctions in Greek are:

- **και** 'and' (optionally reduced to **κι** before a word beginning with a vowel in colloquial usage)
- **ή** 'or'
- **είτε** 'or else; either . . . or . . .'
- **ούτε** 'nor; neither . . . nor . . .'
- **αλλά, μα** 'but'
- **όμως** 'however'

For the use of these conjunctions see section 10.21.

In addition, **και** is very commonly used before a noun phrase, an emphatic pronoun, an adjective, an adverb or a prepositional phrase to mean 'too, also':

1   Ήρθε κι η Μαρία (noun phrase).
    Mary came *too*.

2   Έχουμε καινούριο σπίτι. Είναι και μεγάλο.
    We've got a new house. It's big *too*.

3   Είχαμε κι εδώ βροχές (adverb).
    We had rain here *too*.

4   Είχαμε και στην Αθήνα βροχές (prepositional phrase).
    We had rain in Athens *too*.

Before numerals accompanied by the definite article, **και** may have the sense of 'both' or 'all':

5   και τα δυο παιδιά
   both of the children

6   κι οι τρεις μας
   all three of us (masc./fem.)

After numerals, **και** (pronounced with heavy stress) can mean 'at least':

7   Είναι τριάντα και.
   (S)he's *at least* thirty.

The expression **ε και;** is used to mean 'so what? what of it?' in response to a piece of information (compare the colloquial use in English of 'And . . .?'):

8   – Γύρισε ο μπαμπάς μου. – Ε και;
   'My dad's come back.' 'What of it?'

Και is used in a number of idiomatic expressions, e.g.:

9   Θα είμαστε εμείς κι εμείς.
   It'll just be us (lit. 'We'll be *we and we*').

10   ένας κι ένας (inflected for gender and case)
   hand-picked (i.e. selected for high quality)

Και is also used in the constructions **κι αν, κι ας** 'even if', **αν και, και να** 'although, even though' to introduce concessive clauses (see section 10.14).

The negative conjunction **ούτε** is also used to mean 'not even':

11   ούτε δέκα
   not even ten

9.2 Subordinating conjunctions

Subordinating conjunctions are used to subordinate one clause to another (e.g. 'if', 'when', 'because', 'although'). Of the large number of subordinating conjunctions in Greek the most common are the following (for their uses see sections 10.9–10.19):

- relative particles/pronouns: **που, ο οποίος** 'who, which, that' (section 10.9)
- correlative pronouns and determiners: **όποιος** 'whoever', **ό,τι** 'what(ever)', **όσος** 'however much; as much . . . as' (section 10.9)
- correlative adverbs: **όπου** 'where(ever)', **όποτε** 'whenever', **όπως** 'however', **όσο** 'however much; as much as' (section 10.9)

- interrogative conjunction: **αν** 'if, whether' (section 10.10.1)
- interrogative pronouns and determiners: **ποιος** 'who', **τι** 'what', **πόσος** 'how much/many' (section 10.10.2)
- interrogative adverbs: **πού** 'where', **πότε** 'when', **πώς** 'how', **πόσο** 'how much', **γιατί** 'why' (section 10.10.2)
- complementizers: **να** 'to', **ότι, πως, που** 'that' (section 10.2)
- dubitative conjunction (used with verbs of fearing, uncertainty or doubt): **μήπως** 'in case; lest' (section 10.12.1)
- conditional conjunctions: **αν, εάν, άμα** 'if', **εφόσον** 'provided that', **είτε . . . είτε** 'whether . . . or . . .', **εκτός (κι) αν** 'unless' (section 10.13)
- concessive conjunctions: **ακόμη κι αν, κι ας** 'even if', **αν και, παρ' όλο που, μ' όλο που** 'even though' (section 10.14)
- adversative conjunctions: **αντί να** 'instead of', **χωρίς να** 'without' (sections 8.3.1 and 8.2.14)
- temporal conjunctions: **όταν** 'when', **όποτε** 'whenever', **μόλις**, 'as soon as', **πριν** 'before', **αφού, μετά που** 'after', **ώσπου, μέχρι που/να** 'until', **ενώ, την ώρα που** 'while', **καθώς** 'as', **όσο** 'as long as' (section 10.15)
- manner conjunctions: **όπως, καθώς** 'as' (section 10.16)
- purpose conjunctions: **για να** 'in order to/that' (section 10.17)
- result conjunctions: **που, ώστε** '(so) that' (section 10.18)
- causal conjunctions: **γιατί, διότι** 'because', **επειδή, αφού, μια και/που** 'since' (section 10.19)
- comparative conjunctions: **σαν να** 'as if, as though', **παρά (να)** '(rather) than' (section 10.22)

9.3 Particles

Greek has a variety of very important little words called particles. These words are very versatile in their use, and most of them do not correspond precisely to any words in English. We shall deal with them in seven groups:

- the future particle **θα**
- the subjunctive particles **να** and **ας**
- the negative particles **δεν, μην** and **μη**
- the complementizer and relative particle **που**
- the positive and negative response particles **ναι** and **όχι**
- the deictic particle **να**
- the hortatory particle **για**

9 Conjunctions and particles

Some of the material in this section overlaps with material presented in other sections, but since the particles are so important, some repetition is justified.

9.3.1 The future particle θα

Θα is used before any finite verb form, and can be separated from it only by weak pronouns. The prime use of θα is to express actions that are expected to take place in the future. The use of the two aspects of the future tense (the perfective future consisting of θα followed by the dependent, and the imperfective future consisting of θα followed by the present tense) is covered in section 6.5. The use of the conditional (consisting of θα followed by the imperfect tense) and the perfect conditional (consisting of θα followed by the pluperfect tense) is also covered in the same section.

Apart from its use in future and conditional expressions, θα can be used to express probability. It can appear with any form of the verb in this use, but the most typical forms of the verb it occurs with are the simple past (1), the perfect (2) and the pluperfect (3). Such expressions are the equivalent of English 'must' or 'must have' when referring to probability rather than obligation. The verb tense used is the same as if the speaker was talking about something that definitely happened:

1 *Θα του έδωσε εκείνος τα λεφτά.*
   He must have given him the money himself
   (cf. του έδωσε 'he gave him').

2 *Θα έχει βρέξει, γιατί τα φύλλα είναι βρεμένα.*
   It must have rained, because the leaves are wet
   (cf. έχει βρέξει 'it's rained, it's been raining').

3 *Θα είχε βρέξει, γιατί τα φύλλα ήταν βρεμένα.*
   It must have rained, because the leaves were wet
   (cf. είχε βρέξει 'it had rained, it had been raining').

9.3.2 The subjunctive particles να and ας

As we have said in sections 6.4 and 6.20, the subjunctive mood of the verb is formed by any finite verb form (other than the imperative) preceded by one of the subjunctive particles **να** and **ας**. Verbs introduced by one or other of these particles are negated by **μην** rather than **δεν**. These particles cannot be separated from the verb by any item other than the negative particle **μην** and by weak pronouns.

In main clauses **να** is used with any person of the verb to introduce suggestions, wishes and requests (see section 10.3), and certain types of commands and prohibitions (see section 10.4):

4 Να σου τα δώσω.
   Let me give them to you (offer or promise).

5 Να σου τα δώσω;
   Should I give them to you? (offer in the form of a question)

6 Να μου τα δώσεις.
   You should give them to me (suggestion, request or command).

7 Να μην του τα δώσει.
   (S)he shouldn't give them to him (prohibition or negative request).

It is often used with the imperfect tense to express unfulfilled wishes:

8 Αχ, να σ' έβλεπα!
   Oh, if only I could see you!

Να is often used after question words in questions that do not necessarily expect an answer:

9 Τι να κάνουμε;
   What are we to do? (frequently used either in its literal meaning or in the sense of 'there's nothing we can do about it')
   (cf. Τι θα κάνουμε; 'What shall we do?')

10 Πού να πήγε, άραγε;
   Where can (s)he/it have gone, I wonder?
   (cf. Πού πήγε; 'Where has (s)he/it gone?')

11 Πού να το ξέρω;
   How am I supposed to know? (lit. 'Where to I-know it?')
   (cf. Πού το ξέρεις; 'How do you know?')

Να introduces a wide variety of subordinate clauses, usually as the subject or complement of a verb. In almost all cases the verb in the **να**-clause is in the dependent or the present tense. Typical uses are:

- after verbs of wanting (12), hoping (13), promising (14), suggesting (15) and trying (16), and in fact in most cases where English uses the infinitive ('to' + verb);

9 Conjunctions and particles

- after the verb **μπορώ** 'I can' (in any person, number and tense except the perfect tenses: 17) and the impersonal verb **πρέπει** 'it is necessary' (which exists only in the present, past and conditional: 18–20);
- after verbs of perception such as **ακούω** 'I hear, listen', **βλέπω** 'I see', **παρακολουθώ** 'I watch', **αισθάνομαι** 'I feel', **φαντάζομαι** 'I imagine' (21) (in almost all cases the verb in the **να**-clause is in the present tense);
- after the verbs **αρχίζω** 'I begin' (22), **σταματώ** and **παύω** 'I stop' (23), and **συνεχίζω** and **εξακολουθώ** 'I continue' (24) (the verb in the **να**-clause is always in the present tense).

12 Ήθελα να του μιλήσω επειγόντως.
I wanted to speak to him urgently.

13 Ελπίζω να έρθω αύριο.
I hope to come tomorrow.

14 Υποσχέθηκε να μη μου χαλάσει τα σχέδια.
(S)he promised not to spoil my plans.

15 Πρότεινε να πάμε μαζί στο πάρτι.
(S)he suggested that we (should) go to the party together.

16 Προσπαθούσε να βρει λύσεις για όλα τα προβλήματά του.
(S)he was trying to find solutions to all his problems.

17 Μπόρεσα να κάνω ό,τι ήθελα.
I was able to do what(ever) I wanted.

18 Πρέπει να φύγουμε αμέσως.
We must leave immediately.

19 Έπρεπε να φύγουμε αμέσως.
We had to leave immediately.

20 Θα έπρεπε να φύγουμε αμέσως.
We should leave immediately.

21 Τον άκουσα να λέει πολλά δυσάρεστα πράγματα.
I heard him say many unpleasant things.

22 Άρχισαν να τρέχουν.
They started running.

23 Σταμάτησε να βρέχει.
It stopped raining.

24 Συνέχισε να διαβάζει.
    (S)he went on reading.

Να-clauses can also be used in indirect questions:

25 Δεν ξέραμε τι να κάνουμε.
    We didn't know what to do.

They can also be used as the complement of a noun (26) or adjective (27):

26 Είναι καθαρή ανοησία να υποφέρεις έτσι.
    It's pure stupidity (for you) to suffer like this.

27 Είναι δυνατόν να μη με θυμούνται;
    Is it possible (that) they don't remember me?

Να can also be used after certain prepositions (αντί, για, δίχως, μέχρι, σαν, χωρίς: see sections 8.2, 8.3, 10.15 and 10.17).

While we are presenting the particle να, something should be said about certain special uses of πρέπει and the impersonal form μπορεί followed by να. In this and the following paragraphs we are not concerned with the ordinary use of the impersonal verb πρέπει to express obligation ('I must, I should') and the personal verb μπορώ to express ability ('I can, I am able'). Instead, we are dealing with uses that are similar to the uses of θα in expressions other than future and conditional expressions (see 9.3.1).

Like θα (and like English 'must'), πρέπει να can be used to express probability rather than obligation. Typically, the verb in the να-clause is in the simple past, the perfect (28) or the pluperfect, but it can be in any tense (e.g. the present: 30). The sentence can be negated by the use of the appropriate negative particle in either the main clause or the να-clause (29).

28 Είδα φώτα στο σπίτι τους. Πρέπει να έχουν γυρίσει από τις διακοπές.
    I saw lights in their house. They must have come back from holiday.

29 Δεν έχει φώτα στο σπίτι τους. Δεν πρέπει να έχουν γυρίσει (or Πρέπει να *μην* έχουν γυρίσει) ακόμα από τις διακοπές.
    There are no lights in their house. They mustn't/can't have come back from holiday yet.

30 Πρέπει να γυρίζουν τώρα από τις διακοπές.
    They must be on their way back from holiday now.

As well as expressing ability, **μπορεί** (when it is used in the third person singular of the present tense) can express possibility (like English 'may': 31). In fact, **μπορεί** can be used on its own to mean 'maybe'.

31 Μπορεί να έχουν γυρίσει από τις διακοπές.
    Maybe they've come back from holiday/They may have come back from holiday.

When used with a negative particle, **μπορεί να**-constructions mean different things depending on which verb is negated:

32a Μπορεί να *μην* έχουν γυρίσει από τις διακοπές.
     They *may not* have come back from holiday.

  b *Δεν* μπορεί να έχουν γυρίσει από τις διακοπές.
     They *can't* have come back from holiday.

Ας is used with any verb form to express commands, permission, suggestions or wishes. Unlike **να**, it is used only in main clauses:

33 Ας αφήσουμε αυτό το θέμα.
    Let's leave this subject.

34 Ας φωνάζει ο Πέτρος όσο θέλει.
    Let Peter shout as much as he likes.

In comparison with **να**, expressions with **ας** tend to be less pressing, since **ας** combines the sense of command with that of permission, or even indifference:

35 Ας έρθουν αν θέλουν.
    Let them come if they want.

36 Ας μη μου τα δώσει, αφού δεν θέλει.
    Let him/her not give them to me, since (s)he doesn't want to.

Ας is frequently used after **και (κι)** in concessive clauses (see also section 10.14):

37 Μάλλον θα γίνει πόλεμος, κι ας μην το θέλουμε.
    War will probably happen, even if we don't want it (to).

Ας may be used with the imperfect tense to express a wish that something had happened in the past:

38 Ας μην τον άκουγες.
    If only you hadn't listened to him/You shouldn't have listened to him.

9.3.3 The negative particles δεν, μην and μη

Verbs in the indicative are negated by **δεν**, while verbs in the subjunctive (i.e. verbs preceded by **να** or **ας**) are negated by **μην**:

39   Δεν θα έρθει.
     (S)he won't come.

40   Να μην έρθει.
     (S)he shouldn't come.

Μην may drop the final **-v** before certain letters (see section 1.6).

Apart from its use in negative clauses after **να** or **ας**, **μην** may be used to introduce negative commands (see section 10.4). In these uses it cannot be separated from the verb except by weak pronouns.

When negating items other than verbs, **μη** does not take a final **-v** (see section 10.7.7). It can also be used on its own (without final **-v**) in a single-word sentence to mean 'Don't!'

9.3.4 The complementizer and relative particle που

Που has three chief functions. It may introduce a complement clause (41: see section 10.12), a result clause (42: see section 10.18), or a relative clause (43: see sections 4.7 and 10.9).

41   Λυπάμαι *που* δεν μπόρεσα να έρθω στο πάρτι.
     I'm sorry (*that*) I wasn't able to come to your party.

42   Φώναξα τόσο πολύ *που* δεν μπορώ να μιλήσω.
     I shouted so much (*that*) I can't speak.

43   Ο άντρας *που* ήρθε είναι ο πεθερός μου.
     The man *who* came is my father-in-law.

9.3.5 The positive and negative response particles ναι and όχι

Ναι and **όχι** are used in responses to mean 'yes' and 'no' respectively. In addition, **όχι** can be used to negate any part of speech (see section 7.2, examples 30–2) or a whole clause (section 10.5.1).

9.3.6 The deictic particle να

The deictic particle **να** (spelt the same as the subjunctive particle) is used as the equivalent of English 'there' when pointing out something. It can be used on its own, or followed by a noun phrase (44) or a weak personal pronoun (45; see section 4.1) in the nominative.

44 Να το πρόβλημα!
    That's the problem!

45 Να τος!
    There he is!

9.3.7 The hortatory particle για

The hortatory particle για (spelt like the preposition) is used colloquially to express extra encouragement before an imperative form of the verb:

46 Για κάτσε!
    Do sit down!

Chapter 10
The clause

10.1 Types of clause

The clause is a syntactic unit that consists of a subject (explicit or implicit) and a verb phrase. The term 'sentence' may be used to refer either to a simple clause or to a larger unit, containing more than one clause. Clauses and sentences may be either main or subordinate. According to their function and syntactic characteristics, main clauses are subdivided into the following types:

- statements (section 10.2)
- suggestions, wishes, requests and promises (section 10.3)
- commands and prohibitions (section 10.4)
- yes/no questions (section 10.5)
- wh- questions (section 10.6)
- negative clauses (section 10.7)
- exclamations (section 10.8)

Main clauses

10.2 Statements

A statement is in the indicative mood (see section 6.4). In statements the verb is not introduced by the particles **να** or **ας** and is negated by **δεν** 'not':

1 Το καινούριο αεροδρόμιο *είναι* πολύ ωραίο.
  The new airport *is* very beautiful.

2 Η Ειρήνη *θα πάει* στην Αθήνα τον Δεκέμβρη.
  Irene *will go* to Athens in December.

3 Το τελευταίο του βιβλίο *δεν μου άρεσε* καθόλου.
  I *didn't like* his last book at all.

10.3 Suggestions, wishes, requests, promises, etc.

A main clause expressing a suggestion, wish, request, promise, etc. is in the subjunctive mood. In other words, the verb is introduced by the particle **να** or **ας** and is negated by **μην**:

1 *Να την προσέχεις!*
 You should take care of her!

2 *Αχ και να ήμουνα τώρα στην Κρήτη!*
 If only I was in Crete now!

3 *Να σας ζητήσω μια χάρη;*
 May I ask a favour of you?

4 *Να μην το πείτε σε κανέναν.*
 You shouldn't tell anybody about this.

5 *Ας μην τον άκουγες.*
 You shouldn't have listened to him.

6 *Να τον φέρει ο πατέρας του.*
 Let his father bring him.

10.4 Commands and prohibitions

A positive command may be expressed by using the imperative mood of the verb, which has distinct forms (see sections 6.8–6.12). Sometimes the particle **για** introduces an imperative sentence to add encouragement (see section 9.3.7). A negative command (a prohibition) is expressed by **μην** with or without the particle **να**, as in (5) and (7):

1 *Φέρε μου ένα ποτήρι νερό.*
 Bring me a glass of water.

2 *Σωπάστε επιτέλους!*
 Be quiet at last!

3 *Για φέρε μας και λίγα παγάκια.*
 Do bring us some ice too (please).

4 *Ετοιμάσου γρήγορα!*
 Get ready quickly!

5 *Μην ετοιμάζεσαι τόσο νωρίς.*
 Don't get ready so early.

6   *Να έρθει αμέσως.*
    (S)he should come immediately.

7   *Να μην τον διακόπτετε όταν μιλάει.*
    Don't interrupt him when he's speaking.

10.5 Yes/no questions

Yes/no interrogative sentences seek the answer 'yes' or 'no'. Whereas in English these questions are characterized by an inversion of the subject and verb ('Are you coming?'), in Greek they are characterized simply by the question intonation (rise of the voice pitch followed by a slight fall at the end of the sentence; see section 1.9). Sometimes they are accompanied by the particles **άραγε** 'I wonder' or **μήπως** 'could it be the case that', which reduce the directness of the question and make it perhaps more polite. The verb in yes/no interrogative sentences may be either in the indicative (1, 2, 5, 6) or in the subjunctive (3–4):

1   *Πήρες νέα από τον Γιάννη;*
    Have you had any news from John?

2   *Η Μαίρη θα 'ρθει φέτος στην Αγγλία;*
    Will Mary come to England this year?

3   *Να τον καλέσουμε κι αυτόν;*
    Should we invite him too?

4   *Τι λες; Να μην τον πάρουμε μαζί μας;*
    What do you think? Shouldn't we take him with us?

5   *Μήπως σε ενόχλησε η συμπεριφορά του;*
    Did his behaviour bother you, by any chance?

6   *Άραγε θα πάνε διακοπές μαζί;*
    Will they go on holiday together, I wonder?

10.5.1 Alternative yes/no questions

These consist of a positive interrogative clause and a negative interrogative clause (or simply the particle **όχι** 'no'), separated by the conjunction **ή** 'or':

7a *Τον αγαπάς ή δεν τον αγαπάς;*
    Do you love him or don't you love him?

 b *Τον αγαπάς ή όχι;*
    Do you love him or not?

10.5.2 Leading yes/no questions

These are formed by adding the tag question **έτσι δεν είναι;** or **δεν είναι έτσι;** at the end of a statement:

8   Ο Γιώργος αποφάσισε να μείνει, *έτσι δεν είναι;/δεν είναι έτσι;*
    George decided to stay, *didn't he?*

10.6 Wh- questions

These sentences use the appropriate question word to ask a question about one constituent of the sentence. Question words are the pronouns and determiners **ποιος** 'who, which', **τι** 'what', and **πόσος** 'how much', and the adverbs **πού** 'where', **πώς** 'how', **γιατί** 'why', **πόσο** 'how much' and **πότε** 'when'. Examples 8–10 illustrate the use of determiners with nouns. Note that the verb of such questions may be in the indicative, as in examples 1–3 and 5–9, or in the subjunctive, as in examples 4 and 10:

1   *Ποιος λέει αυτές τις ανοησίες;*
    Who says these silly things?

2   *Ποιον θα ψηφίσεις;*
    Who will you vote for?

3   *Τι της έκανε τόση εντύπωση;*
    What made such an impression on her?

4   *Πού να πάμε για διακοπές;*
    Where should we go for a holiday?

5   *Γιατί δεν σου αρέσει ο Θεοδωράκης;*
    Why don't you like Theodorakis?

6   *Πότε θα γίνουν εκλογές;*
    When will the elections take place?

7   *Πόσους θα καλέσεις στο πάρτι σου;*
    How many will you invite to your party?

8   *Ποιο βιβλίο δεν πρόλαβες να διαβάσεις;*
    Which book didn't you manage to read?

9   *Ποιανού παιδιού ο πατέρας είναι δικηγόρος;*
    Which child's father is a lawyer?

10 *Σε ποιο φίλο σου να δώσω το γράμμα;*
 Which friend of yours should I give the letter to?

Note that in questions involving prepositions the preposition must precede the appropriate question word or phrase. Unlike in English, the two elements (preposition and wh- word) cannot be separated (see example 10). Here are some further examples:

11 *Με ποιο φίλο της μάλωσε;*
 Which friend of hers did she quarrel *with*?

12 *Από πού τα αγόρασες αυτά τα ωραία παπούτσια;*
 Where did you buy those beautiful shoes *from*?

13 *Για ποια με περνάς;*
 Who do you take me *for*? (female speaker)

10.6.1 Multiple questions

As in English, it is possible to question more than one constituent in a sentence, but only one of these may appear at the beginning of the sentence (14–15) unless the two are co-ordinated (16):

14 *Τι να ρωτήσω ποιον;*
 What should I ask *of whom*?

15 *Σε ποιον να δώσω τι;*
 To whom should I give *what*?

16 *Γιατί και με τι λεφτά θα αγοράσεις αυτοκίνητο;*
 Why and *with what money* will you buy a car?

10.7 Negation

As in the case of questions, negation may apply to the whole sentence or to one of its constituents.

10.7.1 Sentence negation

A sentence is negated by one of the two negative particles **δεν** or **μην**. For indicative sentences the negative particle is **δεν**, which is placed before the future particle **θα** (2); for subjunctive sentences the negative particle is **μην**, which is placed after the particles **να** or **ας** (3–4):

1 Ο χειμώνας εφέτος δεν ήταν βαρύς.
   Winter this year *wasn't* severe.

2 Ο Κώστας δεν θα της το συγχωρήσει αυτό.
   Kostas *won't* forgive her for this.

3 Να μην πιστεύεις όσα σου λένε.
   You *shouldn't* believe what they tell you.

4 Ας μην τον καλέσουμε λοιπόν.
   Let's *not* invite him, then.

A negative command or suggestion may be expressed with or without the particle **να**:

5 (Να) μη με διακόπτεις τώρα.
   Don't interrupt me now.

6 (Να) μην κάθεσαι τόση ώρα στον ήλιο.
   Don't sit in the sun so long.

A single-word negative command is expressed with the prohibitive particle **μη!** 'don't!'

10.7.2 Negative interrogative sentences

These sentences consist of a negative sentence pronounced with an interrogative intonation:

7 Δεν θα ξανάρθει στην Ελλάδα;
   Won't (s)he come to Greece again?

8 Να μην του δώσω λίγα λεφτά;
   Shouldn't I give him some money?

10.7.3 Negation with indefinite pronoun, determiner or adverbial

A non-specific indefinite pronoun (section 4.6) or adverbial (**πουθενά** 'nowhere, anywhere', **ποτέ** '(n)ever', **καθόλου** '(not) at all'), accompanied by a negative particle, can be used to form a negative sentence:

9 Δεν της μίλησε κανείς στο πάρτι.
   No one spoke to her at the party.

10 Κανένα από τα παιδιά του δεν του μοιάζει.
   None of his children takes after him.

11 Σε *κανένα* φίλο του *δεν* έχει εμπιστοσύνη.
He *doesn't* trust *any* of his friends.

12 (Να) *μην* ξανάρθεις *ποτέ*!
Don't ever come back!

13 (Να) *μην* πάτε *πουθενά* τέτοια ώρα.
You shouldn't go anywhere at such a time.

The indefinite items, such as those in italics above, have an indefinite meaning when used in positive or negative questions and commands:

14 Θα της μιλήσει άραγε *κανείς* στο πάρτι;
Will *anybody* speak to her at the party, I wonder?

15 Δεν θα πάρετε και *κανένα* σοκολατάκι;
Won't you take *a* little chocolate?

16 Πάρε *κανένα* παλτό μαζί σου.
Take *a* coat with you.

17 Πήγατε *πουθενά* χθες;
Did you go *anywhere* yesterday?

These indefinite items have a negative meaning in sentences containing **χωρίς** 'without' (18–19). They also have a negative meaning if they are in embedded subjunctive clauses following a negated main verb (20–21):

18 Εδώ διαβάζει *χωρίς* να τον ενοχλεί *κανένας*.
Here he can read *without anyone* bothering him.

19 Ήρθε *χωρίς* να κρατάει *τίποτα*.
(S)he came *without* bringing *anything*.

20 *Δεν* θέλει να μάθει *τίποτα*.
(S)he *doesn't* want to learn *anything*.

21 *Δεν* περιμένει να 'ρθει *κανείς φίλος* του.
He *doesn't* expect *any friend* of his to come.

When these indefinite items are used as single-word replies to a preceding question, they also have a negative meaning:

22 – Σε ποιον τα λες αυτά;
Who are you telling these things?

  – Σε κανέναν.
  No one.

Negation

23 –Πότε τελοσπάντων θα σοβαρευτείς;
    When will you ever get serious?

    –Ποτέ.
    Never.

10.7.4 Constituent negation with όχι

The negative particle **όχι** 'not' may be used to negate a word or phrase by being placed in front of this word or phrase.

24 Θα ήθελα να κάνω ένα ταξιδάκι, αλλά *όχι στην Αγγλία*.
    I would like to take a trip, *but not to England*.

25 Η Ελένη αγαπά τον Στέφανο, *όχι τον Κώστα*.
    Helen loves Stephen, *not Kostas*.

26 *Όχι μόνο της αρέσει*, αλλά είναι τρελή γι' αυτόν.
    Not only does she like him, but she's crazy about him.

10.7.5 Constituent negation with ούτε

Constituent negation with **ούτε** 'not even' is exemplified in example 27:

27 Δεν μπορεί *ούτε* δυο βήματα να κάνει.
    (S)he can't take *even* a couple of steps.

10.7.6 Constituent negation with ούτε ... ούτε ...

The expression **ούτε ... ούτε ...** is used in negative sentences accompanying any word or phrase:

28 Δεν τον είδα *ούτε* τη Δευτέρα *ούτε* την Τρίτη.
    I didn't see him *either* on Monday *or* on Tuesday.

29 Δεν μου αρέσει *ούτε* να σε βλέπω *ούτε* να σ' ακούω.
    I don't like *either* seeing you *or* hearing you.

10.7.7 Constituent negation with μην and μη

The negative particle **μην** is generally used to negate gerunds (30–31), while the negative particle **μη**, without final ν, is used to negate nouns (32–33) and adjectives (34), and occurs in some idiomatic expressions (35) (see also section 9.3.3).

30 *Μην ξέροντας ποιος είναι, του μίλησε κάπως απότομα.*
   Not knowing who it was, (s)he spoke to him rather abruptly.

31 *Θα κάνεις αυτό που σου λέω θέλοντας και μη (θέλοντας).*
   You will do what I say whether you like it or not.

32 *Τα προϊόντα αυτά είναι πιο ακριβά για τους μη Ευρωπαίους.*
   These products are more expensive for non-Europeans.

33 *Η αίθουσα αυτή είναι για τους μη καπνιστές.*
   This room is for non-smokers.

34 *για μη σοβαρούς λόγους*
   for non-serious reasons

35 *Και μη χειρότερα!*
   May it not get any worse (= God forbid)!

10.8 Exclamations

These are expressions indicating surprise, both positive and negative, delight, admiration, etc. They are pronounced with a high pitch, which remains high throughout the exclamatory construction. Typical exclamations are introduced by **τι** 'what' or **πόσο** 'how much', usually followed by an adjective or an adverb, sometimes followed by a clause introduced by **που** 'that'.

Τι όμορφα τα μάτια της Μαίρης!
How beautiful Mary's eyes are!

Τι όμορφη που είναι η Ελένη!
How beautiful Helen is!

Πόσο άσχημα συμπεριφέρεται!
How badly (s)he behaves!

Τι κρίμα που χωρίσανε!
What a pity they split up!

10 The clause

Subordinate clauses

10.9 Relative clauses

Relative clauses are subordinate clauses that modify nouns. They are introduced by the relative pronoun phrase **ο οποίος** 'who, which, that' or by the indeclinable particle **που** (same meanings). In formal discourse **ο οποίος** is preferred, while in casual discourse **που** is more frequent. Even in casual speech, **ο οποίος** is preferred when its syntactic function in the relative clause requires the genitive or when it is in a prepositional or adverbial phrase. Relative clauses can be divided into restrictive or non-restrictive. A restrictive relative clause provides necessary information for the identification of the noun to which it refers, while a non-restrictive relative clause adds some extra information as an afterthought. The second type is set off by pauses or commas. Examples 1–3 are restrictive relative clauses, while 4–5 are non-restrictive:

1 Ο κύριος *ο οποίος* ήρθε να με δει ήταν συμφοιτητής σου.
   The gentleman *who* came to see me was a fellow student of yours.

2 Διάβασες το βιβλίο *που* σου δάνεισα;
   Have you read the book (*that*) I lent you?

3 Πήγαμε και είδαμε το έργο *για το οποίο* μας μίλησε η Μαρία.
   We went and saw the film (*that*) Mary spoke to *us about*.

4 Ο Καβάφης, *ο οποίος/που* είναι από τους πιο δημοφιλείς ποιητές μας, έγραφε σε γλώσσα μικτή.
   Cavafy, *who* is one of our most popular poets, wrote in a mixed language.

5 Φέρανε μαζί τους και τον Γιάννη, *ο οποίος/που* είναι ανυπόφορος.
   They also brought John along, *who* is unbearable.

Note that the relative pronoun or particle can never be omitted, as it sometimes can be in English.

It is possible, especially in cases of non-restrictive relative clauses, to find the relative phrase followed by a second instance of the noun it modifies, as in example 6:

6 Πήγαμε να δούμε τη Σοφία την περασμένη Κυριακή, *η οποία Σοφία* έχει γίνει πολύ κομψή.
Last Sunday we went to see Sophie, *who* has become very elegant.

Relative clauses

The relative phrase may be the object of a preposition (3 and 7–9). In such cases the relative phrase **ο οποίος** follows the preposition:

7 Αυτοί είναι οι άνθρωποι *από τους οποίους* πήραμε πληροφορίες.
These are the people (*that*) we got information *from*.

8 Ποιοι είναι αυτοί *με τους οποίους* τσακώνεσαι;
Who are these people (*that*) you are quarrelling *with*?

9 Το σχολείο είναι το κτήριο *δίπλα στο οποίο* είναι η εκκλησία.
The school is the building *next to which* is the church.

When the relative phrase in the genitive case depends on a noun, it may either precede or follow the noun:

10a Ο φίλος μου, *του οποίου* η μητέρα είναι δασκάλα . . .
  b Ο φίλος μου, η μητέρα *του οποίου* είναι δασκάλα . . .
My friend, *whose* mother is a teacher . . .

10.9.1 Relative clauses introduced by που

The indeclinable particle **που** may be used to introduce a relative clause, in which case it can refer to the subject (11), the direct object (12), or the indirect object (13):

11 Ποιος είναι ο συγγραφέας *που* πήρε το Νόμπελ πέρσι;
Who is the author *who* got the Nobel last year?

12 Θα πάω να δω τη γιατρό *που* μου σύστησες.
I will visit the (female) doctor (*who*) you recommended to me.

13 Ο νεαρός *που* (*του*) δώσανε την υποτροφία την άξιζε.
The young man *who* they gave the scholarship *to* deserved it.

In relative clauses introduced by **που**, where the particle refers to anything other than the subject, the appropriate weak pronoun may appear in the relative clause. This is optional for direct objects (14), but fairly regular with indirect objects (13) and adverbial phrases (15).

14 Θα πάω να δω μια γιατρό *που* μου (*τη*) σύστησε ένας καλός μου φίλος.
I will visit a (female) doctor *who* a good friend of mine recommended to me.

15 Η κοπέλα *που κοντά της* κάθεται ο Νίκος είναι η γυναίκα του.
The girl *near whom* Nick is sitting is his wife. (Cf. the equivalent construction with ο οποίος in 9 above)

Relative clauses indicating place, time or instrument can be introduced with που with no accompanying weak pronoun. Their function is inferred from the context:

16 Το σπίτι *που* ζήσαμε τόσα χρόνια γκρεμίστηκε.
The house (*that*) we lived *in* for so many years has been demolished.

17 Τον καιρό *που* ήμουνα φοιτητής έμενα με τον θείο μου.
At the time (*when*) I was a student I lived with my uncle.

18 Στο μουσείο βρίσκεται η πένα *που* έγραψε το πρώτο του μυθιστόρημα.
The pen *with which* he wrote his first novel is in the museum.

To make the function of relative clauses introduced by που clearer it is possible to use a prepositional phrase after it:

19 Το σπίτι *που μέσα σ' αυτό ζήσαμε* ... (= 16)

20 η πένα *που μ' αυτήν έγραψε* ... (= 18)

Relative clauses may be followed by the indicative, as in all the examples given above, or by the subjunctive. Typically relative clauses are in the subjunctive when the main clause is negative or interrogative, or when the main verb expresses a wish, as in the following sentences:

21 Δεν ξέρω κανέναν *ο οποίος/που* να μην αγαπάει τα λεφτά.
I don't know anybody *who* doesn't like money.

22 Ξέρεις κανένα μαγαζί *που* να πουλάει εφημερίδες;
Do you know a shop *that* sells newspapers?

23 Θέλω ένα φίλο *στον οποίο/που* να μπορώ να έχω εμπιστοσύνη.
I want a friend *whom* I can trust.

In these cases the relative clauses indicate 'of the kind that'.

10.9.2 Free relative clauses

In free relative clauses the relative clause does not modify a noun. These clauses are introduced either by the correlative pronouns **όποιος, οποιοσδήποτε** 'anyone', **ό,τι, οτιδήποτε** 'anything', **όσος** 'as much as' or by the correlative adverbs **όπου** 'wherever', **όποτε** 'whenever', **όπως** 'however', **όσο** 'as much as'. Examples 24a and 25a illustrate the use of free relatives as pronouns, while 24b and 25b show their use as determiners (see also section 4.7):

24a Εκεί βρίσκεις *ό,τι/οτιδήποτε* ζητά η ψυχούλα σου.
There you can find *whatever* your heart desires.

 b Εκεί βρίσκεις *ό,τι φαγητό* ζητά η ψυχούλα σου.
There you find *whatever food* your heart desires.

25a Κουτσομπολεύει *όποιονλοποιονδήποτε* συναντήσει.
 b Κουτσομπολεύει *όποιον άνθρωπο* συναντήσει.
(S)he gossips about *anyone* (s)he may meet.

26 Στο σπίτι της, *όπου/οπουδήποτε* κοιτάξεις, θα δεις λουλούδια.
In her house, *wherever* you look you will see flowers.

When the relative clause is the direct object of a verb and the phrase containing the pronoun or determiner is the subject of the relative clause introduced by **όποιος**, the case of **όποιος** is the accusative rather than the expected nominative. This occurs when the relative clause follows the main clause.

27 Συμπαθεί μόνο *όποιον* την κολακεύει.
She likes only *whoever* flatters her.

28 Φοβάται *οποιονδήποτε* την πλησιάζει.
She is afraid of *anyone who* approaches her.

A free relative clause may also be introduced by the correlative pronoun and determiner **όσος** 'as much as':

29 Σου έφερα σύκα να φας *όσα θέλεις*.
I brought you figs so you can eat *as many as* you want.

30 Όσοι δεν φέρουν την εργασία τους εγκαίρως τους απορρίπτει.
(S)he fails *those who* do not bring their work on time.

31 Όσο κι αν τον βασανίζει, αυτός την αγαπά.
No matter how much she tortures him, he loves her.

A relative clause introduced by όσος may be followed by another clause introduced by τόσος:

32 Όσα μου ζητήσεις, τόσα θα σου δώσω.
    I will give you *however many* you ask for.

Free relatives are also found with prepositional and adverbial phrases:

33 Με όποιον μιλήσεις, το ίδιο θα σου πει.
    Whoever you speak to, they'll tell you the same thing.

34 Όπως του μιλήσεις, έτσι θα σου μιλήσει κι αυτός.
    He will speak to you *as* you speak to him.

All correlative words may be followed by the expression κι αν or και να which emphasizes indefiniteness, as in 31 above and the examples below:

35 Εγώ θα σε περιμένω όποτε κι αν έρθεις.
    I will wait for you *no matter when/whenever* you come.

36 Όπου και να πάω, αυτήν συναντώ.
    No matter where/wherever I go I meet her.

37 Όσο κι αν επιμένεις δεν θα με πείσεις.
    No matter how much/however much you insist, you will not persuade me.

10.10 Indirect questions

Indirect questions follow main verbs of asking, wondering, etc., or expressions equivalent to these.

10.10.1 Questioning the whole sentence

An indirect question concerning the truth or falsity of a whole clause is introduced by the conjunction αν 'whether' or μήπως 'by any chance'. The verb is in the indicative:

1 Δεν με ρώτησαν ποτέ *αν* με ενοχλεί η μουσική τους (ή όχι).
   They never asked me *whether* their music bothers me (or not).

2 Απορώ *αν* καταλαβαίνει τίποτα.
   I wonder *whether* (s)he understands anything.

3 Αναρωτιέται *μήπως* της λένε ψέματα.
   She's wondering *whether by any chance* they're lying to her.

> Indirect questions

An indirect question may be in the subjunctive without the introductory conjunction **αν** or **μήπως**, as in example 4. These indirect questions are introduced by **να** because the direct speech equivalent sentence is a deliberative question (**Να τον παντρευτώ ή όχι;** 'Should I marry him or not?'):

4 Με ρώτησε πολλές φορές *να τον παντρευτεί ή όχι*.
   She asked me several times *whether she should marry him or not*.

10.10.2 Questioning one constituent

If the constituent questioned is a noun phrase it is introduced by the appropriate question word (see section 10.6) used either on its own, as a pronoun (5), or as a determiner followed by the noun (6):

5 Απορώ *ποιος* πήγε και του τα είπε.
   I wonder *who* went and told him.

6 Δεν ξέρω *ποιον υπάλληλο* θα απολύσουν.
   I don't know *which employee* they will fire.

7 Αναρωτιέται *ποιανού* πρέπει να δώσει το αυτοκίνητο.
   (S)he is wondering *who* (s)he should give the car *to*.

If the questioned constituent is in the genitive and is part of another noun phrase, the question word may either precede or follow that noun phrase:

8a Ρώτησαν *ποιανού/τίνος ο πατέρας* ήταν γιατρός.
    They asked *whose father* was a doctor.

b   Ρώτησαν *ο πατέρας ποιανού* ήταν γιατρός.
    They asked *whose father* was a doctor.

Indirect questions may also refer to prepositional and adverbial phrases:

9   Δεν μας εξήγησαν *με ποιο δικαίωμα* τα κάνουν αυτά.
    They didn't explain to us *by what right* they do these things.

10 Ρώτησέ την *από ποιο μαγαζί* πήρε τα παπούτσια της.
    Ask her *which store* she bought her shoes *from*.

An indirect question about someone's profession or other quality is introduced by **τι** 'what':

11 Αναρωτιέμαι *τι είναι* ο κ. Παπαδάκης, καθηγητής ή γιατρός;
    I wonder *what* Mr Papadakis *is* – a teacher or a doctor?

Moreover, if the question concerns some quality or characteristic of a noun, the indirect question may be introduced by **τι είδους** + noun, or more colloquially **τι σόι** + noun 'what sort of x':

12 Απορώ *τι είδους άνθρωπος* είναι αυτός τελοσπάντων.
I wonder *what sort of man* he is after all.

13 Πες μου λοιπόν *τι σόι αδερφός* είναι αυτός.
Now tell me *what kind of brother* he is.

The verb in an indirect question may be either in the indicative, as in the examples above, or in the subjunctive, as below:

14 Ας μας πει εκείνη *ποιον να καλέσουμε*.
Let her tell us *who to* invite.

15 Ρώτησέ τον *από ποιο δρόμο να πάμε*.
Ask him *which way we should* go.

10.11 Indirect commands

The difference between direct and indirect positive commands is that, whereas for the former the verb is typically in the imperative mood, for the latter it is in the subjunctive:

1 Του ζήτησε *να την αφήσει* ήσυχη.
She asked him *to leave her* in peace.

2 Τον παρακαλέσαμε *να τη συνοδεύσει* στο χορό.
We asked him *to accompany her* to the dance.

In a direct negative command (prohibition), as described in section 10.4, the particle **να** is optional, but it is obligatory in indirect negative commands:

3 Τον διέταξε *να μη* μιλάει.
(S)he ordered him *not to* speak.

4 Απαιτώ *να μη* με διακόπτεις.
I demand *that you do not* interrupt me.

10.12 Complement clauses

Complement clauses may accompany a verb (1a–c), a noun (2) or an adjective (3):

1a Μου *έλεγε ότι* δεν του αρέσουν τα ψάρια.
    He *was telling me that* he doesn't like fish.

 b Η Ειρήνη *θέλει να* σπουδάσει μουσική.
    Irene *wants to* study music.

 c *Λυπήθηκα* πολύ *που* στενοχωρήθηκε ο Στέφανος.
    I *was* very *sorry that* Stephen got upset.

2   Δεν του αρέσει η *ιδέα να* παντρευτούν τόσο γρήγορα.
    He doesn't like the *idea of* them getting married so soon.

3   Είναι *σίγουρος ότι* τον αδικούν.
    He's *sure that* they're being unfair to him.

Each of these constructions will be described in detail below.

10.12.1 Complement clauses as objects of a verb

These clauses may be divided according to the mood of their verb into indicative clauses and subjunctive clauses.

- Indicative clauses

There are three varieties of indicative clauses according to the complementizer that introduces them and the type of main verb that governs them:

(a) Indicative clauses following verbs of saying, thinking, believing, etc. are introduced by **ότι** or **πως** 'that', as in example 4;
(b) Indicative clauses following verbs expressing psychological states (joy, sorrow, regret, etc.) are introduced by **που** (5);
(c) Indicative clauses following verbs expressing fear are introduced by **μήπως**. **Μήπως** is not a negative particle. Clauses introduced by **μήπως** are negated by **δεν** (compare 6a and 6b).

4a 'Ολοι πιστεύουν *ότι/πως* ο πόλεμος θα συνεχιστεί.
    Everybody believes (*that*) the war will continue.

 b Μου είπε *ότι/πως* δεν σε ξέρει.
    (S)he told me *that* (s)he doesn't know you.

5a Μετάνιωσε *που* της είπε την αλήθεια.
    (S)he regretted telling (lit. 'that (s)he told') her the truth.

 b Λυπήθηκε *που* δεν κατάφερε να τον δει.
    (S)he was upset (*that*) (s)he didn't manage to see him.

6a Ανησυχώ *μήπως* του συνέβη κάτι.
    I'm worried (*that*) something *may* have happened to him.

b   Ανησυχώ *μήπως δεν* έρθει.
    I'm worried (*that*) (s)he *may not* come.

Note that, unlike the English 'that', the complementizers **ότι/πως**, **που** and **μήπως** cannot be omitted.

- Subjunctive clauses

Complement clauses in the subjunctive follow verbs of wishing, hoping, planning, requesting, promising, etc. They are introduced by the subjunctive particle **να** and are negated by **μην**:

7 Θα θέλαμε απλώς *να* της μιλήσουμε.
   We would just like *to* speak to her.

8 Θα φροντίσω *να* έρθω νωρίς.
   I'll take care *to* come early.

9 Ελπίζω *να μην* αργήσει ο Γιάννης.
   I hope (*that*) John *won't* be late.

Subjunctive complement clauses also follow verbs expressing perception, such as 'hear', 'see', 'feel', etc. In similar circumstances English may use the -ing form of the verb.

10 Τον είδαμε *να περπατάει* πολύ βιαστικός.
   We saw him *walking* in a great hurry.

11 Δεν θα ακούσεις την Κλεία *να παραπονιέται* ποτέ.
   You'll never hear Clea *complaining*.

12 Την ένιωσα *να τρέμει*.
   I felt her *trembling*.

Some verbs of saying, thinking etc. that normally take an **ότι**-clause may also be followed by a **να**-clause. The difference between these two is that the **ότι**-clause implies more objective judgement while the **να**-clause implies more subjective, more emotional judgement, coloured with a degree of wishing:

13 Πιστεύω *ότι θα* μας πληρώσουν την άλλη Δευτέρα.
   I believe (*that*) they *will* pay us next Monday.

14 Πιστεύω *να* μας πληρώσουν την άλλη Δευτέρα.
   I believe (*that*) they *might* pay us next Monday.

After verbs of perception we may also find an **ότι**-clause, as in examples 15 and 16. However, here the verb implies information rather than direct perception:

Complement clauses

15 *Ακούσαμε ότι πούλησε και το σπίτι.*
    We heard that (s)he sold the house too.

16 *Είδες λοιπόν ότι είχα δίκιο;*
    You see (lit. 'Did you see') now that I was right?

The verbs **ξέρω** 'I know' and **μαθαίνω** 'I learn' may also be followed either by an **ότι**-clause, in which case they convey knowledge as information (17–18), or by a **να**-clause, in which case they convey knowledge as ability or skill (19–20):

17 *Έμαθε ότι της έλεγαν ψέματα.*
    She found out (that) they were lying to her.

18 *Ξέρει ότι είναι πολύ καλός στη δουλειά του.*
    He knows (that) he's very good at his work.

19 *Έμαθε να μη δίνει και πολλή σημασία στα λόγια του.*
    (S)he learned not to pay much attention to his words.

20 *Ξέρει να φτιάχνει πολύ νόστιμα ντολμαδάκια.*
    (S)he knows how to make very tasty dolmadakia.

Sometimes a complement clause may co-occur with a neuter weak pronoun attached to the main verb. This happens more frequently with indicative clauses introduced by **ότι**, and sometimes with subjunctive clauses introduced by **να** or indicative clauses introduced by **που**:

21 *Δεν το κατάλαβα ότι ήθελες να μου μιλήσεις.*
    I didn't realize (that) you wanted to speak to me.

22 *Το μετάνιωσες ότι/που ήρθες;*
    Have you regretted coming?

23 *Το ήθελε πολύ να τον συναντήσει.*
    (S)he wanted very much to meet him.

10.12.2 Complement clauses with impersonal verbs or impersonal expressions

Impersonal verbs such as **φαίνεται** 'it seems', **πειράζει** 'it matters, it bothers', **αρέσει** 'it pleases', etc., and impersonal expressions such as **είναι καλό** 'it's good', **είναι λυπηρό** 'it's sad', **είναι σωστό** 'it's right', **είναι** κρίμα 'it's a pity', etc. take a complement clause as their subject. This clause may be introduced with either **ότι, που** or **να** depending on the meaning of the main verb:

24 *Μου φαίνεται ότι θα αργήσουν πάλι.*
    It seems to me (that) they'll be late again.

25 *Τον πειράζει που του μιλάει έτσι απότομα.*
    It bothers him that (s)he speaks to him so sharply.

26 *Σου αρέσει να ταξιδεύεις;*
    Do you like to travel?

27 *Είναι φανερό ότι η κατάσταση θα χειροτερέψει.*
    It's obvious that the situation will get worse.

28 *Είναι πιθανόν να φύγουμε την Κυριακή.*
    It's likely (that) we'll be leaving on Sunday.

29 *Είναι κρίμα που δεν θα συναντηθούμε τελικά.*
    It's a pity (that) we won't meet after all.

10.12.3 Complement clauses governed by adjectives and nouns

A complement clause may be governed by either an adjective (30–32) or a noun (33–34):

30 *Είναι λυπημένος που θα φύγει.*
    He's *sad that* he is leaving.

31 *Είναι συνηθισμένη να την περιποιούνται.*
    She's *used to* being pampered.

32 *Είναι σίγουρη ότι την παρακολουθούν.*
    She's *certain (that)* they're following her.

33 *Ζει με τον φόβο ότι θα της κάνουν διάρρηξη.*
    She lives with *the fear that* she'll be burgled.

34 *Έχει μεγάλη χαρά που θα τον ξαναδεί.*
    (S)he's very *happy (that)* (s)he's going to see him again.

10.12.4 Clauses functioning as noun phrases

A complement clause functioning as the subject (35a and 36) or object (35b) of a verb is introduced by the neuter definite article **το**. If the clause is the object, the verb in the main clause may be accompanied by the neuter weak pronoun **το**. The definite article preceding the complement clause is generally found when the complement clause is placed at the beginning of the sentence:

35a *Το ότι είναι ξεροκέφαλος είναι γνωστό σε όλους.*
It is known to everybody *that* he is stubborn.

b *Το ότι είναι ξεροκέφαλος το ξέρουν όλοι.*
Everybody knows (*that*) he is stubborn.

36 *Το να προσπαθείς να τον πείσεις είναι μάταιο.*
It's futile to try *to* convince him.

Clauses functioning as noun phrases can also occur as objects of prepositions:

37 *Δεν θα τον πείσεις με το να γκρινιάζεις συνέχεια.*
You won't persuade him *by* grumbling all the time.

38 *Με το που τον είδε να μπαίνει, έγινε κατακόκκινη.*
The moment she saw him coming in, she turned bright red.

10.13 Conditional constructions

Conditional constructions consist of a conditional clause (if-clause), referred to as the protasis, and a main clause, referred to as the apodosis. Conditional clauses are typically introduced by **αν**, **εάν**, **άμα** (all meaning 'if'), **έτσι και** 'if so much as', **είτε ... είτε ...** 'whether ... or ...', **σε περίπτωση που** 'in the event that', or **εφόσον** 'provided that'. Other more elaborate means of introducing the protasis are **εκτός** (**κι**) **αν** 'unless', (**ακόμη**) **κι αν** 'even if', **έστω κι αν** 'even if'. The negative particle in conditional clauses introduced by the conjunctions or expressions listed above is **δεν**. A protasis may occasionally be introduced by the subjunctive particle **να**, in which case the verb is negated by **μην**. The protasis may either precede or follow the apodosis. Conditional constructions may be divided into factual and counterfactual.

10.13.1 Factual conditional clauses

In a factual conditional construction, if the condition stated in the protasis is fulfilled, it follows that what the main clause (the apodosis) describes is, has been, will be or can be fulfilled also. In the protasis of factual conditionals the verb may be in any tense or aspect other than the pluperfect, and the apodosis may contain a verb in any form. Examples of factual conditionals are presented in the following sentences:

1 *Αν προσπαθείς να τον πείσεις, κάνεις μεγάλο λάθος.*
   If you're trying to persuade him, you're making a big mistake.

2 *Αν (θα) τον παρακαλέσεις θα σου κάνει τη χάρη.*
   If you ask him, he'll do you the favour.

3 *Να τον δεις τώρα θα τον λυπηθείς.*
   If you see him now, you'll feel sorry for him.

4 *Αν συναντήθηκαν, μάλλον θα μίλησαν και γι' αυτό το θέμα.*
   If they met, they most probably spoke about this matter too.

5 *Έτσι και της χαμογελάσει γλυκά τον συγχωρεί αμέσως.*
   If he so much as smiles at her sweetly, she immediately forgives him.

6 *Είτε του μιλάς είτε δεν του μιλάς, το ίδιο κάνει.*
   Whether you speak to him or don't speak to him, it makes no difference (lit. 'it makes the same').

7 *Αν σε πείραξε αυτό που είπα, σου ζητώ συγνώμη.*
   If you got upset by what I said, I ask your forgiveness.

8 *Άμα σε ενοχλεί ο καπνός, άνοιξε το παράθυρο.*
   If the smoke bothers you, open the window.

9 *Αν τελειώσετε νωρίς ελάτε να μας δείτε.*
   If you finish early come and see us (lit. 'so that you see us').

10.13.2 Counterfactual conditionals

In counterfactual conditionals the protasis expresses a situation which has not been realized in the past or is not being realized in the present and as a consequence the content of the apodosis is also not realized or cannot be realized. In the protasis of counterfactual conditionals, the verb is either in the imperfect or the pluperfect, while in the apodosis the verb is either in the conditional or the perfect conditional. If the sentence refers to the past, any of these verb forms may be used (10). If the sentence does not refer to the past, only the imperfect and conditional may be used; thus a conditional sentence that uses the imperfect and the conditional may refer equally to the past or the present or the future (11–13).

10a *Αν έστελνε εκείνο το γράμμα θα τον είχε πείσει.*
  b *Αν είχε στείλει εκείνο το γράμμα θα τον έπειθε.*
  c *Αν είχε στείλει εκείνο το γράμμα θα τον είχε πείσει.*
     If (s)he had sent that letter (s)he would have persuaded him.

11 *Αν έστελνε εκείνο το γράμμα θα τον έπειθε.*
    If (s)he sent that letter (s)he would persuade him OR
    If (s)he had sent that letter (s)he would have persuaded him.

12 *Αν καταλάβαινες τη στενοχώρια μου δεν θα μιλούσες έτσι.*
    If you understood my distress you wouldn't speak like this OR
    If you had understood my distress you wouldn't have spoken like that.

13 *Δεν θα τον παντρευότανε ποτέ αν δεν τον αγαπούσε.*
    She would never marry him if she didn't love him OR
    She would never have married him if she didn't love him.

10.14 Concessive clauses

Concessive clauses express a concession on the part of the speaker. They are indicative subordinate clauses introduced by the following expressions: **αν και** 'although, even though', **παρά το ότι, παρ' ότι, παρ' όλο που, παρ' όλον ότι, μολονότι, μ' όλο που, παρά το γεγονός ότι** 'in spite of the fact that'. The concessive clause usually precedes the main clause, but it is also possible for the main clause to precede the concessive clause.

1 *Αν και δεν διαβάζει πολύ, ξέρει πολλά πράγματα.*
   Although (s)he doesn't read much, (s)he knows a lot.

2 *Παρ' όλο που τον προειδοποιήσαμε, δεν μας άκουσε.*
   Although we warned him, he didn't listen to us.

3 *Παρά το ότι έχει πολλά λεφτά, τσιγκουνεύεται πολύ.*
   In spite of the fact that (s)he has a lot of money, (s)he's tight-fisted.

Concessive clauses may also be introduced by **κι ας** 'even though'. These are negated by the particle **μην**.

4 *Μου αρέσει πολύ αυτό το σπίτι, κι ας είναι μικρό.*
   I like this house very much, even though it's small.

5 *Εκείνη αποφάσισε να πάει, κι ας μην είχε πρόσκληση.*
   She decided to go even though she didn't have an invitation.

10.15 Temporal clauses

Temporal clauses state whether the action of the verb of the main clause takes place before, will take place after or takes place at the same time as that of the main clause. The most common conjunction to introduce a temporal clause is **όταν** 'when'. Other temporal expressions are **σαν** 'when', **όποτε, οπόταν** 'whenever', **οπότε** 'at which point', **τώρα που** 'now that', **τότε που** 'at the time that', **αφού μετά που** 'after', **αφού, αφότου, από τότε που** 'since', **ώσπου** 'until', **ενώ, όσο, ενόσω, την ώρα που** 'while', **καθώς** 'as', **μόλις** 'as soon as', **εφόσον** 'as long as', **πάνω που** 'just as'. The conjunctions **όταν, μόλις, αφού, όποτε** may be followed by the dependent when not referring to the past (3–5). **Ενώ, όσο, ενόσω, την ώρα που** are typically followed by the present or imperfect (6). **Πριν** and **προτού** 'before' combine only with the dependent, with or without **να** (7). **Μέχρι** 'until' is followed by **που** and the indicative when the temporal clause refers to a real action (8). **Ώσπου** and **μέχρι** 'until' may be followed by **να** when the temporal clause refers to a potential rather than a real action (9).

1 *Όταν λείπει η γάτα χορεύουν τα ποντίκια!*
  When the cat's away the mice will play!

2 *Όταν διάβασε το γράμμα του συγκινήθηκε πολύ.*
  When (s)he read his letter (s)he was very moved.

3 *Αφού τελειώσεις, πάρε με τηλέφωνο.*
  After you finish, call me.

4 *Όποτε το αποφασίσεις έλα.*
  Come whenever you decide.

5 *Μόλις τον δει θα καταλάβει ότι είναι θυμωμένος.*
  As soon as (s)he sees him (s)he'll realize that he's angry.

6 *Την ώρα που έπινε τον καφέ του, του εξήγησα το πρόβλημα.*
  While he was drinking his coffee, I explained the problem to him.

7 *Πρέπει να μιλήσεις με τον Νίκο πριν (να) πουλήσεις το σπίτι.*
  You must speak to Nick before you sell the house.

8 *Έτρωγε μέχρι που έσκασε.*
  (S)he kept on eating until (s)he burst.

9 *Θα επιμένω μέχρι να σε πείσω.*
  I will persist until I persuade you.

10.16 Clauses of manner

These clauses describe the manner in which the action of the verb happens, will happen or happened. They are typically introduced by the manner conjunctions **όπως** and **καθώς** 'as', or the expressions **έτσι που** 'in such a way', **όπως κι αν** 'in whatever way'. These conjunctions and expressions are followed by a verb in the indicative.

1   Τα πράγματα είναι δυστυχώς *όπως* μου τα περιέγραψες.
    Matters are unfortunately *as* you described them to me.

2   Μαγείρεψε τις αγγινάρες *έτσι που* της είχε δείξει η γιαγιά της.
    She cooked the artichokes *as* her grandmother had shown her.

3   *Όπως κι αν* το δούμε το πράγμα, η Ειρήνη έχει δίκιο.
    No matter *how* we look at it, Irene is right.

10.17 Clauses of purpose (final clauses)

Purpose (or final) clauses are typically introduced by **για** 'for' followed immediately by the particle **να**. No other word may intervene between the two. After verbs of motion **για** may be omitted.

1   Την καλέσαμε και εκείνη *για να* μην παραπονιέται.
    We invited her too *in order to* prevent her complaining (lit. 'in order that she not complain').

2   Ήρθε (*για*) *να* την δει αλλά εκείνη έλειπε.
    (S)he came *to* see her but she was out.

10.18 Clauses of result

Result clauses are frequently introduced by **που** 'that' or **ώστε** 'so that' followed by a verb in the indicative or subjunctive. In such sentences the main clause often contains the quantitative and qualitative words **τόσος** 'so much' (3) or **τέτοιος** 'such', or the adverb **έτσι** (or **ούτως** in more formal usage) or the prepositional phrase **με τέτοιο τρόπο** 'in such a way' (4–5).

1   Δεν πρέπει να της λέμε τίποτα *ώστε να* αποφασίσει μόνη της.
    We mustn't say anything to her *so that* she can decide on her own.

2   Δεν βρίσκει παπούτσια *που να* της κάνουνε.
    She can't find shoes *that will* fit her.

3   Έχει πει *τόσα ψέματα που* κανείς δεν τον πιστεύει πια.
    He has told so many lies (*that*) nobody believes him any more.

4   Έχτισαν το σπίτι *έτσι* (or *με τέτοιο τρόπο*) *που να* αντέχει στους σεισμούς.
    They built the house *in such a way that* it will withstand earthquakes.

5   Θα σου εξηγήσουμε την κατάσταση *έτσι* (or *ούτως*) *ώστε* να έχεις μια πλήρη εικόνα.
    We'll explain the situation to you *in such a way that* you will have a complete picture.

Note that the **που** or **ώστε**, unlike English 'that' in (3), cannot be omitted. The meaning of result may also be expressed by **για να**:

6   Πρέπει να είσαι πολύ τυχερός *για να* βρεις τέτοιο φίλο.
    You must be very lucky *to* find such a friend.

10.19 Clauses of cause

These are introduced by a variety of conjunctions, namely **γιατί** or more formal **διότι** 'because', **καθώς** 'as', **επειδή** 'because', **αφού, εφόσον, μια και** 'since', followed by a verb in the indicative. When a clause expressing cause is introduced by **γιατί** or **διότι** it generally follows the main clause (1). When it is introduced by one of the other conjunctions it can either precede or follow the main clause (2–5).

1   Δεν θα σας πληρώσουμε, *γιατί/διότι* δεν έχουμε λεφτά.
    We won't pay you, *because* we don't have any money.

2   *Επειδή* δεν κοιμήθηκε χθες το βράδυ, νιώθει πολύ κουρασμένος.
    Because he didn't sleep last night, he feels very tired.

3   *Αφού* σου ορκίστηκε, πρέπει να τον πιστέψεις.
    Since he gave you his word, you have to believe him.

4 Κάνε λοιπόν ό,τι θέλεις, *αφού* επιμένεις τόσο πολύ.
  Do what you like then, *since* you insist so much.

5 *Μια και* είσαι τώρα εδώ, έλα να με βοηθήσεις.
  As you are here now, come and help me.

Other syntactic phenomena

10.20 Word order, topicalization and focusing

10.20.1 Word order

Unlike English, Greek is a highly inflected language. This means that the subject and object of a clause are normally clearly indicated by the form of the noun phrases that make up the subject and object; the subject is in the nominative case, while the direct object is in the accusative. For this reason, the word order of Greek is far more flexible than English.

In English the two sentences below do not mean the same thing:

1a The dog bit Michael.
 b Michael bit the dog.

It is the word order that distinguishes the meaning of these two sentences: in English, the subject normally precedes the verb, while the object normally follows it.

In Greek, since subject and object are distinguished by their form, word order is far less crucial for the meaning of the sentence. This means that the following five sentences have approximately the same meaning:

2a Ο σκύλος (nom.) δάγκωσε τον Μιχάλη (acc.).
 b Τον Μιχάλη δάγκωσε ο σκύλος.
 c Τον Μιχάλη ο σκύλος τον δάγκωσε.
 d Δάγκωσε ο σκύλος τον Μιχάλη.
 e Δάγκωσε τον Μιχάλη ο σκύλος.
   The dog bit Michael.

10.20.2 Topicalization and focusing

When we speak, we often use sentences that convey completely new information. For instance, if we are beginning a conversation about something that the other person knows nothing about, we may say something like,

'Did you hear what happened?', followed by a sentence like 1a above. In this case, 1a would convey totally new information. More often, though, we combine words or phrases that refer to what has already been mentioned in the conversation with words and phrases that convey new information. For instance, the person we are talking to may know that the dog bit someone, but may be uncertain who this was. In English we have different ways of distinguishing new information from already known information; we can place heavy stress on the new element (3a), and we can optionally place it in an 'It is/was . . . that . . .' construction (3b).

3a The dog bit *Michael* (with heavy stress on 'Michael').
 b It was *Michael* (that) the dog bit.

The same applies if we want to make it clear which animal (e.g. the dog rather than the cat) bit Michael:

4a *The dog* bit Michael (with heavy stress on 'dog').
 b It was *the dog* that bit Michael.

If it is the verb that we want to emphasize (if, for instance, the other person doubts or denies that the dog bit Michael, or if the action is presented as a complete surprise), we can use the auxiliary 'do/did' with the verb (5a) or we can use an adverb such as 'actually' (5b):

5a The dog *did* bite Michael.
 b The dog *actually bit* Michael.

In examples (3–5) the element in italics, i.e. the new information that is emphasized, is called the focus. Conversely, any noun phrase that is already known and agreed on by the speakers is called the topic of the sentence. The topic in example 3 is 'the dog', in 4 it is 'Michael', while in 5 both 'the dog' and 'Michael' are topics.

In Greek, as in English, heavy stress is used to indicate the focus of a sentence, but constructions such as 'It is/was . . . that . . .' are not frequently used, and there is no equivalent in Greek of the use of 'do/did' as an auxiliary verb. Instead, Greek uses an important device for indicating topic and focus, namely the use or non-use of weak pronouns referring to the object.

In examples 2a and 2d above, in which the order is subject-verb-object or verb-subject-object and there is no weak pronoun, we have a sentence that could be used after saying 'Did you hear what happened?', that is, a sentence that consists of entirely new information and therefore one that has no topic and no focus.

A weak pronoun can be used together with an object noun phrase to show that the object is the topic and that the focus is some other element in the sentence (usually the subject or the verb, but sometimes an adverbial). A weak pronoun that refers to the object of a clause is called a doubling pronoun. This is the case with example 2c on p. 229. In this sentence 'Michael' is the topic, while the focus may be either 'the dog' or 'bit', depending on which of these elements is heavily stressed. Thus 2c might be translated in any of the following ways:

Word order, topicalization and focusing

6   It was *the dog* that bit Michael.

7a The dog *did* bite Michael.
 b The dog *actually bit* Michael.

Conversely, in 2b on p. 229, where the object is placed first but there is no doubling pronoun, the object is the focus. Thus example 2b could be translated as:

8   It was *Michael* (that) the dog bit.

If we wanted to make Michael into the topic (as in example 6), we would have to use a doubling pronoun:

9   Τον Μιχάλη *τον δάγκωσε ο σκύλος*.

Indirect objects behave in exactly the same way as direct objects as far as topicalization and focusing are concerned:

10 *Του Γιάννη* δεν θα δώσουνε αύξηση.
    It's *John* they won't give a pay rise to.

11 Του Γιάννη *δεν θα του δώσουνε αύξηση*.
    They won't give a pay rise to John.

To sum up, the most neutral word order in Greek tends to be either subject-verb-object or verb-subject-object. If we want to place particular emphasis on some element of the sentence, we can introduce a doubling pronoun that refers to the object to show that we are emphasizing some element other than the object; this element is usually the subject or the verb, but it can be an adverbial, as in 12 below:

12a Τον Μιχάλη τον δάγκωσε *χθες* ο σκύλος.
  b Ο σκύλος τον δάγκωσε *χθες* τον Μιχάλη.
    The dog bit Michael *yesterday* **or** It was *yesterday* (that) the dog bit Michael [as opposed to today].

In such cases, the object may optionally be placed before the verb, as in 12a. Conversely, if we want to place particular emphasis on the object, we can place the object before the verb and omit the doubling pronoun, as in 2b on p. 229.

10.21 Co-ordination

It is possible to co-ordinate any constituents, whether they be clauses, phrases or simple words. The most common conjunctions marking co-ordination are **και** 'and' (**κι** before a word beginning with a vowel), **ή**, **είτε ... είτε ...** 'either ... or ...', **αλλά** or the more colloquial **μα** 'but', **ούτε ... ούτε ...** 'neither ... nor ...', and **όμως** 'however'. Όμως is used for co-ordinating only clauses; it may appear either between the two clauses (7a), or at the end of the second item (7b), or between the phrases of the second member of the co-ordination (8).

10.21.1 Co-ordination of clauses:

1 Αύριο θα δω τον Γιάννη *και* θα του μιλήσω για σένα.
   Tomorrow I'll see John *and* I'll speak to him about you.

2 Θα τηλεφωνήσω στον Νίκο *αλλά* δεν θα τον καλέσω εδώ.
   I'll telephone Nick *but* I won't invite him here.

3 Τελικά θα μου πεις τι συμβαίνει *ή* να ρωτήσω την Ελένη;
   Finally will you tell me what's going on, *or* should I ask Helen?

4 Εγώ πάντως θα πάω, *είτε* έρθεις *είτε* δεν έρθεις.
   In any case I will go, *whether* you come *or* not.

5 *Ούτε* έφαγα *ούτε* ήπια τίποτα από χθες.
   I have *neither* eaten *nor* drunk anything since yesterday.

6 Της το είπα *μα* δεν θέλει να το πιστέψει.
   I told her *but* she doesn't want to believe it.

7a Θα σε περιμένω στο γραφείο, *όμως* μην καθυστερήσεις.
 b Θα σε περιμένω στο γραφείο, μην καθυστερήσεις *όμως*.
    I'll be waiting for you at the office *but* don't be late.

8 Θα φάμε μαζί, τον λογαριασμό *όμως* θα τον πληρώσω εγώ.
   We'll eat together *but* I'll pay the bill.

Co-ordination

10.21.2 Co-ordination of other constituents:

9 Θα αγοράσω το κίτρινο πουκάμισο *και* τη μαύρη τσάντα.
   I will buy the yellow shirt *and* the black bag.

10 Πρέπει να διαλέξεις τον Σπύρο *ή* εμένα.
   You have to choose Spiros *or* me.

11 Δεν της μίλησε η Μαρία *αλλά* η Ελένη.
   It wasn't Mary *but* Helen who spoke to her.

12 Μου αρέσει με *ή* (και) χωρίς λάδι.
   I like it with *or* without oil.

The co-ordinating conjunctions **και**, **ούτε**, **είτε** and **ή** may appear before both of the elements that are connected:

13 Θέλουνε *και* την πίτα ολόκληρη *και* τον σκύλο χορτάτο.
   They want *both* the dog well fed *and* the pie whole (i.e. they want to have their cake and eat it).

14 Δεν είναι *ούτε* ψηλός *ούτε* κοντός.
   He's *neither* tall *nor* short.

15 Δεν ξέρω τι να κάνω. *Ή* θα το πουλήσω *ή* θα το χαρίσω.
   I don't know what to do. *Either* I'll sell it *or* I'll give it away.

In the above examples the conjunction is pronounced with heavy stress.

The co-ordinating conjunction **και** may also be used in the place of a subordinating conjunction. Some of these uses are exemplified below:

- **Και** may replace **να** or **που** after verbs of perception:
  16a Τους άκουσα *και* ψιθυρίζανε *instead of*
   b Τους άκουσα *να* ψιθυρίζουνε *or*
   c Τους άκουσα *που* ψιθυρίζανε.
     I heard them whispering.

- **Και** may replace **να** after verbs of beginning (**αρχίζω**) or continuing (**συνεχίζω** or **εξακολουθώ**):

    17a Άρχισαν *και* τον παρακολουθούσαν *instead of*
    b   Άρχισαν *να* τον παρακολουθούν.
        They started following him.

    18a Συνέχιζε *και* μας έλεγε ψέματα *instead of*
    b   Συνέχιζε *να* μας λέει ψέματα.
        He continued to lie to us.

- **Και** may express result:

    19a Τι κάνει *και* είναι τόσο αντιπαθητικός; *instead of*
    b   Τι κάνει *ώστε να* είναι τόσο αντιπαθητικός;
        What does he do *to* be so unlikeable?

- **Και** may replace a relative clause:

    20a Μπήκε μέσα ένας νεαρός *και* φορούσε ωραίο κοστούμι *instead of*
    b   Μπήκε μέσα ένας νεαρός *που* φορούσε ωραίο κοστούμι.
        In came a young man (*who* was) wearing a beautiful suit.

- **Και** may express reason:

    21a Κλείσε την τηλεόραση *και* θέλω να κοιμηθώ *instead of*
    b   Κλείσε την τηλεόραση *γιατί* θέλω να κοιμηθώ.
        Switch off the TV *because* I want to sleep.

- **Και** may express a condition:

    22a Κάνε μου αυτή τη χάρη *και* θα σου δώσω ό,τι θέλεις *instead of*
    b   *Αν* μου κάνεις αυτή τη χάρη θα σου δώσω ό,τι θέλεις.
        Do this favour for me *and* I will give you whatever you want.

10.22 Comparison

Comparison may be expressed by means of the comparative form of an adjective or adverb. The second member of the comparison is introduced either by the preposition **από** + accusative (1), or by the genitive case of a weak pronoun (2). **Παρά** may also introduce the second member of the comparison, which is in the same case as the first member (3). **Παρά** is also used when the elements compared are not noun phrases but clauses (4), prepositional phrases (5) or adverbials (6):

Comparison

1 Αυτή την εποχή ο σολομός είναι *ακριβότερος από* τον μπακαλιάρο.
   At this time of the year salmon is *more expensive than* cod.

2 Η Ελένη είναι κατά πολύ *μεγαλύτερή του*.
   Helen is far *older than him*.

3 Είναι *καλύτερα* να μας συνοδεύει ο Νίκος *παρά* ο Μιχάλης.
   It's better that Nikos escorts us *rather than* Michael.

4 Προτιμώ να του κάνω το χατίρι *παρά* να τον ακούω να κλαίει.
   I prefer to do what he wants *than to* hear him cry.

5 Δουλεύω *πιο καλά* στο γραφείο *παρά* στο σπίτι.
   I work *better* in the office *than* at home.

6 *Καλύτερα* να έρθεις σήμερα *παρά* αύριο.
   It's better that you come today *than* tomorrow.

The second member of the comparison may be omitted if it is easily understood:

7 Νομίζω ότι έτσι είναι *καλύτερα*.
   I think that it's *better* this way.

For the comparative form of adjectives and adverbs see sections 3.44 and 7.6 respectively.

10.22.1 Correlative comparison

Correlative comparison indicates that the two elements possess a quality to the same degree. The first part is introduced by the adverb **όσο** 'as much as' and the second by the adverb **τόσο** 'so much', or by the correlative pronoun and determiner **όσος** and the quantitative pronoun and determiner **τόσος**:

8 'Όσα άστρα έχει ο ουρανός, *τόσες* ευχές σου δίνω.
   I give you *as many* wishes *as* the sky has stars.

9 'Όσο πιο γελαστός είναι, *τόσο περισσότερο* νευριάζει η Καίτη.
   The more cheerful he is *the more* Kate gets irritated.

10 Όσο πιο πολλά κερδίζει, τόσο πιο τσιγκούνης γίνεται.
The more he earns the stingier he becomes.

10.22.2 Equation

In equation the two members compared are identical with respect to a certain property. The second member of the equation is introduced by **σαν**, **όπως**, **ως** or **όσο**. Σαν is followed by the accusative when the second member of the comparison is a definite noun phrase (11–12), or the nominative when it is indefinite (13):

11 Το πεπόνι αυτό είναι γλυκό *σαν* το μέλι.
This melon is sweet *like* honey.

12 Ο Νίκος είναι έξυπνος *σαν* τον πατέρα του.
Nick's clever *like* his father.

13 Γελάει *σαν* χαζός.
He's laughing *like* an idiot.

If **σαν** precedes a **να**-clause, it has the meaning 'as if':

14 Με κοιτάζει *σαν να* μη με έχει ξαναδεί.
(S)he's looking at me *as if* (s)he hasn't seen me before.

If the second member of the equation is introduced by **ως** the meaning is 'in one's capacity as' rather than 'like':

15 Σου μιλάω *ως ειδικός* στο θέμα αυτό.
I'm speaking to you *as a specialist* in this subject.

Όπως introduces the second member of the equation in the nominative case:

16 Ο Παύλος είναι τεμπέλης *όπως (κι) εσύ*.
Paul is lazy *like you*.

17 Περπατάει αργά *όπως η χελώνα*.
(S)he walks slowly *like a tortoise*.

It is also possible to express equation by placing **τόσο** before the first member of the equation and **όσο** before the second. The first element of the equation may be omitted, as in example 20:

18 Με συγκινεί *τόσο* η κλασική μουσική *όσο* και η μοντέρνα.
Classical music moves me *as much as* modern.

19 Είναι άραγε *τόσο* αδιάφορος *όσο* θέλει να δείχνει;
Is he *as* indifferent *as* he wants to appear, I wonder?

20 Δεν είναι σοβαρή *όσο* εσύ.
She's not *as* serious *as* you.

10.23 Reflexive expressions

Languages use special means for expressing a situation in which the subject of the sentence is both the actor of the verb and the patient (i.e. the recipient of the action). There are three ways of achieving this in Greek: (a) by the reflexive expression **ο εαυτός μου** 'myself', (b) by a passive verb form, or (c) by the verbal prefix **αυτο-** attached to a passive verb form.

(a) The definite article **ο** and the noun **εαυτός** 'self' of the reflexive phrase **ο εαυτός μου** 'myself' appear most frequently in the accusative case when the reflexive expression is the direct object of the verb, as in examples 1–2. The reflexive expression may also occur in a prepositional phrase (3–4). The definite article and the noun **εαυτός** are normally in the singular even when the possessive pronoun is in the plural (2):

1 Πρέπει να φροντίζεις *τον εαυτό σου*.
You must look after *yourself*.

2 Μόνο *τον εαυτό τους* κοιτάζουν και κανέναν άλλο.
They only look after *themselves* and no one else.

3 Πρέπει να έχεις εμπιστοσύνη μόνο *στον εαυτό σου*.
You should only trust *yourself*.

4 Η Μαρία έχει μεγάλη ιδέα *για τον εαυτό της*.
Mary has a very high opinion *of herself*.

(b) The passive verb form expresses reflexivity for some verbs of grooming or bodily care, especially when the subject is human:

5 Πρέπει να *ντύνεσαι* ζεστά τον χειμώνα εδώ.
You must *dress* warm in the winter here.

6 Θα *λουστώ* και θα 'ρθω.
I'll *wash my hair* and I'll come.

7 Πάλι *χτενίζεσαι*;
Are you *combing your hair* again?

(c) A few reflexives can be formed with the prefix **αυτο-** attached to the passive verb:

8   Ο άνθρωπος αυτός *αυτοκαταστράφηκε*.
    This man *destroyed himself*.

10.24 Reciprocal expressions

Reciprocal expressions in Greek are used to express the English equivalent of 'one another'. There are three ways of achieving this: (a) by the reciprocal periphrasis **ο ένας τον άλλο** 'each other' or by the preposition **μεταξύ** followed by a weak pronoun in the genitive, (b) by a passive verb form, or (c) by the prefix **αλληλο-** attached to a passive verb form.

(a) The reciprocal periphrasis consists of two phrases: **ο ένας** 'the one' and **τον άλλο** 'the other'. It is used with verbs expressing mutual feelings or actions motivated by these feelings. The first phrase (**ο ένας**) is in the nominative case, while the second (**τον άλλο**) appears in the gender and case appropriate to its meaning and syntactic content:

1   Οι δυο αυτοί φίλοι αγαπούν πολύ *ο ένας τον άλλο*.
    These two friends love *each other* very much.

2   Εμείς οι γυναίκες πρέπει να βοηθούμε *η μία την άλλη*.
    We women must help *each other*.

3   Συναγωνίζονται *ο ένας με τον άλλο (OR μεταξύ τους)*.
    They compete *with each other*.

4   Συχνά δίνουν λεφτά *ο ένας στον άλλο*.
    They often give money *to each other*.

The two parts of the reciprocal expression may be separated, the first functioning as the subject while the other is either in the accusative and functions as the object (5), or is in a prepositional phrase (6). In such constructions the verb in the sentence containing the reciprocal periphrasis is in the singular:

5   Το πρόβλημα είναι ότι *ο ένας* αντιπαθεί *τον άλλο*.
    The problem is that *the one* dislikes *the other*.

6   Δεν έχει *ο ένας* εμπιστοσύνη *στον άλλο*.
    They do not trust *one another* (lit. 'The one does not have trust in the other').

(b) Some verbs which express feelings or actions motivated by feelings may be used in the plural form of the passive with a reciprocal meaning:

> **Impersonal uses of verbs**

7   Ο Νίκος και η Όλγα *αγαπιούνται* πολύ.
    Nick and Olga *love each other* very much.

8   Δεν τους είδα ποτέ να *φιλιούνται*.
    I've never seen them *kiss (each other)*.

(c) The prefix **αλληλο-** can be attached to the plural of the passive forms of a small number of verbs to give a reciprocal meaning:

9   Οι καλοί φίλοι *αλληλοϋποστηρίζονται*.
    Good friends *support one another*.

10.25 Impersonal uses of verbs

In English impersonal verbs appear with either 'it' or 'there' as their subject, e.g. 'it's raining', 'it seems Mary will be late', 'there's a lot of noise in here'. In Greek impersonal verbs have no subject and they appear in the third person singular. In addition to the verbs that are only impersonal (see section 6.6), there are several other verbs that may be used impersonally. Impersonal uses of verbs include the following:

- Weather verbs, e.g. **βρέχει** 'it is raining', **χιονίζει** 'it is snowing':

    1   Από τον Οκτώβριο *βρέχει* σχεδόν κάθε μέρα.
        Since October *it's been raining* almost every day.

- The impersonal **έχει** (lit. 'it has'):

    2   *Έχει* πολλούς ανθρώπους εκεί μέσα.
        There are a lot of people in there.

- Verbs such as **φαίνεται** 'it seems', followed by either an **ότι**- or a **να**-clause, and **πρόκειται** 'be going to' followed by a **να**-clause:

    3   *Φαίνεται* ότι δεν την πιστεύουν.
        It seems that they do not believe her.

    4   *Φαίνεται* να μην είναι ευχαριστημένος.
        He *does not seem* to be pleased.

    5   Δεν *πρόκειται* να τον ξεχάσει.
        (S)he's not *about to* forget him.

10
The clause

- The verb **αρέσει** 'it pleases', followed by a **να**-clause, is accompanied by a personal pronoun in the genitive to express the meaning of the English expression 'I like':

    6   *Μου αρέσει να σε ακούω να μιλάς.*
        I like to hear you talk.

    7   *Του αρέσει να ακούει μουσική.*
        He likes listening to music.

- The modal verbs **πρέπει** 'it must', **μπορεί** 'it is possible':

    8   *Πρέπει να τους καλέσουμε.*
        We *must* invite them.

    9   *Μπορεί να μην ήταν αυτός ο φταίχτης.*
        Maybe he wasn't the culprit.

Chapter 11

Word formation

Throughout its long history Greek has always had a great facility for creating new words, either by modifying existing words by means of a suffix or a prefix, or by combining two or more word stems to form a compound. The great richness of the Greek language (as well as its role as a source of lexical borrowings in other languages) is due in large measure to the ease with which new words can be formed. In the following sections we can give only a very small selection of the various ways of forming words which have created the vocabulary of contemporary Greek. The process does not stop: many of the elements given in our examples continue to be productive in the formation of new words.

11.1 Suffixation

Many nouns are formed from verbs by the addition of a suffix to the verb stem, e.g.

-της (masculine nouns for the person or appliance that carries out the action of the verb), e.g. προπονητής 'trainer' (from προπονώ), τραγουδιστής 'singer' (τραγουδώ), κλέφτης 'thief' (κλέβω), παρατηρητής 'observer' (παρατηρώ), μετρητής 'meter' (μετρώ), υπολογιστής 'computer' (υπολογίζω) (see section 3.10 for the declension of these nouns);

-τήρας (masculine nouns for implements etc.), e.g. ανεμιστήρας 'fan, ventilator' (from ανεμίζω), αναπτήρας 'lighter' (ανάβω), συνδετήρας 'paper clip' (συνδέω) (section 3.9: Type (a));

-ση, -ξη, -ψη (feminine nouns denoting the action of the verb), e.g. απάντηση 'answer' (from απαντώ), παρατήρηση 'observation' (παρατηρώ), επιφύλαξη 'reservation' (επιφυλάσσω), χώνεψη 'digestion' (χωνεύω) (section 3.17);

**11
Word formation**

-μα (neuter nouns denoting the action or result of the verb), e.g. **διάβασμα** 'reading' (from **διαβάζω**), **σημείωμα** 'note' (**σημειώνω**), **βοήθημα** 'help, aid' (**βοηθώ**) (section 3.25);

-σιμο, -ψιμο, -ξιμο (neuter nouns denoting an action), e.g. **πλύσιμο** 'washing' (from **πλένω**), **γράψιμο** 'writing' (**γράφω**), **τρέξιμο** 'running' (**τρέχω**) (section 3.26).

Feminine nouns corresponding to masculine ones in **-της** have the suffix -τρια or -τρα, e.g. **διευθύντρια** 'female director', **καθαρίστρια** 'female cleaner', **παρουσιάστρια** 'female presenter', **ποιήτρια** 'female poet', **φοιτήτρια** 'female student', **ράφτρα** 'female dressmaker' (section 3.14: type (b)).

Other suffixes for nouns referring to females include:

-ισσα, e.g. **βασίλισσα** 'queen' (masculine **βασιλιάς**), **γειτόνισσα** 'woman neighbour' (**γείτονας**), **πριγκίπισσα** 'princess' (**πρίγκιπας**), **Σπαρτιάτισσα** 'Spartan woman' (**Σπαρτιάτης**) (section 3.14: type (b));

-ίνα (with implications of familiarity, or sometimes depreciation, when referring to professional women), e.g. **βουλευτίνα** 'woman member of parliament' (from **βουλευτής**), **δικηγορίνα** 'female lawyer' (**δικηγόρος**) (see also section 3.20 for the use of the masculine forms to refer to women);

-ίδα, e.g. **ηρωίδα** 'heroine' (from **ήρωας**), **Αμερικανίδα** 'American woman' (**Αμερικανός**), **Ελληνίδα** 'Greek woman' (**Έλληνας**) (section 3.14: type (a)).

Nouns denoting abstract concepts or qualities are often feminine, with suffixes such as:

-ιά, e.g. **ζεστασιά** 'warmth', **ομορφιά** 'beauty' (section 3.14: type (b));

-άδα, e.g. **εξυπνάδα** 'intelligence', **φρεσκάδα** 'freshness' (section 3.14: type (a));

-οσύνη, e.g. **δικαιοσύνη** 'justice', **ευγνωμοσύνη** 'gratitude', **καλοσύνη** 'kindness' (section 3.15);

-ότητα or -ύτητα, e.g. **δυνατότητα** 'possibility', **ικανότητα** 'capability', **ταχύτητα** 'speed' (section 3.14: type (a)).

Words denoting ideologies, beliefs, artistic movements and scientific phenomena often have the suffix **-ισμός**, with masculine gender, corresponding to English nouns in -ism, e.g. **θετικισμός** 'positivism', **μαγνητισμός** 'magnetism', **ρεαλισμός** 'realism', **ρατσισμός** 'racism', **σοσιαλισμός** 'socialism'.

The place where an action or business is carried out can have the following suffixes:

- **-είο**, e.g. **ταχυδρομείο** 'post office', **φαρμακείο** 'pharmacy' (section 3.21: type (a));

- **-ήριο**, e.g. **καθαριστήριο** 'cleaner's', **δικαστήριο** 'law court', **εργαστήριο** 'laboratory, workshop', **γυμναστήριο** 'gymnasium' (section 3.21: type (a)).

Among the many suffixes used to form adjectives, or to modify the meaning of existing adjectives, we may note:

- **-ένιος** or **-ινος** (indicating the material from which something is made), e.g. **σιδερένιος** 'iron', **μαλαματένιος** 'of gold', **μάλλινος** 'woollen', **ξύλινος** 'wooden';

- **-ικός, -ικος** and **-ιακός**, e.g. **ανδρικός** 'male, masculine', **γαλλικός** 'French', **μαζικός** 'mass', **συμπαθητικός** 'pleasant', **ψεύτικος** 'false', **οικογενειακός** 'of the family';

- **-ινός** (usually indicating time or place), e.g. **σημερινός** 'today's, present-day', **καλοκαιρινός** 'summer', **διπλανός** 'adjacent, next';

- **-τός** (usually indicating the result of a verb, with passive meaning), e.g. **γραπτός** 'written', **τηγανητός** 'fried', **μικτός** 'mixed';

- **-ούτσικος** ('to a moderate extent'; compare English -ish), e.g. **καλούτσικος** 'quite good', **μεγαλούτσικος** 'biggish'.

Diminutives express small size, familiarity, affection or, sometimes, depreciation. The suffixes which are used to form diminutives from nouns include the following:

- **-άκης** (attached to the stem of masculine nouns), e.g. **κοσμάκης** 'ordinary person, "man in the street"', but mainly used for proper names, such as **Μανολάκης** 'Manolis' (see section 12.2 for further examples);

- **-ούλης** (for masculine nouns), e.g. **πατερούλης** 'daddy'; this suffix is often attached to adjectives, e.g. **γλυκούλης** 'sweetie', **μικρούλης** 'youngster' (see section 3.40 for the declension);

- **-ούλα** (attached to the stem of feminine nouns), e.g. **αδερφούλα** 'little sister', **βαρκούλα** 'little boat', **λεξούλα** 'little word', **στιγμούλα** 'brief moment';

- **-ίτσα** (attached to the stem of feminine nouns), e.g. **μπιρίτσα** 'little beer', **ωρίτσα** '(an) hour (or so)', and often for feminine proper names such as **Ελενίτσα** 'Helen' (see section 12.2 for further examples);

Suffixation

**11
Word
formation**

-άκι (neuter diminutives mainly, but not exclusively, derived from neuter nouns), e.g. **αδερφάκι** 'little brother', **καφεδάκι** 'small coffee', **μεζεδάκι** 'snack', **παιδάκι** 'small child', **σπιτάκι** 'little house' (see section 3.23).

Augmentatives express large size or admiration, and can be formed with the following suffixes:

-α (feminine), e.g. **κουτάλα** 'big spoon', **μπουκάλα** 'big bottle';

-άρα (feminine), e.g. **αυτοκινητάρα** 'big car', **κοιλάρα** 'big belly';

-αράς or -ακλάς (masculine, denoting the male possessor of a quality), e.g. **δουλευταράς** 'hard worker', **κλεφταράς** 'big thief', **κοιλαράς** 'big-bellied person', **φωνακλάς** 'loud-mouth' (see section 3.13: type (a));

-αρος (masculine), e.g. **παίδαρος** 'big (handsome) lad', **σκύλαρος** 'great big dog' (see section 3.11: type (b)).

Finally, we note some suffixes which are frequently used to form verbs (usually from nouns or adjectives):

-ίζω, e.g. **βουρτσίζω** 'I brush', **εκσυγχρονίζω** 'I modernize', **προγραμματίζω** 'I programme';

-ώνω, e.g. **κουμπώνω** 'I button', **μαλακώνω** 'I soften', **τσεπώνω** 'I pocket';

-άρω or -ίρω (added to stems of words borrowed from other languages), e.g. **παρκάρω** 'I park' (see section 6.14 (w) for further examples and the formation of other verb forms);

-οποιώ, e.g. **αξιοποιώ** 'I develop, exploit', **τροποποιώ** 'I modify', **τυποποιώ** 'I standardize'.

11.2 Prefixation

The most commonly used prefixes are prepositions, including some Ancient Greek ones which no longer exist as independent prepositions. For a list of these prepositional prefixes see section 6.23. Each prefix has a wide range of meanings that cannot be detailed here. Often the same basic verb is prefixed with different prepositions to express different meanings. Thus **δίνω** 'I give' (usually in the form **-δίδω**) appears with different prefixes in, for example, **αποδίδω** 'I give back, attribute', **διαδίδω** 'I give out, disseminate', **εκδίδω** 'I issue, publish', **μεταδίδω** 'I transmit', **παραδίδω** 'I hand over', **προδίδω** (or **προδίνω**) 'I betray', and with two prefixes in **ανταποδίδω** 'I give in return'. For each of these verbs there is a corresponding feminine noun: **απόδοση** 'yield, rendering', **διάδοση** 'dissemination', **έκδοση** 'issue, publication', **μετάδοση** 'transmission', **παράδοση** 'surrender, tradition', **προδοσία** 'betrayal', **ανταπόδοση** 'repayment'.

Prepositional prefixes are found in various parts of speech (verbs, nouns, adjectives, adverbs). The main ones which are still productive are the following (with examples of each):

ανα- or **επανα-** ('re-'): **αναπαλαίωση** 'restoration' (lit. 'making old again'), **επανεκλέγω** 'I re-elect';

αντι- ('in place of', 'vice-', or 'against', 'anti-'): **αντιπρόεδρος** 'vice-president', **αντικομμουνιστικός** 'anticommunist';

απο- ('de-', 'dis-'): **αποσύνθεση** 'decomposition', **απολυμαντικό** 'disinfectant';

δια- ('inter-'): **διαδίκτυο** 'internet', **διακρατικός** 'interstate' (adj.), **διασύνδεση** 'interconnection';

εκ- and **εξ-** before a vowel (denotes the process of change): **εκσυγχρονισμός** 'modernization', **εξουδετερώνω** 'I neutralize';

κατα- ('very much'): **κάτασπρος** 'very white', **καταβρέχω** 'I soak, drench';

μετα- ('after', 'post-'): **μεταμοντερνισμός** 'postmodernism', **μεταπολεμικός** 'post-war';

προ- ('before', 'pre-'): **προκριματικός** 'preliminary [round of competition]', **προπολεμικός** 'pre-war';

συν- ('joint', 'co-'): **συμμαθητής** 'fellow pupil', **συνυπάρχω** 'I co-exist';

υπερ- ('over', 'trans-', 'super-'): **υπερατλαντικός** 'transatlantic', **υπερπαραγωγή** 'overproduction', **υπερφυσικός** 'supernatural';

υπο- ('under', 'sub-'): **υποδιευθυντής** 'undermanager', **υποσύνολο** 'subtotal'.

Negative adjectives are normally formed with the prefix **α-** (**αν-** before a vowel), which can be compared with English 'un-', 'in-', 'im-', etc. There is often a shift of stress: the negative adjectives normally have stress on the third syllable from the end. The positive and negative forms may also have differences in their endings. Some examples:

γνωστός (well-)known   **άγνωστος** unknown
όμοιος similar   **ανόμοιος** dissimilar

πιθανός probable   απίθανος improbable
σχετικός related   άσχετος unrelated, irrelevant
τίμιος honourable   άτιμος dishonourable
φυσικός natural   αφύσικος unnatural
χρήσιμος useful   άχρηστος useless

Other common prefixes include:

ξανα- ('again', 're-' prefixed to verbs): ξαναρχίζω 'I begin again', ξανα-διαβάζω 'I reread';

ξε- (prefixed to verbs, gives the opposite meaning; cf. English 'un-'): ξεμπαρκάρω 'I disembark', ξεδιψώ 'I quench my thirst', ξεντύνω 'I undress';

μεγαλο- ('big'): μεγαλοεπιχειρηματίας 'big-businessman';

μικρο- ('small'): μικροπράγματα 'little things, trifles';

νεο- ('new', 'neo-'): νεοφασισμός 'neo-Fascism', νεόπλουτος 'newly rich';

πολυ- ('much', 'multi-'): πολυπολιτισμικός 'multicultural', πολυεκατομ-μυριούχος 'multimillionaire'.

11.3 Compound formation

In this section we shall give some examples of compounds formed from two (or more) separate words, a phenomenon which is very widespread in Greek and which continues to produce new words. The elements that make up a compound are typically linked by the vowel -o-. The first type of compound consists of words that link two elements which belong to the same part of speech (nouns, adjectives, verbs), where the resulting word combines the meaning of both:

- Compounds of two nouns: αντρόγυνο 'married couple' (άντρας and γυναίκα), γυναικόπαιδα 'women and children' (γυναίκες and παιδιά), μαχαιροπίρουνο 'knife and fork' (μαχαίρι and πιρούνι), ονοματεπώνυμο 'name and surname' (όνομα and επώνυμο), Σαββατοκύριακο 'weekend' (Σάββατο and Κυριακή).
- Compounds of two adjectives: ασπρόμαυρος 'black and white' (άσπρος and μαύρος), μακρόστενος 'long and narrow' (i.e. 'oblong') (μακρύς and στενός).

- Compounds of two verbs: **αναβοσβήνω** 'I flash on and off' (**ανάβω** and **σβήνω**), **ανεβοκατεβαίνω** 'I go up and down' (**ανεβαίνω** and **κατεβαίνω**), **ανοιγοκλείνω** 'I open and close' (**ανοίγω** and **κλείνω**), **πηγαινοέρχομαι** 'I come and go' (**πηγαίνω** and **έρχομαι**).

There are very many compounds belonging to various parts of speech, in which the two elements may be a noun and a verb, two nouns, an adjective and a noun, etc. Here we can only give a very small number of examples:

- noun and verb: **βιβλιοδεσία** 'book-binding', **μυθιστοριογράφος** 'novelist', **νομοθετώ** 'I legislate', **σταυροκοπιέμαι** 'I cross myself, make the sign of the cross', **φυλλομετρώ** 'I leaf through, browse', **χρονοτριβώ** 'I waste time';
- two nouns: **ανεμόμυλος** 'windmill', **ηλιοβασίλεμα** 'sunset', **κλειδαρότρυπα** 'keyhole', **ροδόνερο** 'rosewater', **ταυρομαχία** 'bullfight', **τερματοφύλακας** 'goalkeeper', **τυρόπιτα** 'cheese pie', **χαρτοπαίκτης** 'card-player';
- adjective and noun: **αγριογούρουνο** 'wild boar', **κοκκινομάλλης** 'red-haired', **στενόμυαλος** 'narrow-minded', **ψηλομύτης** 'snobbish' (lit. 'high-nosed');
- adjective (or adverb) and verb: **γελοιογραφία** 'cartoon', **κοντοστέκομαι** 'I stop short', **ξεροβήχω** 'I clear my throat';
- adjective and passive perfect participle: **μαυροντυμένος** 'dressed in black', **φρεσκοβαμμένος** 'freshly painted', **χοντροκομμένος** 'roughly cut'.

Compound formation

Chapter 12

Conversational features

12.1 Politeness and familiarity

Below we give the most important and most commonly used politeness markers in Greek.

12.1.1 The polite (formal) plural

The second person plural (instead of the second person singular) is used to a single addressee in the following circumstances:

- When the addressee is unknown or unfamiliar to the speaker, such as a passer-by (1) or a taxi-driver (2):

    1   Σας παρακαλώ, μου *λέτε* τι ώρα είναι;
        Please can *you tell* me what time it is?

    2   *Μπορείτε* να *σταματήσετε* στην άλλη γωνία, *σας* παρακαλώ;
        Can *you stop* at the next corner, please?

- When the addressee is older or of higher status than the speaker:

    3   Θα *είστε* στο γραφείο *σας* αύριο να *σας* φέρω την εργασία μου;
        Will *you be* at *your* office tomorrow so I can bring *you* my essay?

    4   Αν *είστε* κουρασμένος *ελάτε* να *καθίσετε* εδώ.
        If *you are* tired come and sit here.

In all the above examples the pronouns and the verbs in italics are in the second person plural in spite of the fact that the person addressed is a single individual. Notice, however, that in example 4 the adjective predicate **κουρασμένος** 'tired', which also refers to the same individual, is not in the plural but in the singular.

Politeness and familiarity

12.1.2 Diminutives

Greek often uses the diminutive forms of nouns and adjectives with linguistic acts like offers, compliments and requests, as a device to show affection or to minimize the imposition placed by the speaker on the addressee:

5 Πάρτε ένα *μπισκοτάκι* (παρακαλώ).
   Please take *a biscuit*.

6 Μας φέρνετε μια *μπιρίτσα* ακόμη και *λίγο κρασάκι* (παρακαλώ);
   Can you bring us one more *beer* and *a little wine* please?'

7 Το *κρασάκι* είναι *ξινούτσικο*, ή μου φαίνεται;
   The *wine* is *a little sour*, or is it my imagination (lit. 'or does it seem to me?')?

8 Ωραία *μπλουζίτσα*, σου πηγαίνει τέλεια.
   A lovely *blouse*. It suits you perfectly.

12.1.3 The adverb λίγο

In requests the adverb **λίγο** may be used to lessen the imposition on the addressee:

9 Έλα *λίγο* αύριο να τα πούμε.
   Why not come tomorrow so that we can have a chat.

10 Πέστε μου *λίγο* το όνομά σας.
    Tell me your name, *please*.

12.1.4 Να-clause

A **να**-clause may be used to express polite suggestions and polite requests:

11 *Να* σε βλέπουμε πιο συχνά.
    We *would like* to see you more often.

12 *Να* σε ρωτήσω κάτι;
    May I ask you something?

13 *Να πάτε μέχρι το περίπτερο και να στρίψετε δεξιά.*
    You *should* go as far as the kiosk and then turn right.

12.1.5 Present tense of the verb

The second person singular or plural of the present tense is used in interrogative utterances to express polite requests. It is equivalent to 'can you, could you?', for example:

14 *Ανοίγεις λίγο το παράθυρο;*
    Can you *open* the window, please?

15 *Φέρνετε το τηλέφωνο πιο κοντά;*
    Could you *bring* the telephone closer?

12.1.6 Παρακαλώ 'please'

All requests may be accompanied by the word **παρακαλώ**, which can be placed at the beginning or the end of the utterance or between major phrases:

16 *Παρακαλώ περάστε από το γραφείο μου την Τρίτη το πρωί.*
    Please come by my office on Tuesday morning.

17 *Μου δίνετε το βιβλίο σας, παρακαλώ;*
    Can you give me your book, *please*?

18 *Μου φέρνετε παρακαλώ κι ένα καφεδάκι;*
    Can you bring me a coffee too, *please*?

If the word **παρακαλώ** is preceded by the plural pronoun **σας** (**σας παρακαλώ**) it becomes more formal. **Παρακαλώ** is also used as the response to **ευχαριστώ** 'thank you':

19 – *Σας ευχαριστώ πολύ.*
    Thank you very much.

    – *Παρακαλώ.*
    You're *welcome* (lit. 'please').

An alternative to **παρακαλώ** as a response to 'thank you' is the expression

Να 'στε καλά. 'Be in good health'.

12.1.7 The verb μπορώ

The second person plural of the verb **μπορώ** in the present or in the conditional is used to introduce more formal requests:

20 *Μπορείτε να μας φέρετε και τον λογαριασμό, παρακαλώ;*
    Can you bring us the bill too, please?

21 *Θα μπορούσατε να μου κάνετε αυτή τη χάρη, παρακαλώ;*
    Could you do me this favour, please?

12.1.8 The conditional θα ήθελα

The conditional of **θέλω** 'I want', namely **θα ήθελα**, is more polite than the present:

22 *Θα ήθελα ένα βιβλίο για δώρο.*
    I would like a book for a present.

12.1.9 Familiarity

The items **βρε, ρε, μωρέ** 'hey you' are used to attract the attention of someone with whom the speaker is fairly familiar. They may optionally be followed either by **συ** 'you' or by the first name of the addressee in the vocative, or by phrases such as **παιδί** 'child' or **παιδί μου** 'my child', **παιδιά** 'children', or others in the vocative. (For pet names see section 12.2.)

23 *Ρε συ, πού πήγες χθες;*
    Hey you, where did you go yesterday?

24 *Μωρέ Γιάννη, τι λες να κάνουμε;*
    Hey John, what do you suggest we do?

25 *Ελάτε και από δω, βρε παιδιά.*
    Come this way, *you guys*.

12.2 Proper names and pet names

Many Greeks are normally known by a first name that is slightly different from their official name, which is used for official purposes such as identity cards. Here are some common examples:

Official form	Everyday form	English equivalent (if any)
Αθανάσιος	Θανάσης	
Αλέξανδρος	Αλέκος	Alexander
Αλέξιος	Αλέξης	
Αναστάσιος	Τάσος	
Αντώνιος	Αντώνης	Anthony
Βασίλειος	Βασίλης	Basil
Βασιλική	Βάσω	
Γεώργιος	Γιώργος	George
Δημήτριος	Δημήτρης	
Ειρήνη	Ρένα	Irene
Εμμανουήλ	Μανόλης, Μάνος	Emmanuel
Ευάγγελος	Βαγγέλης	
Ευγενία	Τζένη	
Ευφροσύνη	Φρόσω	
Θεοδώρα	Δώρα, Ντόρα	
Θεόδωρος	Θόδωρος	Theodore
Ιουλία	Τζούλια	Julie, Julia
Ιφιγένεια	Τζένη	
Ιωάννα	Γιάννα	Joanna
Ιωάννης	Γιάννης	John
Κωνσταντία/ίνα	Ντίνα	
Κωνσταντίνος	Κώστας, Ντίνος	Constantine
Μιλτιάδης	Μίλτος	
Μιχαήλ	Μιχάλης	Michael
Νικόλαος	Νίκος	Nicholas
Ουρανία	Ράνια	
Παναγιώτα	Γιώτα	
Παναγιώτης	Πάνος, Τάκης	
Σπυρίδων	Σπύρος	
Στυλιανή	Στέλλα	
Στυλιανός	Στέλιος	
Σωτήριος	Σωτήρης	
Χαράλαμπος	Μπάμπης	

In addition, within the family and among close friends, people (especially, but not only, children) may be talked about and addressed affectionately with forms that incorporate diminutive endings (see section 11.1), such as the following:

Proper names and pet names

Base form	Diminutive form
Άννα	Αννούλα
Βασίλης	Βασιλάκης
Γιάννα	Γιαννούλα
Γιάννης	Γιαννάκης
Γιώργος	Γιωργάκης
Δήμητρα	Δημητρούλα
Δημήτρης	Δημητράκης
Ελένη	Ελενίτσα
Κατερίνα	Κατερινιώ
Κώστας	Κωστάκης
Μαρία	Μαρούλα
Μιχάλης	Μιχαλάκης
Νίκος	Νικολάκης (from the alternative familiar form Νικόλας)
Παναγιώτης	Παναγιωτάκης

There are many more variations than this, both in the everyday forms and in the diminutive forms. Usage depends entirely on the individuals themselves and their family and close friends, and some people prefer to be known by their official name. The following is a sample of alternative names by which many people are normally known; notice that some alternative forms may correspond to more than one base form:

12 Conversational features

Base form	Alternative form
Αθηνά, Ιωάννα	Νανά
Αναστασία	Τασούλα
Βασιλική	Βούλα, Βίκυ, Κούλα
Γεωργία	Ζέττα
Δήμητρα	Ρούλα, Ρίτσα
Δημήτρης	Μήτσος, Μίμης
Ελένη	Λένα
Θανάσης	Θάνος, Νάσος, Σούλης, Σάκης
Θόδωρος	Θοδωρής
Καλλιόπη, Πηνελόπη	Πόπη
Κατερίνα	Κάτια, Καίτη
Κυριακή	Κούλα
Κώστας	Κωστής
Μαρία	Μάρω, Μάρια, Μάρα, Μαίρη
Μιχάλης	Μίκης
Χαράλαμπος	Χάρης, Λάμπης

Greek women's surnames are based on the genitive form of their father's or husband's surnames. They are indeclinable. Certain types of feminine surname normally appear in an archaic form (this is illustrated in the following examples of names with masculine forms in -ίδης, -ιάδης, and in stressed vowel + -της):

Masculine	Feminine
Μητσάκης	Μητσάκη
Μητσάκος	Μητσάκου
Μητσόπουλος	Μητσοπούλου

254

Πετρίδης	Πετρίδου (or Πετρίδη)
Αναστασιάδης	Αναστασιάδου (or Αναστασιάδη)
Πολίτης	Πολίτου (or Πολίτη)

With the feminine form **Μητσοπούλου** (with shift of stress as in the genitive form of nouns like **άνθρωπος**) compare the normal genitive of the masculine form, **Μητσόπουλου** (without shift of stress, as in nouns like **καλόγερος**); see section 3.11 (type (b)).

12.3 Greetings and wishes

The standard greetings for different times of the day are:

καλημέρα good morning
καλησπέρα good evening
καληνύχτα good night

When used formally, or to more than one person, these greetings can be followed by the plural of the weak second-person pronoun **σας**, e.g. **καλημέρα σας** 'good morning to you'.

Other greetings of a less formal kind include:

γεια σας hello OR goodbye (γεια σου, when addressed to one person whom you know well)
χαίρετε hello OR goodbye
αντίο goodbye
(να πας) στο καλό! goodbye (lit. 'may you go to the good')

Conversations often begin with:

Τι κάνεις; *(plural or formal* **Τι κάνετε;**) How are you?
Πώς είσαι/είστε; How are you?
Τι γίνεσαι OR Πώς τα πας; How are you getting on?
Πώς πάει; How's it going?

Welcomes and formal introductions:

12 Conversational features

Καλώς ήλθατε! OR **Καλώς ορίσατε!** Welcome!

When addressed to one person you know well, the forms are **Καλώς ήλθες!** OR **Καλώς όρισες.** The normal reply is:

Καλώς σας βρήκα! (formal or to several people) OR **Καλώς σε βρήκα!** (familiar, to one person) Good to see you!
Να σας συστήσω τον φίλο μου Θάνο Πετρόπουλο. May I introduce my friend Thanos Petropoulos.
Χαίρω πολύ. Pleased to meet you.
Χάρηκα πολύ. Pleased to have met you OR Nice to see/hear you (at the end of a meeting or phone conversation).

There are many wishes of a more or less standard kind that use the adjective **καλός** 'good' with an appropriate noun. These expressions are in the accusative case:

καλό βράδυ! have a good evening!
καλή εβδομάδα! have a good week! (said at the start of the week)
καλό μήνα! have a good month! (said at the start of the month)
καλή διασκέδαση! have a good time!, enjoy yourself!
καλή όρεξη! enjoy your meal!, *bon appétit!*
καλή επιτυχία!/καλή τύχη! good luck!
καλό ταξίδι! have a good journey!
καλές διακοπές! have a good holiday!
καλό χειμώνα! have a good winter! (said at the end of the summer holiday period)
καλά Χριστούγεννα! happy Christmas!
καλό Πάσχα! happy Easter!
καλή χρονιά! happy New Year!

Birthday wishes and wishes on someone's name day (i.e. the feast day of the saint after whom a person is named) can be expressed by:

χρόνια πολλά! happy birthday! (lit. 'many years'; the same phrase also serves as a general wish for festivals such as Christmas, Easter and New Year)
να τα εκατοστήσεις! Long life! (lit. 'may you make them a hundred [years]')

Expressions used in toasts include:

γεια μας! cheers (lit. 'health to us'), or more formally **στην υγειά μας!**
εις υγείαν! good health

Some other wishes:

συγχαρητήρια! congratulations!
(και) εις ανώτερα! to your continued success! (lit. 'and to higher [things]')
να σας ζήσει! may (s)he live long for you! (addressed to a parent when a child's birth is announced, or on special family occasions, or when a child is discussed)
με γεια! lit. 'with health!' (to a person who has something new, such as clothes)
περαστικά! get well soon!
περαστικά του/της I hope (s)he will get well soon
συλλυπητήρια/τα συλλυπητήριά μου (my) condolences
και του χρόνου! here's to next year! (referring to an annual event)

Appendices

1 Correspondence table of pronouns, determiners and adverbs

	Pronouns and determiners		Adverbs			
	Masc./fem./neut.[1]	Neuter only[1]	Place	Time	Manner	Quantity
Indefinite (specific)	κάποιος some(one)	κάτι something	κάπου somewhere	κάποτε once, at some time	κάπως in some way, somehow	κάπως somewhat
Indefinite (non-specific)	κανένας any/no(one)	τίποτα any/no(thing)	πουθενά anywhere, nowhere	ποτέ (n)ever	καθόλου (not) at all	καθόλου (not) at all
Interrogative[2]	ποιος who, which πόσος how much/many	τι what πόσο how much	πού where	πότε when	πώς how	πόσο how much
Demonstrative	αυτός this εκείνος that	αυτό this εκείνο that	εδώ here εκεί there	τώρα now τότε then	έτσι in this/that way	

Quantitative demonstrative	τόσος so much/ many	τόσο so much				τόσο so much
Qualitative demonstrative	τέτοιος such, this/that kind of				έτσι in such a way	
Relative	που, ο οποίος who, which		όπου where	όταν when	όπως, καθώς as	
Correlative	όποιος, οποιοσδήποτε whoever όσος, οσοσδήποτε as much/many as	ό,τι, οτιδήποτε whatever	όπου, οπουδήποτε wherever	όποτε, οποτε- δήποτε whenever οπότε at which point	όπως, οποσδήποτε however, whichever way	όσο, οσο- δήποτε as much as, however much
Universal	καθένας each one	καθετί each thing	παντού everywhere	πάντα always	πάντως in any case	
Distributive	κάθε each, every					
Contrastive	άλλος other, (someone) else	άλλο other, (something) else	αλλού elsewhere	άλλοτε at another time	αλλιώς otherwise, another way	άλλο more, further

1. i.e. when used as pronouns.

2. Also reason: γιατί 'why'.

Appendices

2 Some abbreviations in common use

Below we give a list of abbreviations that are commonly used in Greece and Cyprus, with their English equivalents. When abbreviations referring to institutions are used, they appear in the same gender as the chief noun of the full name, e.g. **η Δ.Ε.Η., ο Ο.Τ.Ε., το Κ.Τ.Ε.Λ.** Where the abbreviation is commonly pronounced, we give the pronunciation in square brackets.

Α	=	ανατολικός (east(ern))
αγ.	=	άγιος/αγία (saint)
Α.Ε.	=	ανώνυμος εταιρεία (limited company)
Α.Ε.Κ. [áek]	=	Αθλητική Ένωση Κωνσταντινουπόλεως [an Athens football team]
αι.	=	αιώνας (century)
Α.Κ.Ε.Λ. [ak'él]	=	Ανορθωτικό Κόμμα Εργαζόμενου Λαού [a Cypriot political party]
αρ.	=	αριθμός (number)
Αφοί	=	Αδελφοί (Brothers, Bros)
Β	=	βόρειος (north(ern))
ΒΑ	=	βορειοανατολικός (north-east)
ΒΔ	=	βορειοδυτικός (north-west)
Γ.Γ.	=	γενικός γραμματέας (general secretary)
Γ.Ε.Σ. [jes]	=	Γενικό Επιτελείο Στρατού (General Staff of the Greek Army)
γρ.	=	γραμμάριο (gram(s))
Γ.Σ.Ε.Ε. [jeseé]	=	Γενική Συνομοσπονδία Εργατών Ελλάδας (General Trade Unions Federation of Greece)
Δ	=	δυτικός (west(ern))
Δ.Ε.Η. [deí]	=	Δημόσια Επιχείρηση Ηλεκτρισμού [Greek electricity authority]
δηλ.	=	δηλαδή (that is, i.e.)
δις [δis]	=	δισεκατομμύριο (billion)
Δ.Σ.	=	διπλωματικό σώμα (diplomatic corps)
Ε.Ε.	=	Ευρωπαϊκή Ένωση (European Union)
Ε.Ε.Σ.	=	Ελληνικός Ερυθρός Σταυρός (Greek Red Cross)
εκ.	=	εκατομμύριο (million) *or* εκατοστό (centimetre(s))

Some abbreviations in common use

Ε.Κ.Α.Β. [εκάν]	=	Εθνικό Κέντρο Άμεσης Βοήθειας (National First-Aid Centre)
ΕΛ.ΑΣ. [elás]	=	Ελληνική Αστυνομία (Greek Police)
ΕΛ.ΤΑ. [eltá]	=	Ελληνικά Ταχυδρομεία (Greek Postal Service)
Ε.Μ.Υ. [émi]	=	Ελληνική Μετεωρολογική Υπηρεσία (Greek Meteorological Service)
Ε.Ο.Τ. [eót]	=	Ελληνικός Οργανισμός Τουρισμού (Greek Tourism Organization)
Ε.Σ.Υ. [esí]	=	Εθνικό Σύστημα Υγείας (National Health Service)
Ε.Τ. [et]	=	Ελληνική Τηλεόραση [Greek state television service]
Ε.ΥΔ.Α.Π. [ejδáp]	=	Εταιρεία Υδάτων Αθήνας-Πειραιά (Athens–Piraeus Water Company)
Η/Υ	=	ηλεκτρονικός υπολογιστής (computer)
Η.Π.Α.	=	Ηνωμένες Πολιτείες της Αμερικής (United States of America)
Ι.Κ.Α. [íka]	=	Ίδρυμα Κοινωνικών Ασφαλίσεων (Greek state social security organization)
κ.	=	κύριος/κυρία (Mr/Mrs)
κ.ά.	=	και άλλα (and other people/things, et al.)
κεφ.	=	κεφάλαιο (chapter)
Κ.Κ.Ε. (sometimes pronounced [kukué])	=	Κομμουνιστικό Κόμμα Ελλάδας (Greek Communist Party)
κλπ.	=	και λοιπά (etc.)
Κ.Τ.Ε.Λ. [ktel]	=	Κοινό Ταμείο Εισπράξεων Λεωφορείων [Greek national bus service]
κ.τ.λ.	=	και τα λοιπά (etc.)
λ.χ.	=	λόγου χάριν (for instance, e.g.)
μ.	=	μέτρο/μέτρα (metre(s))
μ.μ.	=	μετά το μεσημέρι (p.m.)
Μ.Μ.Ε.	=	μέσα μαζικής ενημέρωσης (mass media)
μ.Χ.	=	μετά Χριστόν (A.D.)
Ν	=	νότιος (south(ern))
ΝΑ	=	νοτιοανατολικός (south-eastern)

ΝΔ	=	νοτιοδυτικός (south-western)
Ν.Δ.	=	Νέα Δημοκρατία (New Democracy [a Greek political party])
Ο.Α.	=	Ολυμπιακή Αεροπορία (Olympic Airways)
Ο.Η.Ε. [oié]	=	Οργανισμός Ηνωμένων Εθνών (United Nations Organization)
Ο.Τ.Ε. [oté]	=	Οργανισμός Τηλεπικοινωνιών Ελλάδας (Greek Telecommunications Organization)
Π.Α.Ο.	=	Παναθηναϊκός Αθλητικός Όμιλος [an Athens football team]
Π.Α.Ο.Κ. [páok]	=	Πανθεσσαλονίκιος Αθλητικός Όμιλος Κωνσταντινουπολιτών [a Thessaloniki football team]
ΠΑ.ΣΟ.Κ. [pasók]	=	Πανελλήνιο Σοσιαλιστικό Κίνημα (Panhellenic Socialist Movement [a Greek political party])
πβ.	=	παράβαλε (compare, cf.)
π.μ.	=	πριν από το μεσημέρι (a.m.)
ΠΡΟ-ΠΟ [propó]	=	Προγνωστικά Ποδοσφαίρου [Greek football pools organization]
π.Χ.	=	προ Χριστού (B.C.)
π.χ.	=	παραδείγματος χάριν (for example, e.g.)
P.I.K. [rik]	=	Ραδιοφωνικό Ίδρυμα Κύπρου (Cyprus Broadcasting Corporation)
σ./σελ.	=	σελίδα (page, p.)
τ.μ.	=	τετραγωνικό μέτρο (square metre(s))
Υ.Γ.	=	υστερόγραφο (postscript, P.S.)
Φ.Π.Α.	=	Φόρος Προστιθέμενης Αξίας (Value Added Tax, V.A.T.)
χλμ.	=	χιλιόμετρο (kilometre(s))
χφ.	=	χειρόγραφο (manuscript, ms.)

Glossary of grammatical terms

Note: This glossary should be used in conjunction with the Index of grammatical categories and concepts, which refers to the specific pages of the Grammar where these terms are discussed. Words in italics are terms that are defined in the glossary.

accusative	see *case*
active	when a *verb* is in the active voice its *subject* is the person or thing doing the action (cf. *passive*)
adjective	a word that denotes a property or characteristic of a *noun* (**ένα μεγάλο τραπέζι** 'a *big* table')
adverb	a word indicating manner, time, place or quantity (**Έλα γρήγορα** 'come *quickly*', **έλα αύριο** 'come *tomorrow*', **έλα δω** 'come *here*', **πολύ καλός** '*very* good')
adverbial	an *adverb* or any phrase or *clause* that functions as an adverb
adverbial phrase	an *adverb* on its own or modified by another adverb
agent	the entity carrying out the action of the *verb* (the term is usually applied to the noun phrase after **από** with passive verbs: **Τιμήθηκε** *από την κυβέρνηση* '(S)he was honoured *by the government*')
alveolar	a consonant sound made with the blade of the tongue in contact with the alveolar ridge (the bony ridge behind the upper teeth), such as English and Greek [n]
apodosis	the *clause* in a *conditional sentence* that expresses the action that takes place if the condition expressed in the *protasis* is fulfilled (**Αν έρθεις στο**

Glossary of grammatical terms

πάρτι, **θα δεις τον Γιάννη** 'If you come to the party, *you'll see John*')

article — a word placed before a *noun* to limit, individualize or give definiteness to the *noun phrase*; there are two kinds of article: definite (**ο, η, το** 'the') and indefinite (**ένας, μια, ένα** 'a(n)')

aspect — grammatical property of *verbs* that indicates whether the action is presented as completed (*perfective*), as progressive or repeated (*imperfective*), or as a past action seen in relation to some other time (*perfect*)

augment — the *prefix* added to certain *verb stems* to make certain forms of the past tenses (**έχασα** 'I lost')

augmentative — a special form of a *noun*, formed with a *suffix* and expressing large size or admiration (**κοιλάρα** 'big belly') (cf. *diminutive*)

bilabial — a consonant sound made by contact between the two lips, as in English and Greek [p] and [m]

case — one of the forms of a *noun*, *adjective*, *pronoun*, *numeral* or *article* indicating the *syntactic* function of the noun phrase in the *clause*; the nominative case indicates the *subject*, the accusative the *direct object*, and the genitive normally the *indirect object* or the possessor of a *noun*; the vocative is used for addressing someone or something

clause — a *syntactic* unit consisting of at least a finite *verb* (i.e. a verb that is not a *gerund*, *participle* or *non-finite*); a clause may be a main clause (a clause that can stand independently as a *sentence*) or a subordinate clause (a clause whose meaning depends on another clause)

comparative — see *degree*

complement clause — a *clause* that completes meaning of a *verb*, *noun* or *adjective* (see section 10.3)

complementizer — a word (in Greek **ότι, πως, που**) that introduces a *complement clause*

compound — a word made up of two *stems* (**μαχαιροπίρουνα** 'knives and forks')

conditional — *tenses* of the *verb* formed by **θα** + *imperfect* or *pluperfect* to express actions that would take place if certain conditions were fulfilled (**θα έχανα** 'I would lose', **θα είχα χάσει** 'I would have lost');

	also *sentences* that express conditions (**Αν έρθεις στο πάρτι, θα δεις τον Γιάννη** 'If you come to the party, you'll see John')
conjunction	a word that links phrases or *clauses* (**και** 'and', **αν** 'if', **όταν** 'when')
declension	the pattern of endings by which a *noun*, *adjective*, *pronoun*, *determiner*, etc indicates number, *gender* and *case*
defective verb	a *verb* that has only *imperfective aspect* (**έχω** 'I have')
degree	Greek distinguishes four degrees of comparison in *adjectives* and *adverbs*: positive (**ωραίος** 'lovely'), comparative (**ωραιότερος** or **πιο ωραίος** 'lovelier'), relative superlative (**ο ωραιότερος** or **ο πιο ωραίος** 'the loveliest') and absolute superlative (**ωραιότατος** 'very lovely')
dental	a consonant sound formed by placing the tip of the tongue near or against the top teeth, as Greek [s], [t] and [l]
dependent	the *perfective* non-past form of the *verb* (**χάσω**)
deponent verb	a *verb* without *active* forms but with active meaning (**κοιμάμαι** 'I sleep')
determiner	a word that is not an *adjective* or *numeral* but accompanies a *noun* (e.g. **κάθε** 'each', **κάποιος** 'some', **κανένας** 'any; no'); most Greek determiners may also act as *pronouns*
diminutive	a special form of a *noun*, formed with a *suffix* and normally expressing small size or affection (**καφεδάκι** 'small coffee')
direct object	a weak *pronoun* or *noun phrase* in the *accusative* case indicating the person or thing that the action of the *verb* is done to
enclisis	phenomenon whereby a second stress develops on a *noun*, *verb*, etc. stressed on the third syllable from the end when it is followed by a weak *pronoun* (**ο δάσκαλός μας** 'our teacher')
finite	any *verb* form that indicates both person and number
flap	a consonant sound formed by a single rapid contact between two vocal organs (e.g. between tip of tongue and *alveolar* ridge in Greek [r])

Glossary of grammatical terms

Glossary of grammatical terms

focus	the part of the *sentence* that carries the main stress and constitutes the most important emphasis or contrast
fricative	a consonant sound made by the movement of air between two vocal organs placed very close together (e.g. English [f], [v]) (cf. *plosive*)
genitive	see *case*
gerund	an uninflected *non-finite verb* form that functions as an *adverbial* (τρέχοντας 'running')
imparisyllabic	a noun that has an additional syllable in the plural
imperative	*verb* form used to express a positive command (γράψε! 'write!')
imperfect	the *imperfective* past form of the *verb* (έγραφα 'I was writing, I used to write')
imperfective	the *aspect* of the *verb* that presents an action as being progressive or repeated
impersonal verb	a *verb* in the third person singular which has no *subject*
indicative	the *mood* of a *verb* that typically makes a statement that can be judged as either true or false; it may also ask a question to which there is potentially a definite answer; the indicative is negated with δεν and does not combine with the *particles* να and ας
indirect object	a weak *pronoun* or *noun phrase* denoting the entity to or for which the action denoted by the *verb* is done (***Της** το έδωσα* 'I gave it *to her*', *το έδωσα **στη Μαρία*** 'I gave it *to Mary*')
indeclinable	a *noun*, *adjective* or *pronoun* that does not change form to indicate number, gender, case.
inflection	(a) the way a declinable word (*noun*, *adjective*, *pronoun*, *determiner*, *verb*) changes form to indicate number, gender, *case*, person and *tense*; (b) the endings of words that indicate these categories
intransitive verb	a *verb* that does not normally have an *object* (βήχω 'I cough', κάθομαι 'I sit')
labial	any of the *bilabial* and *labiodental* consonants
labiodental	a consonant sound made by the passage of air between the lower lip and the upper teeth, as in English and Greek [f] and [v]
linking verb	a verb that links the *subject* with the *subject predicate* (typically the verb είμαι 'I am')

liquid	the English and Greek consonant sounds [l] and [r]	Glossary of grammatical terms
main clause	see *clause*	
modifier	any word, phrase or *clause* that limits the meaning of a *noun, verb, adjective* or *adverb*	
mood	a set of formal contrasts and *semantic* differences indicating the way in which the speaker wishes to present the information of the sentence, as a statement of fact (*indicative*), a wish, hope, expectation, plan, etc. (*subjunctive*), or an order (*imperative*)	
nasal	a consonant sound made when the air is released through the nose, as in English and Greek [m] and [n]	
nominative	see *case*	
non-finite	a *verb* form that does not display number and person; in particular, the form used with έχω to form the *perfect aspect* (έχω γράψει 'I have written')	
noun	a word that denotes a thing, person, place, process, concept, etc. (τραπέζι 'table', Μάρκος 'Mark', κίνηση 'motion', ιδέα 'idea')	
noun phrase	a phrase consisting of a *noun* (alone or accompanied by *article, adjective, determiner*, etc.) or a *pronoun* (ο καλύτερος ποδοσφαιριστής 'the best footballer', εσύ 'you')	
numeral	a word expressing number; cardinal numerals are the basic forms (ένας 'one', δύο 'two'), while ordinal numerals express order or sequence (πρώτος 'first', δεύτερος 'second')	
object	a *noun phrase* or *pronoun* that indicates an entity that is acted upon by the *subject* (see *direct object* and *indirect object*)	
object predicate	an *adjective* phrase or *noun phrase* that refers to an *object* (**Τον θεωρούν χαζό** 'They consider him *stupid*')	
palatal	a consonant sound made when the tongue touches or approaches the hard palate, such as the first sound in Greek χιόνι or English *huge*	
parisyllabic	a *noun* that has the same number of syllables in the plural as in the singular	

Glossary of grammatical terms

participle   a form of the *verb* used as an *adjective* (**κουρασμένος** 'tired')

particle   one of a number of small words, including those preceding the *verb* (the *subjunctive* particles **να** and **ας**, the future particle **θα** and the negative particles **δεν** and **μην**)

passive   when a *verb* is in the passive voice its *subject* is not the person or thing doing the action but the person or thing acted upon (cf. *active*)

perfect   (i) an *aspect* of the *verb* consisting of the present or *imperfect* forms of **έχω** followed by the *non-finite*; it refers to a past action that is presented in relation to some other time; (ii) *a tense* of the *verb* consisting of the present forms of **έχω** followed by the *non-finite* (**έχω γράψει** 'I have written')

perfective   the *aspect* of the *verb* that presents an action as being complete (cf. *imperfective*)

plosive   a consonant sound produced when a complete closure in the vocal tract is suddenly released (as in English [p], [b], [t]) (cf. *fricative*)

pluperfect   a *tense* of the *verb* formed with the past forms of **έχω** followed by the *non-finite*; it is used to express the completion of an action before a specified past time (**είχα γράψει** 'I had written')

prefix   a component of a word added to the front of a *stem* (***προπολεμικός*** '*pre*-war')

preposition   a word placed before a *noun phrase* that typically indicates time, place or manner ('at', 'on', 'with')

pronoun   a word that has the function of a *noun phrase*; it may be an emphatic personal pronoun (**εμένα** 'me'), a weak personal pronoun (**με** 'me'), or some other kind of pronoun (**ποιος;** 'who?', **κάποιος** 'someone', **κανένας** 'no one; anyone'); most Greek pronouns other than personal pronouns may also act as *determiners*

protasis   the *clause* in a *conditional sentence* that expresses the condition that must be fulfilled if the action of the *verb* in the main clause (the *apodosis*) is to take place (*Αν έρθεις στο πάρτι, θα δεις τον Γιάννη* '*If you come to the party*, you'll see John')

Glossary of grammatical terms

quantifier	a word that expresses quantity (e.g. όλος 'all', πολύς 'much')
question word	a *pronoun* or *determiner* (ποιος, 'who', τι 'what', πόσος 'how much') or *adverb* (πού, 'where', πότε 'when', γιατί 'why') that is used to introduce questions
reduplication	a *prefix* added to some verbs in the passive perfect *participle*, usually formed by repeating the initial consonant of the stem and adding ε (πεπεισμένος 'convinced')
semantic	regarding the meaning of words, phrases, etc.
semi-deponent verb	a *verb* that has only *passive* forms in the *imperfective aspect* and only *active* forms in the *perfective aspect* (κάθομαι 'I sit', κάθισα 'I sat') (cf. *deponent verb*)
sentence	a *syntactic* unit that expresses a complete meaning and consists of one or more *clauses*
sibilant	the consonant sounds [s] and [z]
simple past	the *perfective* past form of the *verb* (έγραψα 'I wrote')
stem	the part of an inflected word (*noun*, *verb*, *adjective*, etc.) to which *prefixes* and *suffixes* are added
subject	the *noun phrase* denoting the person or thing doing the action of an *active verb* (Ήρθε η Μαρία 'Mary came') or undergoing the action of a *passive verb* (Η Μαρία τραυματίστηκε 'Mary was injured')
subject predicate	an *adjective* phrase or *noun phrase* referring to a *subject* by means of a *linking verb* (Ο Νίκος είναι πολύ έξυπνος 'Nick's very clever', Ο Νίκος είναι δάσκαλος 'Nick's a teacher')
subjunctive	the *mood* of the *verb* that typically presents the action as wished for, hoped for, expected, planned, etc.; the subjunctive is marked by the particles να and ας, and is negated by μην
subordinate clause	see *clause*
suffix	a component of a word added to the end of a *stem* (παλαιότερος 'older')
superlative	see *degree*
syntactic	regarding the way words, phrases, etc. are joined to make phrases, *clauses* and *sentences*

Glossary of grammatical terms

tense	grammatical property of a *verb* that primarily refers to the time of the action; in this book we make two different types of distinction between tenses: (a) the general categories of past and non-past; and (b) the specific verb-forms present, *imperfect*, *simple past*, future, *perfect*, etc.
topic	the person or thing about which something is said (cf. *focus*)
transitive verb	a *verb* that may have an *object* (**βλέπω** 'I see')
velar	a consonant sound made with the back of the tongue against the soft palate, as in English and Greek [k] and [g]
verb	a word that denotes an action or a state (**γράφω** 'I write', **υπάρχω** 'I exist')
vocative	see *case*
voice	see *active* and *passive*
voiced consonant	a consonant sound produced with vibration of the vocal cords (e.g. [d], [m], [v], [z])
voiceless consonant	a consonant sound produced without vibration of the vocal cords (e.g. [t], [f], [s])

Some recommended books for further study

Coursebooks

Τα νέα ελληνικά για ξένους. Aristoteleio Panepistimio Thessalonikis, Idryma Manoli Triantafyllidi, 3rd ed. Thessaloniki 1998. Workbooks and cassettes available.

K. Arvanitakis and F. Arvanitaki, *Επικοινωνήστε ελληνικά*. Deltos, new ed. Athens 2002. A complete course in three volumes, with cassettes and workbooks.

G. Babiniotis and others, *Ελληνική γλώσσα. Εγχειρίδιο διδασκαλίας της ελληνικής ως δεύτερης ξένης γλώσσας*. Idryma Meleton Lambraki, 2nd ed. Athens 1995. Written primarily for the needs of returning migrants, and entirely in Greek, this is an attractive course which links grammar with information about Greek culture. There is also a supplementary volume with vocabulary and outlines of grammar in English. A cassette is available separately.

G. Catsimali and others, *Ελληνικά με την παρέα μου*. Vol. 1. Organismos Ekdoseos Didaktikon Vivlion, Athens 1999. This is a fast course intended for students who already know some Greek. A second volume will appear soon.

G. Catsimali and other, *Ελληνικά από κοντά: 20 (γλωσσικά) μυστήρια για τον επιθεωρητή Σαχίνη... κι εσένα*. E.DIA.M.ME., Rethymno, 2001. This book explains and provides practice for various grammatical phenomena of Greek which present difficulties.

D. Dimitra and M. Papacheimona, *Ελληνικά τώρα 1 + 1*. Nostos, 5th ed. Athens 2002. This is an excellent basic course, with cassettes and workbook, more suitable for class use than private study. There is also a second volume: *Ελληνικά τώρα 2 + 2*.

Some recommended books for further study

D. A. Hardy, *Greek Language and People*. BBC Books, London 1983 (with cassettes). The material is attractively presented, but formal grammar is kept to a minimum.

S. Vogiatzidou, *Learning Modern Greek as a Foreign/Second Language: a Communicative Approach*. University Studio Press, Thessaloniki 2002. A well-illustrated course, with workbook and three cassettes.

N. Watts, *Colloquial Greek: A Complete Language Course*. Routledge, London and New York 1994. A step-by-step course with clear presentations of grammar, accompanied by two cassettes.

Grammars

D. Holton, P. Mackridge and I. Philippaki-Warburton, *Greek: A Comprehensive Grammar of the Modern Language*. Routledge, London 1997, reprinted with corrections 1999 and 2002. A full descriptive grammar of the modern language.

C. Klairis and G. Babiniotis, Γραμματική της Νέας Ελληνικής. Δομολειτουργική – επικοινωνιακή. Ellinika Grammata, Athens 1996– . So far only three (of the projected six) volumes of this advanced grammar have appeared. It is based on contemporary language teaching theory and aims at a full description of the morphological and syntactic structures of the modern language.

P. Mackridge, *The Modern Greek Language: A Descriptive Analysis of Standard Modern Greek*. Oxford University Press, Oxford 1985. This is not a reference grammar as such, but presents and analyses a wide range of material illustrating current usage. It is aimed at more advanced learners.

M. A. Triandaphyllidis, *Concise Modern Greek Grammar*. Translated by John B. Burke. Aristotle University of Thessaloniki, Thessaloniki 1997. A translation of the abridged version (1974) of the 'official' grammar of 1941. The 1974 adaptation continues to be used in the Greek educational system, despite the fact that it has not been substantially updated to reflect contemporary usage.

Dictionaries

J. T. Pring, *The Pocket Oxford Greek Dictionary*. Oxford University Press, Oxford 1982, reissued 2000. A compact two-way dictionary for basic use.

D. N. Stavropoulos, *Oxford Greek–English Learner's Dictionary*. Oxford University Press, Oxford 1988. This is the best available small dictionary for translation from Greek to English; it includes reliable information about forms, usage and idioms.

D. N. Stavropoulos and A. S. Hornby, *Oxford English–Greek Learner's Dictionary*. Oxford University Press, 2nd ed. Oxford 1998. This is an adaptation of the *Oxford Advanced Learner's Dictionary*, and therefore intended primarily for the use of Greek-speaking learners of English. However, it is also quite useful for English-speaking learners of Greek.

There are also three large-format monolingual dictionaries suitable for advanced learners and native speakers:

Λεξικό της κοινής νεοελληνικής. Aristoteleio Panepistimio Thessalonikis, Institouto Neoellinikon Spoudon, Thessaloniki 1998.

G. Babiniotis, *Λεξικό της νέας ελληνικής γλώσσας, με σχόλια για τη σωστή χρήση των λέξεων*. Kentro Lexikologias, Athens 1998.

E. Kriaras, *Νέο ελληνικό λεξικό της σύγχρονης δημοτικής γλώσσας, γραπτής και προφορικής*. Ekdotiki Athinon, Athens 1995.

Some recommended books for further study

Index of grammatical categories and concepts

This index is intended to be used in conjunction with the table of contents. Many of the terms below are defined in the Glossary of grammatical terms. Bold numbers refer to the pages where these items are most thoroughly treated.

abbreviations **260–2**
accents **14–15**, 140, 187; *see also* stress
accusative *see* case
active *see* voice
adjectives 19, 23–4, 42–3, **54–67**, 68, 75–6, 79, 88–9, 91, 93–6, 99–104, 109, 147–8, 170, 173, 175, 177–9, 193, 199, 210–11, 218–19, 222, 243–7, 249; comparative 54, **63–7**, 75–6, 90, 104, 173, 234–6; declension of **54–65**; indeclinable 63–4; stress of 10–11, 54–6, 59–60, 62, 64–5, 245–6; superlative 54, **63–7**, 75–6, 90, 173; use of 67, **83–6**
adverbial phrases 115–16, 169–80, 212–13, 217
adverbs 80, 86–8, 90, 104, 112–13, 148, **169–80**, 190, 193, 211, 231–2, 235, 245, 247; comparative 172–3, 179–80, 234–5; formation of 170, **177–9**; indefinite **208–10**; interrogative 14, 170–2, 195, **206–7**; of manner 169–70, 173; of place 169–71, 173–4, 176, 179, 182–7, 189, 191–2; of quantity 169, 172–3, 175, 180; of time 169, 171–5, 179, 182; stress of 11; superlative 172–3, 179–80
agent 119, 183
agreement 19, 23, 26–7, 67–8, 83, 94, 109, 116–17, 148, 185
alphabet **1–2**, 53, 105, 107
alveolar 5–7
aorist xi
apodosis 223–4
apostrophe 15, 91
articles 19, 23, 39, 42, 68; definite 9–10, 14, 19–20, 25–6, 64, 68, 74, **77–81**, 83, 89 92–5, 97, 100–4, 110, 130, 183, 187–8, 190, 193, 222–3; forms of 25–7; indefinite 20, **25–6**, 77, **81**, 101, 108; uses of 77–83
aspect 117, **118**, 120, 125, 196; *see also* verbs
augment **152–3**, 154; internal 141, 153; syllabic 128, 132, 135, 138 152; vocalic 152–3
augmentatives **244**

bilabials 4–5

capital letters 14–16
case 19, 24, 26–7, 54, 63, 67, 79, 83, 91, 94–5, 97, 100, 104–5, 109, 147–8, 229, 236, 238; accusative 20–2, **68–72**, 75–6, 88–9, 113–16, 184, 190, 215, 235, 256; forms of 25–63; genitive 20–1, 68, **72–7**, 88, 90, 94, 113–15, 176, 181, 184, 186–7, 189–90, 217, 235, 254; nominative 20–2, 68–9, 116, 202; uses of **68–77**; vocative 17, 20–1, 77; *see also* adjectives, agreement, nouns
clauses 175, 189, **203–40**; adverbial 115; comparative **235**; complement 19–20, 80, 86, 201, **218–23**; concessive 185, 194, **225**; conditional 82, 98, **123–4**, 190, **223–5**, 234; imperative 98; indicative 118, 219–21; main 118, 193, 200, **203–11**; noun **19–20**, 80, 222–3; of cause **228–9**; of manner **227**; of purpose **227**; of result 201, **227–8**, 234; relative 20, 93, 99–100, 201, **212–15**, 234 (free relative 100, **214–15**); subjunctive 98, 220–1; subordinate 118, 169, 194–5, **212–29**; temporal 186, 190, **226**

Index of grammatical categories and concepts

colloquial usage 8, 72, 76–7, 89, 91, 94, 97, 99, 104, 110, 126–32, 147, 168, 183, 188, 193–4, 212, 218, 232
commands 17, 129, 179, 197, 200–1, 204–5, 208; indirect 218; *see also* prohibitions
comparative *see* adjectives *and* adverbs
comparison 76, 90, 183, 187–8, **234–7**
complementizer *see* **μήπως, ότι, που, πως**
compound words 33, 45, 60, 154, 241, **246–7**
conditional *see* clauses, tense
conjugation *see* verbs
conjunctions 122, 187, 190, 193–5, 223, 225–8; co-ordinating **193–4**; subordinating **194–5**; *see also individual conjunctions in Index of Greek words*
consonants 1–2, 4–9, 25–6, 128, 130, 147, 152; combinations of (in pronunciation) 7–8, (in writing) 3, 5, 6–8
co-ordination 81, 193–4, 207, **232–4**

dash 17
dative *see* case
decimals 16
declension *see* adjectives, articles, determiners, nouns, pronouns
deletion of consonants 9; of vowels 9–10, 14
demonstratives 19, 78, 91, 92–4, 103; qualitative 93; quantitative 94
dentals 4–6, 143
dependent **122**, 123, 129–30, 133, 136–41, 154, 196–7, 226
deponent *see* verbs
determiners 23–4, 67, **87–104**; distributive 101; *see also* pronouns *and individual determiners in Index of Greek words*
diacritics 15
diaeresis 15
diminutives 33, 41, 46, **243–4, 249,** 253
direct speech 17

emphasis 87, 94, 117, **229–32**
enclisis 11, 89
equation 81, **236–7**
exclamations 76, 88, 211

feminine *see* gender
flaps 5–6
focus **229–32**
formal usage 4, 8, 30, 37–8, 40, 45, 77, 99, 127, 134, 141–4, 147, 178, 212, 227–8, 255–7
fricatives 5–6
future *see* tense

gender 19, **22–4**, 26–7, 52–4, 63, 67–8, 77, 83, 91, 94–5, 99–100, 104–5, 109, 116, 147–8, 238, 241–4, 254–5, 260; common 23, 28, 34, **42–3**, 53; *see also* adjectives, agreement, nouns
genitive *see* case
gerund 88, 113, 117, **124**, 130, 134, 136, 139, 210–11
greetings 76, **255–7**

hyphen 17

imperative 10, 113, 129–30, 133–34, 136, 138–9, 141, 154, 202, 204, 218
imperfect *see* tense
imperfective *see* aspect
indicative *see* mood
interrogative *see* adverbs (interrogative), pronouns (interrogative), questions
intonation 11–13, 205, 208

labials 142, 153
labiodentals 5–6
liquids 5–6

masculine *see* gender
mood 112–13, 117–18, **119**, 127, 205, 207, 214, 218–19, 227; indicative 203, 228; subjunctive 141, 204 (forms **151**, uses **195–200**, 204–5, 217–18); *see also* imperative

names 16, 18, 33, 35–6, 38–42, 44, 46, 53, 78, 243, **251–5**
nasals 4–7, 9
negation 9, 98, 82, 97, 112–13, 151, 172, 175–7, 179, 196, 201, 203–4, **207–11**, 214, 223, 245–6; *see also* **δεν** and **μην**
neuter *see* gender
nominative *see* case
non-finite 117, **122–3**, 150–1, 154
noun phrases 23–4, 87, 92, 104, 114, 116, 181–2, 184–90, 193, 202, 217, 222–3, 229–31, 235–6; constituents of 19–20; uses of 20–2, **67–83**
nouns 15, **19–24**, 25–7, 60, **67–83**, 84, 87–9, 92, 94–103, 109–10, 148, 174–5, 190, 199, 206, 210–13, 218–1, 222, 241–7; abstract 22, 79; declension of **27–53**; gender of 27–8, 52–3 (*see also* gender); indeclinable 27, 45, **53**; stress of 10–11, 28, 30–3, 36–41, 44–51, 255
number 19, 24, 26, 54, 63, 67–8, 77, 83, 91, 94–5, 97, 99–100, 104, **117–18**, 125, 148, 237, 248–9; *see also* adjectives, agreement, nouns, plural, verbs

275

Index of grammatical categories and concepts

numerals 19, 23–4, 26, 67, 75, 81, 88, 90, 99, 101, 103, **105–11**, 175, 193–4;
cardinal **105–10**; collective 110; multiplicative 109; ordinal 15, **105–7**, 110

objects 82, 87–9, 92, 100, **113–16**, 119, 213, 222–3, 229–32, 238; direct 20–2, 69, **72–3**, 83, 147, 215; indirect 15, 20–1, 72–3, 188; of prepositions 70, 92, 95
obligation 125, 199, 240

palatals 5–7
participles 51, 62; passive perfect 54, 64, 84, 141, **147–9**, **154–68**, 173, 247
particles 112–13, 117–18, 122, 151, **195–202**; *see also individual particles in Index of Greek words*
partitive expressions 182
passive *see* voice
perception, verbs of 220, 233
perfect *see* tense
perfective *see* aspect
permission 200
person 87, 90, 92, 94, 99, 114, **117–18**, 125, 248–9
place *see* time, place and quantity
plosives 4–5, 97
pluperfect *see* tense
plural of politeness 117, 248–50, 255–7; *see also* adjectives, nouns, number, verbs
politeness 205, 250–1; *see also* plural
possession 72, 74, 86; *see also* pronouns, possessive
possibility 200, 240
predicates 20–21, 84, 112, 116, 249; object 70, 116; subject 69, 81
prefixes 241, **244–6**; prepositional 148, **153**, 154, 237–8, 244–5
prepositional phrase 20, 86, 113, 119, 169, **181–92**, 193, 212, 217, 235, 237–8
prepositions 9, 20, 70, 77, 92, 95, 176, **181–92**; *see also individual prepositions in Index of Greek words*
present *see* tense
probability 196, 199
prohibitions 17, 197, 204–5, 218; *see also* commands
pronouns 19, 23, 67–8, 75–6, 81, 84, **87–104**, 117–18; contrastive **102–3**, 179; correlative (forms of 100, uses of 215–16); indefinite **96–9**, 101, 177, **208–9**; intensive 76, **101–2**; interrogative **95–6**, **206–7**, 217–18; personal 24, 102, 181, 187, 189–90, 248 (emphatic 20, 87–9, **91–2**, 94, 113–14, 185, 188, 193; weak 9–11, 15, 72–6, 86, **87–90**, 94, 112–15, 150–1, 176, 182, 186, 196, 202, 213–14, 221, 223, **230–2**, 234–5, 240, 250, 255); possessive 11, 15, 20, 78, **89–90**, 94–5, 237; relative 99–100 (uses of 212–14); universal **101**; *see also* demonstratives, determiners, *and individual pronouns in Index of Greek words*
pronunciation 1–10, 15, 18
protasis 223–4
punctuation 16–18

quantifiers 19, 57, 67, 88, **103–4**, 175; *see also* όλος, ολόκληρος
quantity *see* time, place and quantity
questions 11–12, 82, 88, 97, 170–2, 176–7, 179, 205–9, 214, 250; indirect 199, 216–18
question words 197; *see also* pronouns (interrogative), adverbs (interrogative)

reciprocal expressions **238–9**
reduplication 148
reflexive expressions **237–8**

sibilants 5–6
simple past *see* tense
singular *see* adjectives, number, nouns, verbs
sounds 1–2
spelling 1–8, 18; *see also* accents, capital letters, diacritics
stems, imperfective *and* perfective *see* verbs
stress **10–11**, 12, 14–15, 87, 89, 100, 110, 231–3; *see also* accents, adjectives, nouns, verbs
subjects 20, 69, 83, 87, 92, 112, 117–19, 124, 197, 203, 215, 222–3, 229, 231, 237–8
subjunctive *see* mood
suffixes 38, 43, 63, 65, 110, 177–8, **241–4**
superlative *see* adjectives *and* adverbs

tense 112, 117, **118–25**, 127, 196–7, 199, 223; conditional 120, **123**, **151**, **224–5**, 251; future 118, 120, **123**, 141, 149, 196; future perfect **123**, **151**; imperfect **121**, 123, 125, 134, 151–2, 154, 200, **224–5**; perfect 118, **122**, 123, **150–1**, 154; perfect conditional **124**, **224–5**; pluperfect 118, **122–3**, 124, **151**, **224–5**; present **120–1**, 122–3, 125–6, 134, 136, **154–68**, 250; simple past **121–2**, 122, 146, 142, **154–68**; *see also* dependent *and* verbs

Index of grammatical categories and concepts

time, place and quantity, expressions of 21, 70–2, 74–5, 79–80, 109–11, 115–16, 169–73, 182, 186–8
topic **229–32**

velars 5–6, 143, 153
verbs 9, 15, 20, 22, 24, 48, 62, 69, 72–3, 82, 87, 89, 92, **112–68**, 173, 196–7, 199 202–3, 206, 216, 218–23, 222–3, 227–8, 231–2, 237–48; auxiliary 117–18, **122–3, 150–1**; conjugation of **125–68**; defective 125; deponent 125, 135, 137–8, 142–6, 154; imperfective stems 116, 128–30, 139, **141–7**; impersonal 125, 154, 198–9, **221–2, 239–40**; intransitive 113, 115–16, 147; irregular 126, 139, **154–68**; linking 116; perfective stems of 128, 130, 132, 136, 139, **141–7**, 147, **154–68**; semi-deponent 125; stress of 11, 126–9, 131–2, 134–5, 138, 140–1, 150, 152–3; transitive 113–16; *see also* mood, tense, voice
vocative *see* case
voice 117, **118–19**, 125, 130; passive 237–9; *see also* verbs
vowels 1–4, 6, 9–11, 14–15, 25–6, 49, 91, 97, 130, 134, 141, 153; combinations of (in pronunciation) 4, (in writing) 1, 3, 14

wishes 76, 119, 197, 200, 204, 214, 220, **255–7**
word order **229–32**

Index of Greek words

Here we list a number of important Greek words that are thoroughly treated or frequently mentioned in the *Grammar*.

αλλά 193, 232–3
άλλο(ς) 23, 68, 97, **102–3**, 179
αν 122, 190, 216–17, **223–5**, 227, 234
αν και 225
ανάμεσα 170, 186, 191
απέναντι 170, 191
από 10, 75–6, 91, 181, **182–3**, 185, 190–2, **234–5**
άραγε 205, 237
ας 9, 117, 119, 122, 151, **200**, 201, 203–4, 207–8
αφού 226, **228–9**
για (particle) **202**
για (preposition) 91, 181–2, **183–4**, 190, 202, 227–8
γιατί 206–7, **228**, 234
γύρω 170, 191
δεν 9, 98, 119, 151, 203, 207–8, 219–20, 223, 225
δικός 94, 97
δίπλα 170, 191
εδώ 170, 173–4, 176
είμαι 81, 125, 221; forms of **126**
είτε 193, **223–4**, **232–3**
εκεί 170, 174, 176, 182
εναντίον 181, 184
ένας 26–7, 81, 108
εξαιτίας 181, 184
έξω 170, 191
έτσι 170, 206, 223–4, 227–8
έχω 117–18, **122–3**, 125, **150–1**, 160, 239
ή (conjunction) 14, 193, 205, **232–3**
θα 117–18, 120, 122–4, 141, 151, 199, 207–8
ίδιος 101–2
κάθε 101, 172
καθένας 76, 101
καθετί 101
καθόλου 170, 172, 174, 176–7
καθώς 227–8
και 186, **193–4**, 223–4, 227–9, **232–4**
κάμποσο(ς) 104, 172
κανείς 97–9, 208–9
κανένας 23, 75, 97–9, 101, 103, 110, 183, 208–9
κάποιος 81, 96–7, 99, 103
κάπου 170, 172
κάπως 170, 172
κάτι 93, 96–7
κάτω 170, 174, 179, 191
κι ας 225
κοντά 170, 174, 191
λίγο(ς) 86, 104, 172–4, 179–80, 249
μαζί 170, 191
με 181, **184–5**, 190, 225
μέσα 170, 179, 191
μετά 171, 173, 190, 226
μεταξύ 181, 186, 238
μέχρι 181–2, **186**, 226
μη 208, 210–11
μην 9, 89, 98, 119, 204, 207–8, 210–11, 218, 220–1, 223, 225
μήπως 205, 216–17, **219–20**
μισός 109
μόλις 171, 226
μόνο(ς) 76, **101–2**, 170, 176, 179
μπορώ 198–200, 240, 251
μπροστά 170, 191
να (deictic particle) 88, **201–2**
να (subjunctive particle) 80, 86, 117, 119, 122, 125, 141, 151, 183, **196–200**, 201, 203–9, **217–24**, 226–8, 233–4, 236, 239–40, 249–50
ναι 175, 201
ξέρω 152, 163
ολόκληρος 78

Index of Greek words

όλο(ς) 23, 76, 78, 89–90, **103–4**, 172, 185, 187, 225
όμως 193, **232–3**
ο οποίος 100, **212–14**
όποιος 100, 103, **215–16**
όποτε 171, **215–16**, 226
οπότε 171, 216
όπου 170, **215–16**
όπως 170, 215, 227, 236
όσο(ς) 100, 190, **215–16**, **235–7**
όταν 122, 226
ότι (complementizer) 16, 80, 86, 100, **219–22**, 239
ό, τι (pronoun and determiner) 16, 100, 215
ούτε 193–4, 210, **232–3**
όχι 175, 201, 205, 210
πάνω 170, 174, 187, 191, 226
πάρα 173, 187
παρά 186–7, 225, **234–5**
πέρα 170, 179
πιο 63–5, 71, 86, 173–4, 179, 236
πίσω 170, 179, 191
πλάι 170, 191
ποιος 20, 23, 95–6, 103, 206–7, 209
πολύ(ς) 57–8, 66, 57–8, 86, 94, 104, 172–4, 179–80
πόσο(ς) 95, 172, 206, 211
πότε 171–2, 206, 208
ποτέ 171, 176–7, 208–9
που (relative and complementizer) 14, 99–100, 201, 211, **212–14**, **219–22**, **226–8**, 233–4
πού (question word) 14, 88, 170, 187–8
πουθενά 170, 176–7, 209
πρέπει 125, 198–9, 240
πριν 122, 171, 174, 190, **226**
πως (complementizer) 14, **219–20**
πώς (question word) 14, 170, 206
σαν 81, 181, **187–8**, 226, **236**
σε 10, 21, 25, 73, 115, 181, **188**, 191–2
τέτοιος 93, 99, **227–8**
τι 95, 100, 206–7, 211, 217–18
τίποτα/τίποτε 97–9, 209
τόσο(ς) 94, 103, 172, 174, 216, **227–8**, 235–7
τότε 171, 176, 226
τώρα 171, 176, 182, 226
χωρίς **188–9**, 209
ώσπου 226
ώστε **227–8**, 234

eBooks

A library at your fingertips!

eBooks are electronic versions of printed books. You can store them on your PC/laptop or browse them online.

They have advantages for anyone needing rapid access to a wide variety of published, copyright information.

eBooks can help your research by enabling you to bookmark chapters, annotate text and use instant searches to find specific words or phrases. Several eBook files would fit on even a small laptop or PDA.

NEW: Save money by eSubscribing: cheap, online access to any eBook for as long as you need it.

Annual subscription packages

We now offer special low-cost bulk subscriptions to packages of eBooks in certain subject areas. These are available to libraries or to individuals.

For more information please contact webmaster.ebooks@tandf.co.uk

We're continually developing the eBook concept, so keep up to date by visiting the website.

www.eBookstore.tandf.co.uk